NEW DEVELOPMENTS IN MACROECONOMICS RESEARCH

New Developments in Macroeconomics Research

Lawrence Z. Pelzer
Editor

Nova Science Publishers, Inc.
New York

For permission to use material from this book please contact us:
Telephone 631-231-7269; Fax 631-231-8175
Web Site: http://www.novapublishers.com

NOTICE TO THE READER

Library of Congress Cataloging-in-Publication Data

New developments in macroeconomics research / Lawrence Z. Pelzer (editor).
p. cm.
Includes index.
ISBN 1-59454-663-0
1. Macroeconomics. I. Pelzer, Lawrence Z.

HB172.5.N486 2005
339--dc22

2005024919

Published by Nova Science Publishers, Inc. ✦ New York

Contents

Preface

Macroeconomics is that part of economics that focuses on economic growth and economic fluctuations. In a world under the push and pull of globalization, it becomes crucial for the Developed Countries as well as the Developing Countries. It is necessary for some countries and companies to find the best regions to invest in while it is necessary for others to grow and compete for investment at the same time. This new book brings together an impressive array of research valuable for providing important insight into the international financial currents rippling around the world.

In the first chapter, *The New Millennium: APEC and Emerging China*, M. Ulric Killion discusses the Asia-Pacific Economic Cooperation (APEC) and how it has been universally acknowledged as the major regional economic cooperation organization for the liberalization and facilitation of trade and investment (TILF) in the Asia-Pacific region. However, APEC's role as leader in the Asia-Pacific region is being challenged. In 2004, an emerging China entered into a landmark agreement with ASEAN, which is the 2004 ASEAN-China accord that portends to establish the world's largest free trade area by the year 2010. As a result, the fate of APEC largely became intertwined with the fate of China.

APEC was formed in 1989, and evolved from a regional economic consultative body, into an organization explicitly addressing political concerns in the region. APEC is the by-product of evolving international political economy concerns, from the post-Cold War, post-East Asian financial crisis, to post-9/11 and global threats of mega-terrorism. APEC has suffered a crisis in lack of credibility since the East Asian financial crisis; many perceive that APEC failed to adequately respond to the crisis. However, APEC's credibility has been more harmed by a perceived inability to accomplish the Bogor goals. In 1994, APEC member economies signed the Bogor Declaration, and developed economies pledged to eliminate trade and investment barriers by 2010, while developing economies pledged to eliminate trade and investment barriers by 2020. Some critiques link accomplishing the Bogor goals to APEC's survival and relevancy in the new millennium.

A critique of APEC based solely on the Bogor goals results in a denial of other equally important relevancies, serving as harbingers for survivability and continuing relevancy. In the new millennium, APEC's survival and continuing relevancy will lie in its historical commitment to TILF. However, historical relevancies must also allow for adjustments reflecting new international political economy concerns, such as, global threats of mega-terrorism, the 2004 ASEAN-China accord, termination of the WTO Multi-Fibre Agreement (MFA) of 1974, and what is being dubbed "JACIK," a prospective free trade super mega zone, comprising ASEAN, China, Japan, India and the Republic of Korea. Moreover, survival for APEC in the new millennium means encompassing an explicit economic agenda, in conjunction with an explicit international relations (political) agenda. APEC will survive in the new millennium by incorporating the latter relevancies, which reflect both historical relevancies, and evolving relevancies from changing and dynamic international political economy environments.

In *The Effects of Dollar Fluctuations on Private Consumption in the U.S.,* Magda Kandil and Ida Aghdas Mirzaie examine the effects of the change in the value of the dollar on private consumption in the United States. The empirical model includes disposable income, an index of consumer sentiment, the interest rate, and the real effective exchange rate. Anticipated movements in these determinants are likely to affect planned consumption, while unanticipated changes determine cyclical consumption. Dollar appreciation (depreciation) decreases (increases) consumption of non-tradables, while increasing (decreasing) consumption of tradables. The former channel appears to be more dominant on total consumption. A few exceptions suggest, however, that currency appreciation may be associated with higher values of consumption. This is particularly evident for durable goods, which are likely to constitute a large share of tradables.

In Chapter 3, *Responsiveness to External Developments Through the Trade Channel: New Estimates for the Euro Area*, Daniele Antonucci, and Alessandro Girardi assesses the impact of various external shocks on trade exchanges between the euro area and the rest of the world using cointegration techniques for simulation purposes. The main results are: *i*) non-price competitiveness factors and the real exchange rate affect the euro area trade balance in the long-run. Furthermore, the Marshall-Lerner conditions is strongly rejected; *ii*) extending the sample span over the post-EMU period, i.e. accounting for the introduction of the single currency, the results are qualitatively similar in terms of statistical significance and feedback mechanisms; *iii*) changes in foreign demand and in the price of oil do not exert a statistically significant impact on the trade balance; *iv*) domestic demand and price competitiveness play the main role in explaining trade fluctuations. Moreover, the share of volatility attributable to the former increases over time, while the contribution of the latter remains stable and accounts for the biggest proportion.

Active involvement in international trade and finance is typical of sovereign entities with a track record of significant involvement in the large-scale production of a commodity that is widely consumed and appreciated across international boundaries. However, many economies do not have the tools that recognize budgetary provisions as the totality of policy instruments to address the current macroeconomic realities. This attracts a loss of information on the socio-economic reading of history on past and future interventions. It also results in dramatic changes in social policy, unfolding conflict and dwindling market economy, which threaten and weaken the society with dehumanization and poverty despite huge investments and the often use of irrecoverable resources. There is therefore a need to provide the necessary information to all stakeholders involved in development so as to avert the creation of failed states, unpredictable regimes and the attendant distortion of social and political structures meant for discharging intervention schemes. In *Organic Page Information for International Trade and Finance* Olufemi A. Yesufu and Thomas K. Yesufu show how the market paradigm can be used to obtain the poverty and gender equilibrium (PAGE) information with a view to achieving cooperation, creativity and synergy between stakeholders and intervention programs.

In Chapter 5, *Mathematical Model Stock Market Fluctuations in the Absence of Economic Growth*, Alexei Krouglov presents a mathematical model inferring the stock market fluctuations from the business fluctuations. There are shown the ordinary differential equations describing the fluctuations of equities, derivatives, and second derivatives on the stock market.

These last two decades many authors have pointed out that the way to develop appropriate microfoundations for macroeconomics is not to be found from the study of individuals in isolation but rests in an essential way on studying the aggregate activity resulting from the interaction between different individuals. An alternative approach to the neoclassical paradigm based on individual rationality has been developed. The fundamentals of the models remain individual behaviors described by individual characteristics. However, the assumptions formalized at the individual level are very weak so that individual rationality might even be redundant. The major assumptions rely on the whole population and, more precisely, on the distribution of agents' characteristics. Isabelle Maret, in *The Statistical Approach to the Aggregation Problem* gives an overview of this approach that we call the "statistical approach" 1and to present it in an unified framework with the hope that its assumptions will be more systematically used in macroeconomic models.

Axel Gautier, in *Information Acquisition in Repeated Relationships*, presents a new rationale for delegation. In a repeated relationship, when the principal gives up at time t the control over an action to the better informed agent, the decision taken by the agent signals his private information to the principal. The revelation of information is valuable to the principal only in a context of repeated relation where the principal can use the information at time t+1 to take another decision. In this paper, we present an example where delegation occurs only if the relation lasts for more than one period. In a single period context, if the agent has a bias in favor of one project, he does not have incentives to select a project that is not his preferred one; hence he does not disclose his private information and delegation is not valuable. While in a repeated relationship, it becomes costly for the agent to keep the principal non-informed and this counterbalances the agent's bias for one project. Shared-control (partial delegation) is then the preferred organizational structure when the interaction is repeated. Moreover, shared-control dominates an alternative mechanism where the principal centralizes all the decisions and the information is transferred through a message game.

Previous research has revealed that among adults, behaviors such as smoking, drinking, physical inactivity, and overeating vary procyclically. Additional research finding procyclical fluctuations in mortality from sources such as heart and liver diseases, influenza and pneumonia, and homicide suggest that lifestyles become healthier as economic conditions worsen. In contrast, suicide appears to vary countercyclically. In the last chapter, *Bad Times, Bad Behavior: The Effects of Economic Conditions on Health-Related Behaviors Among High School Students*, Jeff DeSimone extends the hypothesis that economic downturns diminish mental health while otherwise prompting individuals to adopt healthier and less risky lifestyles to adolescents, who are presumably both less responsive to economic conditions and less risk averse than adults. In particular, the author use pooled cross sections of data on high school students from the biennial 1991–2001 Youth Risk Behavior Surveys to examine the relationship between state unemployment rates and a large set of potentially health-reducing behaviors including riding a bicycle and motorcycle without a helmet, not wearing a seat belt, driving while drinking and riding with a drinking driver, carrying a weapon, being involved in physical fights, attempting suicide, using cigarettes, alcohol, marijuana and cocaine, having sex with one or more partners, while drunk or high and without birth control, being under or overweight and not exercising regularly. Controlling for age, grade and race as well as fixed effects for states and years, he finds that, in contrast to the results of many recent studies of adults, almost all risky behaviors examined increase in prevalence as unemployment rises for at least one of the two genders. This suggests that economic downturns affect teenagers psychologically through substantive impacts on them or their families, allow teens more leisure time to engage in risky activities, or reduce their perceived opportunity costs of potential health reductions or entry into the legal system.

In: New Developments in Macroeconomics Research
Editor: Lawrence Z. Pelzer, pp. 1-45
ISBN: 1-59454-663-0

Chapter 1

The New Millennium: APEC and Emerging China

*M. Ulric Killion**
Shanghai International Studies University (P.R.C.)

Abstract

The Asia-Pacific Economic Cooperation (APEC) has been universally acknowledged as the major regional economic cooperation organization for the liberalization and facilitation of trade and investment (TILF) in the Asia-Pacific region. However, APEC's role as leader in the Asia-Pacific region is being challenged. In 2004, an emerging China entered into a landmark agreement with ASEAN, which is the 2004 ASEAN-China accord that portends to establish the world's largest free trade area by the year 2010. As a result, the fate of APEC largely became intertwined with the fate of China.

APEC was formed in 1989, and evolved from a regional economic consultative body, into an organization explicitly addressing political concerns in the region. APEC is the by-product of evolving international political economy concerns, from the post-Cold War, post-East Asian financial crisis, to post-9/11 and global threats of mega-terrorism. APEC has suffered a crisis in lack of credibility since the East Asian financial crisis; many perceive that APEC failed to adequately respond to the crisis. However, APEC's credibility has been more harmed by a perceived inability to accomplish the Bogor goals. In 1994, APEC member economies signed the Bogor Declaration, and developed economies pledged to eliminate trade and investment barriers by 2010, while developing economies pledged to eliminate trade and investment barriers by 2020. Some critiques link accomplishing the Bogor goals to APEC's survival and relevancy in the new millennium.

A critique of APEC based solely on the Bogor goals results in a denial of other equally important relevancies, serving as harbingers for survivability and continuing relevancy. In the new millennium, APEC's survival and continuing relevancy will lie in its historical commitment to TILF. However, historical relevancies must also allow for adjustments reflecting new international political economy concerns, such as, global threats of mega-terrorism, the 2004 ASEAN-China accord, termination of the WTO Multi-Fibre Agreement (MFA) of 1974, and what is being dubbed "JACIK," a prospective free trade super mega

*E-mail address: mulrickillion@netscape.net. All observations and analysis are the author's own and by no means reflect the views of Shanghai International Studies University or its affiliates.

zone, comprising ASEAN, China, Japan, India and the Republic of Korea. Moreover, survival for APEC in the new millennium means encompassing an explicit economic agenda, in conjunction with an explicit international relations (political) agenda. APEC will survive in the new millennium by incorporating the latter relevancies, which reflect both historical relevancies, and evolving relevancies from changing and dynamic international political economy environments.

Introduction

The importance of Asian Pacific Economic Cooperation (APEC) lies in the numbers, in particular, economic data. At the time of the 2004 APEC-Chile summit, APEC comprised twenty-one member economies, spans four continents, represents more than one-third of the world's population (2.6 billion), constitutes over fifty percent of world gross national product (GNP) (US $19,254 billion), and represents more than forty-one percent of global trade.[1]

Nonetheless, APEC has been described as "four adjectives in search of a noun."[2] This statement reflects the understandings and misunderstandings of APEC as an international intergovernmental organization (IGO) and the role of APEC in the global economy, especially in terms of the new millennium. In addition, this statement reflects problems experienced by APEC since its 1989 birth as an international economic cooperation organization, especially defining itself, setting goals, and accomplishing goals such as the Bogor goals. In 1994, APEC member economies signed the Bogor Declaration, which is dubbed the Bogor goals, and developed economies pledged to eliminate trade and investment barriers by 2010, while developing economies pledged to eliminate trade and investment barriers by 2020.[3] The history of APEC lends understanding to how it grew from a simple economic consultative forum into a more complex anomaly in terms of IGOs, its role in promoting multilateral trade as opposed to regionalism, and the prospect of APEC as a major player in the new millennium, which some critiques link to accomplishing the seemingly all-important Bogor goals.

Moreover, given the growing maturity of the People's Republic of China (China) in economics, diplomacy and politics, the fate of APEC may well be contingent on the direction and vision of a maturing Chinese polity. The economic data also reflects the growing importance of China. In 2004, China's export and import figures were estimated at US $325,642 million in exports and US $295,303 million in imports. Notwithstanding growing U.S. – China trade deficit,[4] the leader remains the United States with US $693,103 million in exports and US $1,161,366 million in imports. The estimates in exports and imports for APEC economies demonstrate that China only lags between the economies of the U.S. and Japan, whose trade was estimated at US $417,165 million in exports and US $337,957 million

---

1 *See* APEC OUTCOMES AND OUTLOOKS 2003/2004, Asian-Pacific Economic Cooperation Publication 2004, at 4, [hereinafter 2004 APEC Outcomes].

2 *See* Walden Bello, *APEC: The Unauthorized History*, 18th May 1998, http://www.hk.super.net/~daga/walden01.htm, "To borrow the classic definition of the forum by former Australian Foreign Minister Gareth Evans, APEC is still "four adjectives in search of a noun."

3 APEC ECONOMIC LEADERS' DECLARATION OF COMMON RESOLVE
Bogor, Indonesia, 15 November 1994, Asia-Pacific Economic Cooperation, Member Economies, at http://www.apec.org/apec/.

4 *See* Robert E. Scott, *Soaring Imports of Oil and Chinese Goods Drive Trade Deficits to New Record, Trade Picture*, (Econ. Pol'y Inst.), Aug. 13, 2004 (The deficit rose from $22.7 billion in 1993 to $124 billion in 2003.).

in imports.[5] In 2004, China continued to experience robust economic growth,[6] and most important, in terms of foreign diplomacy, pushed its relations with the Association of Southeast Asian Nations (ASEAN) into a new stage.[7]

An emerging China combining its growing economic strength with the economic potential of ASEAN, challenges APEC's leadership in the Asian region. The ASEAN region has a population of about 500 million, a combined gross domestic product of US $737 billion, and a total trade volume of US $720 billion.[8] On 29 November 2004, China joined ASEAN in signing an agreement that established regional cooperation between them; they paved the way for establishing the world's largest free trade zone, or free trade area (FTA).[9] Whether perceived as good or bad, the fate of APEC became largely intertwined with the fate of China.

APEC is generally regarded as the major forum for facilitating economic growth, cooperation, trade and investment in the Asia-Pacific region,[10] or trade and investment liberalization and facilitation (TILF). APEC from its original inception and membership of twelve economies has expanded to a membership of twenty-one economies.[11] An APEC annual cycle begins and ends with the annual joint ministerial meeting of foreign affairs and trade ministers. Since 1993, there was also added to the annual cycle an annual APEC economic leaders' meeting.[12] APEC is the only IGO in the world operating on the basis of non-binding commitments, open dialogue and equal respect for the views of all participants, or member economies. In comparison with other IGOs, unlike the World Trade Organization

---

5 2004 APEC Outcomes, *supra* note 1, at 18, *citing Current Price GDP, Current GDP per Capita, Exports and Imports*, The APEC Region Trade and Investment 2003.

6 *See* Fu Jing, *Rosy Forecast of Economic Growth*, CHINA DAILY, Nov. 6, 2003, at 2003 WL 57560665; *see also* Lena Lee, *Foreign Investors, Retail Sales Set the Pace in China,* THE ASIAN WALL STREET JOURNAL, Mar. 26, 2004, at A2, at 2004 WL 56592469; *see also China set 7% growth target for 2004,* NEWS GUANGDONG, Dec. 3, 2003, http://www.newsgd.com/business/prospective/200312030031.htm.

7 *See* Editor's Note, *China more mature in Diplomacy*, CHINA DAILY, December 16, 2004; *see also* Association of Southeast Asian Nations, Overview, http://www.aseansec.org/64.htm, "ASEAN was established on 8 August 1967 in Bangkok by the five original Member Countries, namely, Indonesia, Malaysia, Philippines, Singapore, and Thailand. Brunei Darussalam joined on 8 January 1984, Vietnam on 28 July 1995, Laos and Myanmar on 23 July 1997, and Cambodia on 30 April 1999." *Id.*

8 Association of Southeast Asian Nations, Overview, http://www.aseansec.org/64.htm. [hereinafter ASEAN].

9 *See Deal forms free-trade megazone, China, ASEAN sign landmark accord*, SHANGHAI DAILY, 30 November 2004; *see also* T.N. Srinivasan, *Preferential Trade Agreements with Special Reference to Asia*, (Paper presented at the Asian Economic Outlook Workshop, Manila, November 2001), Yale University, January 2002, http://www.econ.yale.edu/~srinivas/PrefTradeAgreements.pdf.
Preferential Trade Agreements (PTAs) are agreements among a set of countries involving preferential treatment of bilateral trade between any two parties to the agreement relative to their trade with the rest of the world. Preferences, however, need not extend to all trade between the two, and the coverage could depend on the type of PTAs. Customs unions and the so-called free trade areas are common forms of PTAs. Members of most PTAs belong to a well-defined geographical area, such as for example, the European Union (EU), North American Free Trade Area (NAFTA) and Association of Southeast Asian Nations (ASEAN). For this reason regional PTAs are called Regional Trade Agreements (RTAs). The most common form of RTAs are the euphemistically named Free Trade Areas (FTAs), with few Customs Unions (CU) which require the partners to maintain a common external trade policy, in addition to free trade with each other.

10 Takeshi Isayama, Commissioner of JPO, Keynote Speech: *APEC Region Intellectual Property Right Protections beyond the Year 2000*, February 22, 1999.

11 2004 APEC Outcomes, *supra* note 1, "The word 'economies' is used to describe APEC members because the APEC cooperative process is predominantly concerned with trade and economic issues, with members engaging one another as economic entities." *Id.*, at 2.

12 *See* Heather Gibb, *Gender Front and Center An APEC Primer*, Chapter 2, in *How APEC Works*, (The North-South Institute 1999), http://www.nsi-ins.ca/ensi/publications/apec/.

(WTO),[13] or other international instruments and treaty bodies, APEC has no international treaty obligations required of its member economies; perhaps it is not even a formal agreement.[14] Decisions made within APEC are reached by consensus. As a result, commitments are undertaken only on a voluntary basis.[15] APEC's management style is characteristically consensus building and a step-by-step approach.[16] As for the four adjectives in search of a noun, an examination of the history of APEC should lend to both the search for and greater understanding of the manifest noun, which describes APEC in the new millennium.

History of APEC

A true historicism of the birth of APEC directly relates to the post-Cold War era. Contrary to the prognostications of Samuel Huntington and his clash of cultures thesis,[17] a post-Cold War era may best be described as one of growing global economic tensions, rather than cultural or ideological tensions.[18] These global economic tensions evolved from fear that at the close of the Cold War (1945-1991), the United States would not be able to resolve its trade disputes with Europe and Japan. In the advent of the U.S. retreating into economic isolationism because of these unresolved disputes, there was fear of the formation of three major tracing blocs based on the dollar, yen and deutschmark, respectively, the U.S., Japan and Germany.[19] The creation of the North American Free Trade Agreement (NAFTA) only heightened these fears.[20] This pre-history of APEC prompted the initiatives of Robert Hawke and others, which eventually led to the formation of APEC. The post-Cold War era has been described as the advent of acceleration in economic regionalization, which was accompanied by a corresponding increase in transnational political interactions that were also associated with regional*ism*.[21] Asia-Pacific regionalism was necessarily defined in terms of the contours of the post-Cold War international political economy.

---

13 Marrakesh Agreement Establishing the World Trade Organization [hereinafter WTO Agreement], The Legal Texts: The Results of the Uruguay Round of Multilateral Trade Negotiations, 1867 U.N.T.S. 154, 33 I.L.M. 1144 (1994).

14 Aziz Choudry, *APEC and Free Trade*, Seminar to Development Studies, Massey University, Palmerston North, Aotearoa/New Zealand, 2 May 1997.

15 About APEC – Asian-Pacific Economic Cooperation, http://www.apecsec.org.sg/apec/about_apec.html.

16 Takeshi Isayama, *supra* note 10.

17 *See* Samuel P. Huntington, THE CLASH OF CIVILIZATIONS AND THE REMAKING OF WORLD ORDER 19 (1996).

18 *See* Tim Harcourt, APEC'S LABOR AGENDA: NEGOTIATING THE FUTURE, at 4-5, Foreword by R. J. L. Hawke, A.C., (2000).

19 *See* Paul Bowles, *APEC: Progress Based on the Wrong Model?*, Canadian Business Economics 48, 57, Fall 1997 (Discussing different definitions for regional blocs.).

20 *See* Lincoln Wright, *APEC--Australia's Pragmatic Asia Policy?*, Japan Policy Research Institute, JPRI Working Paper No. 8: April 1995, http://www.jpri.org/publications/workingpapers/wp8.html, "The initial rationale in Canberra for enmeshing itself with Asia was the fear of being excluded from a regional trade agreement, such as a Yen bloc, as well as from the European Community and a Dollar bloc in the Americas. The creation of NAFTA added to Australia's fear;" *see also generally* North American Free Trade Association, NAFTA Secretariat, Legal text of NAFTA, http://www.nafta-sec-alena.org/DefaultSite/index_e.aspx?CategoryId=42.

21 *See* Mark T. Berger & Mark Beeson, *APEC, ASEAN+3, and American Power: The History and Limits of the New Regionalism in the Asia-Pacific*, at 1, 2003, University of Queensland, Australia, http://eprint.uq.edu.au/archive/00000732/; *see also* Mark Beeson, *Re-thinking Regionalism: Europe and East Asia in Comparative Historical Perspective*, at 3, (This paper was presented at the Oceanic Conference on International Studies, Canberra July 14-16, 2004), Consequently, much recent scholarship about regional

The international political economy of the East Asian financial crisis (1997-98) equally influenced Asia-Pacific regionalism. In the 1970s and 1980s, Japan, South Korea, Taiwan, Hong Kong, and Singapore, followed by Thailand, Malaysia and Indonesia, were being hailed as miracles of capitalist development. In terms of Western taxonomies, dominant interpretations of the making of the East Asian Miracle were linked to the rise and spread of neo-liberalism or economic liberalism, while many commentators used the dynamic new Asian capitalism to support the case for *laissez-faire* economic policies. The post-Cold War period and the miracle economies of Northeast and Southeast Asia were perceived as a challenge to the West. However, the East Asian financial crisis (1997-98) did eventually precipitate changes in the contours of the post-Cold War international political economy.[22]

A third admixture to the forces of international political economy, or macroeconomic forces, were the terrorist attacks on September 11, 2001, or what has been dubbed 9/11, other incidents of mega-terrorism, and the resulting economics of terrorism that ensued. Subsequent to 9/11, a 2002 Organisation for Economic Co-operation and Development (OECD) report on the economics of terrorism found that heightened terrorist threats do have some long-lasting, if diffuse, macroeconomic repercussions.[23] Indeed, the international political economy of the post-9/11 world and new geo-political realities, in conjunction with a general global economic slowdown, posed a challenge to all economies, both Asian and non-Asian economies.[24] The international political economy of the post-Cold War period, the East Asian financial crisis, the events of 9/11, other incidents of mega-terrorism, and resulting economics of terrorism affected the growth of Asian regionalism. APEC in the 1980s and early 1990s seemed the perfect venue for both benefiting from and facilitating a post-Cold War preoccupation with economic development and integration, and managing relations among the miracle economies of East Asia (Northeast Asia and Southeast Asia). However, changing international political economy environments such as a post-East Asian financial crisis and post-9/11 gravely affected the credibility of APEC.[25]

In addition, one should understand just what is, or includes, the region known as the Asia-Pacific. The region does not include South Asia (India, Pakistan, Afghanistan, Bangladesh and Sri Lanka), and Southwest Asia (the Arab Peninsula, Iraq and Iran). More

processes makes a basic distinction between regional*ism* and regional*ization*. In this formulation, regionalism refers to the political process in which states drive cooperative initiatives. Regionalization, by contrast, refers to processes of economic integration which, while they may be influenced by state policies, are essentially the uncoordinated consequence of private sector activities.

22 *See* Mark T. Berger, *Bringing History Back In: The Making and Unmaking of the East Asian Miracle*, Politik und Gesellschaft Online, International Politics and Society 3/1999, at http://www.fes.de/ipg/ipg3_99/artberger.html.

23 *See* ORG. FOR ECON. CO-OPERATION AND DEV. (OECD*)*, Overview of the OECD: What is it? History? Who Does What? Structure of the Organization?, at http://www.oecd.org/document/18/0,2340, en_2649_201185_2068050_1_1_1_1,00.html (OECD's role has been "to build strong economies in its member countries, improve efficiency, hone market systems, expand free trade and contribute to development in industrialised as well as developing countries."); *see also* Patrick Lenain et al., *The Economic Consequences of Terrorism* (Org. for Econ. Co-operation and Dev., Econ. Dept, Working Paper No. 334, 2002), at http://appli1.oecd.org/olis/2002doc.nsf/linkto/ecowkp (2002)20/$FILE/ JT00129726.PDF.

24 *See* Yeo Lay Hwee, *Culture and Civilizations Dialogue*, Lecture Tour of Asia-Europe Foundation (ASEF) on Countering Unilateralism, Preserving Diversity: Dimensions of Asia-Europe Cooperation, December 2-4, 2003, http://www.iias.nl/asem/index.html?http://www.iias.nl/asem/asem2003/ASEM Conference_CulturesCivilizationsDec2003.html.

25 *See* Mark Beeson, *Multilateralism: American Power and East Asian Regionalism*, at 1, Working Paper Series, No 64, City University of Hong Kong, May 2004, http://www.cityu.edu.hk/searc/WP.html (This paper looks at multilateral processes in the Asia-Pacific region and the impact of American foreign policy on them.).

specifically, the Asia-Pacific region comprises East Asia and Southeast Asia, two socio-geographical subsets (along with Oceania, North America and South America) all constituting the pacific basin. It is a region that is larger than Europe. Some consider it as characterized by geographical, historical, cultural and political diversity, while still maintaining a high degree of mutual interaction among its nation-states. The Asia-Pacific is also a region consisting of some Asia nation-states that are grounded in strong tradition, if not ontological bases in tradition, such as China, Japan, Korea and some Southeast Asia nation-states.[26]

Southeast Asian countries emerged from colonialism in the 1950s and 1960s. These countries faced problems of poverty, overpopulation, high birth rates, undeveloped economies and the weight of tradition. For instance, the Malaysian economy was mostly dependent on rubber (40 percent of GDP in the 1950s), with about half of its workforce engaged in the agricultural sector. In the 1980s, these economies underwent restructuring, mostly by shifting from an emphasis on agriculture to industrial development and export-based growth. In addition, many of these economies began to benefit from the transfer of technology such as Japan, Korea and Taiwan. It is a pattern of technology transfer broadly ranging from manufacturing to electronics.[27]

In the 1980s, China became a significant economic partner of most of these ASEAN nation-states. In the mid-1980s, ASEAN nation-states sought to expand exports in the wake of falling commodity prices and growing protectionist sentiment in developed countries. Consequently, expanding economic relations with China ensued. In addition, Japan, under the umbrella of the Fukuda Doctrine (1972), improved its relations with Southeast Asia by forging a special relationship with ASEAN as an organization, which included bilateral relations with ASEAN members.[28]

In comparison to APEC, ASEAN, which was formed in 1967,[29] originally comprised Indonesia, Malaysia, the Philippines, Singapore, and Thailand, and was formed more for political rather than economic reasons. Later joining ASEAN were Brunei in 1984, Vietnam in 1995, and Laos and Myanmar in 1998. Before 1992, ASEAN was mostly concerned with political issues affecting the region. A watershed event in the history of ASEAN was the 1992 summit, when the vision of establishing an ASEAN Free Trade Area (AFTA) was adopted. Consequently, ASEAN shifted from an emphasis on politics to economic cooperation.[30]

In 1989, APEC presented an alternative to ASEAN nations. However, the idea of APEC had to be first borne, and then affected into a regional economic cooperation organization. There are several historical accounts offered in explanation for the beginnings of APEC.

---

26 *See* Tan Tai Yong, *The Post-War History of East and Southeast Asia*, Asia-Europe Environment Forum, ASEF University, 2000, http://www.asef.org/asef-uni/3_infohub/infohub_m_library.html.

27 *Id.*

28 *See* Jiro Okamoto, *Japan's View on "East Asian Economic Zone*," (Institute of Development Economy, Jetro, October 8, 2001), http://www.npf.org.tw/English/Publication/TE/TE-R-090-026.htm, "The "Fukuda Doctrine" declared, among other things, that Japan would never become a military power again, it would pursue mutual confidence building with ASEAN members, and it would assist their economic development as an equal partner;" *see also* Tadahiro Yoshida, *East Asian Regionalism and Japan*, IDE APEC Study Center, Working Paper Series 03/04 – No. 9, March 2004, APEC Study Center Institute of Developing Economies, Jetro, at http://www.ide.go.jp/English/Publish/Apec/pdf/apec15_wp9.pdf, "The Fukuda Doctrine was epoch-making because it signaled Japan's official recognition of the ASEAN nations as friendly partners in Asia. The Fukuda Doctrine was a sign of the growing importance of Asia to Japan."

29 ASEAN, *supra* note 8.

30 *See* Jose L. Tongzon, *The Challenge of Regional Economic Integration: The Vietnamese Perspective*, The Developing Economies, XXXVII-2 (June 1999), 137-61, 137 n.1, *see also* Kernial Singh Sandhu, et al., THE ASEAN READER, Singapore: Institute of Southeast Asian Studies (1992).

Some of these historical accounts are distinctive, while others offer histories that overlap other historical accounts.

In the late 1980s and 1990s, there was a growing inclination towards Pacific regionalism. Regional cooperation in Western developed economies provided ample example and incentive. For instance, there was the deepening European integration or the EC-92 that led to a fear of a fortress Europe, and the U.S. decision to form a preferential trade agreement (PTA) with Canada.[31] In 1980, the Pacific Economic Cooperation Conference (PECC) was formed.[32] PECC was a government-supported private body, and a novel initiative striving for creation of a new regional economic framework. However, ASEAN showed little enthusiasm for its agenda. ASEAN perceived the larger institution alternative as potentially threatening to its integrity and solidarity.

During an earlier 1986 meeting of the PECC, a standing committee created the Trade Policy Forum (TPF) for purpose of regularly reviewing macroeconomic conditions, other conditions in the Asia-Pacific region, monitoring GATT trade round negotiations, and exploring trade policy issues deemed important to the region. Subsequent to APEC being established in 1989, the TPF contributed to APEC's Committee on Trade and Investment (CTI), various sub-fora and expert groups. In 1989, when APEC was established, PECC became the only non-government observer of APEC. The TPF both formally and informally subsequently contributed to the CTI,[33] and other forums, such as, the WTO, Asian Development Bank (ADB)[34] and United Nations Conference on Trade and Development (UNCTAD).[35]

There were other pre-1989 attempts at Asian regionalism. In the late 1960s, although not effected, the concept of a Pacific free trade area (PAFTA) was advanced. In 1966, there was a first meeting of the Southwest Asian Ministerial Conference for Economic Development. In 1968, the Pacific Basin Economic Council was established.[36] In the 1970s, there was also advanced, but not affected, a concept of an Organization for Pacific Trade and Development (OPTD), which many hail as an Asian-Pacific version or clone of the Organization for Economic Cooperation and Development (OECD).[37]

---

31 *See* Maurice Schiff, *Small Is Beautiful: Preferential Trade Agreements and the Impact of Country Size, Market Share, Efficiency, and Trade Policy*, World Bank, Working Paper 1688, October 1966, http://www.worldbank.org/html/dec/Publications/Workpapers/wps1668-abstract.html.

32 Pacific Economic Cooperation Council (PECC), http://www.pecc.org/, "PECC is a unique tripartite partnership of senior individuals from business and industry, government, academic and other intellectual circles."

33 TPF WWW Homepage, http://www.pacific.net.id/content/TPF/public.htm, "Trade Policy Forum is one of the key policy groups of the Pacific Economic Cooperation Council, an organization of business, government and academic."

34 Asian Development Bank (ADB), http://www.adb.org/, "ADB is a multilateral development finance institution dedicated to reducing poverty in Asia and the Pacific."

35 United Nations Conference on Trade and Development (UNCTAD), UNCTAD XI Home, http://www.unctadxi.org/templates/Startpage____4.aspx, "The Member States of UNCTAD gathered in São Paulo, agreed on a Declaration that they called "The Spirit of São Paulo". The decisions adopted at UNCTAD XI, in addition to the Bangkok Plan of Action, form a solid basis to build upon and are essential instruments in the Member State's continued commitment to support UNCTAD in fulfilling its mandate as the focal point within the United Nations for the integrated treatment of trade and development, on the road to its twelfth session in 2008."

36 Japan Ministry of Foreign Affairs, APEC Information, History of Asia-Pacific Cooperation, http://www.mofa.go.jp/policy/economy/apec/1995/info/history.html.

37 *See* David MacDuff & Yuen Pau Woo, *APEC as a Pacific OECD Revisited*, (Paper was prepared for the APEC International Assessment Network (APIAN) and presented to the APEC Study Centres International

There is also a more Asian-specific viewpoint to the history of APEC that contains slight variations from the Hawke-originating theme, which attributes the original idea of APEC to former Prime Minister Robert Hawke of Australia. The issue of an Asian regional trading bloc was of great concern to Asian leaders. In particular, the controversial Malaysian Prime Minister Mahathir Mohamad proposed the formation of an East Asian economic group in response to perceived threats from North America, Europe and Australia. Fearing marginalization, Mahathir invited several East Asian countries to Canberra, Australia to discuss a new regional group. This initial proposal did not include the U.S. and Canada. It was at the insistence of Japan that these North American countries be included, to avoid harming the existing trans-Pacific trading relationship.[38] Moreover, even Hawke's initial proposal did not envision the participation of the U.S. and Canada. Rather, his initial vision focused on the importance of regional cooperation among Australia, New Zealand, South Korea, Japan and the six members of ASEAN.[39] Historically, what became the ASEAN Plus Three group comprises the nations that Mahathir earlier proposed for an East Asian Economic Caucus (EAEC). Practically speaking, the idea of an EAEC evolved into the ASEAN Plus Three group.[40]

Most recognize the origin of ASEAN as dating back to 1989, as a part initiative of Robert (Bob) Hawke, then Prime Minister of Australia (1983-1991), and Australia; part Japan;[41] and others. However, Hawke more than any other source is credited with the initial idea of an economic gathering of nation-states. The stimulus for this meeting was Hawke's January 1989 call for more effective cooperation among Asia-Pacific economies.[42] An APEC declaration from the 1989 meeting contains a special acknowledgement to the people and government of Australia. Conversely, APEC ascribes as its beginning that, "APEC was established in response to the growing interdependence among Asia-Pacific economies and to the need to advance Asia-Pacific economic dynamism and sense of community."[43] Nonetheless, the origin of the APEC forum is mostly attributed to an earlier initiative of Robert Hawke, who as a member of the Australian Labor Party, and a former trade union

Consortium Meeting, Merida, Mexico, May 23-24, 2002; *see also* Merit E. Janow, *APEC: An Assessment*, (Discussion Paper Series, APEC Study Center, Columbia University, January 1997), at 7-9.

38 Bowles, *supra* note 19, at 57-58.

39 Janow, *Id.,* at 8, at footnote 17, "Press reports indicate that Japan's Prime Minister Takeshita wrote Prime Minister Hawke in March supporting the Seoul plan. In April, Hawke sent a senior Australian diplomat, Dick Woolcott on a series of talks throughout Asia on the proposed grouping and its draft agenda." (Internal citations omitted).

40 *See* Edward J. Lincoln, *Taking APEC Seriously*, Policy Brief No. 92, Brookings Institute, December 2001, at 4.

41 Takeshi Isayama, *supra* note 10, During the 1980s, North America and Europe had initiated steps toward regional integration. The question of Asian integration resulted in Japan's Ministry of International Trade and Industry (MITI), which was earlier call the Trade Agency and the Ministry of Commerce and Industry, fearing that the development of regional blocs in North American and Europe would leave the Asia-Pacific region behind others. The MITI established a research group for purpose of debating the future of the Asia-Pacific region, subsequently concluded that an organization such as APEC was needed. This finding paralleled a similar debate that occurred in Australia at about the same time; *see also* Japan Ministry of Economy, Trade and Industry (METI), http://www.meti.go.jp/english/.

42 Chairman's Summary Statement, Asia-Pacific Economic Cooperation, Ministerial Meeting, Canberra, 6-7 November 1989.

43 Canada Foreign Affairs, Canada-APEC, A Brief History of APEC, http://www.dfait-maeci.gc.ca/canada-apec/history-en.asp.

leader, believed in government by consensus.[44] As early as 1983, Hawke envisioned the future of Australia as being intertwined with the Asia-Pacific region.[45]

In 1989, Australia proposed the formation of an intergovernmental forum called APEC. Thereafter, the first APEC meeting of foreign and trade ministers from twelve Asia-Pacific economies was convened in Canberra, Australia. The initial member economies were Australia, Brunei Darussalam, Canada, Indonesia, Japan, the Republic of Korea, Malaysia, New Zealand, the Republic of the Philippines, Singapore, Thailand and the United States. In, 1989, there were six ASEAN members of APEC, being Brunei, Indonesia, Malaysia, Philippines, Singapore, and Thailand. As a result, the original nation-states included ASEAN members, Australia, Canada, Japan, Korea, New Zealand and the U.S. In later years, APEC expanded its members to include Chile, China, Chinese Taipei, Hong Kong, Mexico, Papua New Guinea, Peru, Russia, and Viet Nam.[46]

In order to understand the Bogor goals and how it affects APEC in the new millennium, an APEC history of its annual meetings and minister meetings, including leaders' meetings, should be considered in reference to three historical periods. These periods are the pre-Bogor goals period, Bogor goals period, and post-Bogor goals period. One source described the earlier history of APEC in terms of the historical categorizations of birth and childhood (1989-1991), adolescence (1992-1994), and proliferation and accelerated development (1995-present).[47] However, the present for this source constituted the 1997 APEC summit, and this source could not have reasonably anticipated the directional growth of APEC, especially the growth and evolution manifest in the 2004 APEC-Chile summit. Categorizations built around the Bogor goals are more appropriate, because as previously mentioned some critiques link APEC's survivability and continuing relevancy to the success or failure in accomplishing the Bogor goals.

A more official history, rather than pre-history, of APEC ranges from the first minister meeting at Canberra, Australia in 1989 to the minister meeting and leaders' meeting convened at Santiago, Chile in 2004. Understanding the history of APEC meetings should lend understanding to the importance of the 1994 Bogor goals and issues of survivability and relevancy of APEC in the new millennium.

---

44 National Museum of Australia Home, Prime Ministers of Australia – Hawke, http://www.nma.gov.au /primeministers/12.htm.

45 *See Moves Towards Asianisation: Australia's "Asian Future", and the "Labor" Side of Politics*, The Asianisation of Australia: volume 1, section 8 (Last updated October 2000), *citing* Halliwell, Malcolm, *Fighting over Asia*, (Letter), The Australian, 31 October 1994, p. 8. "In 1994, former Labor prime minister Bob Hawke continued on with his previous pronouncements when he proclaimed that 'I said in my first days as prime minister that Australia's future depended upon becoming more enmeshed with Asia;'" *see also Moves Towards Asianisation: Australia's "Asian Future", and the "Labor" Side of Politics*, The Asianisation of Australia: volume 1, section 8 (Last updated October 2000), *citing* The Sunday Mail, 23 June 1985; cited in: Dique, Dr. J.C.A., *Immigration - A Policy of Perfidy*, Veritas, Bullsbrook, Western Australia, c1985, p. 61.

46 Asia-Pacific Economic Cooperation, Member Economies, http://www.apec.org/apec/member_ economies.html.

47 The leaders of Asian Pacific Economic Cooperation (APEC), APEC FAQ, International Economics, Chinese University of Hong Kong (2000), http://intl.econ.cuhk.edu.hk/topic/index.php?did=16#ref, *citing* Lu Jianren, *Asian Pacific Economic Cooperation and China* (1997) (Discussing relationship between APEC and China). [hereinafter APEC FAQ].

Pre-Bogor Goals Period (1989-1993)

The pre-Bogor goals period comprises the ministerial meetings at Canberra, Australia (1989), Singapore (1990), Seoul, Republic of Korea (1991), Bangkok, Thailand (1992) and Blake, Island, in Seattle, Washington (1993). In addition, this period encompasses the first leaders' meeting convened at Blake Island (1993).

First APEC Ministerial Meeting (Canberra, Australia 1989)

The first APEC Ministerial Meeting is held 6-7 November 1989 at Canberra, Australia.[48] This economic consultation addressed issues of strengthening the multilateral trading system and enhancing the potential for success of the then pending Uruguay trade round, assessing both prospects and obstacles to increasing trade and investment flows in the region, and identifying practical common economic interests. The agenda was relatively simple and reflected APEC's early organizational structure. The Chairman's Summary Statement, at paragraph 17 (Carrying Forward Regional Economic Cooperation), expressed the consensus of member economies that at this stage in the development of APEC it was too early to decide upon a particular organizational structure for a ministerial-level forum and the necessary support needed for this sort of mechanism. Rather, paragraph 21 (Carrying Forward Regional Economic Cooperation), despite preferences of some participants, evidences a consensus that a proper support mechanism will be the by-product of both reflection and evolution of APEC's cooperation process.

APEC defined itself in terms of a consensus-based organization, rather than rules-based organization. The Chairman's Summary Statement, at paragraph 16 (General Principles of Asia-Pacific Economic Cooperation), outlines broad areas that the member economies have in common. Paragraph 16 stresses cooperation, non-informal consultation, and most importantly, consensus. Electing to be a consensus-based organization was possible because of lack of more formally structured organization and APEC's earlier emphasis on cooperation, non-formal consultation, and recognition and respect for all participants, including both differing socio-economic systems and levels of development.

In addition, the issue of China participating in these economic consultations was expressly addressed. Paragraph 24 (Carrying Forward Regional Economic Cooperation) acknowledges the importance of China and the respective economies of Hong Kong and Taiwan to the future prosperity of the region. There was a consensus that it is desirable to further consider the involvement of these three economies in the process of Asia-Pacific Economic Cooperation. While the desirability of China's participation was obvious, it was still problematic. Obtaining the participation in economic consultations of China, more so than either Taiwan or Hong Kong, was imperative to Asia-Pacific regionalism. A problem for APEC was that participation of China posed political problems, and not economic problems, in terms of the participation of the three economies at the same time.

Political problems surrounding the participation of China were also linked to China's bid for resumption of membership in GATT 1947. In 1989, China, unlike other APEC member

48 Chairman's Summary Statement, First APEC Ministerial Meeting, Canberra, Australia, 6-7 November 1989.

economies, was not a member of GATT.[49] Nonetheless, and despite its non-GATT-member status, China in the 1980s had already emerged as a major player in the global economy. At the close of the infamous Cultural Revolution (1966-76), China's trade grew dramatically faster than world trade. China's foreign trade rose from about $20 billion in the 1970s to about $475 billion in 2000, or, comparatively, from 0.6 percent of world trade (1977) to 3.7 percent of world trade (2000).[50]

The problem confronting APEC was how to get the three economies of China, Hong Kong and Taiwan to participate at the same time. In 1947, the Republic of China (ROC) was one of the original members of GATT 1947. However, in 1949, the People's Republic of China (China) was established on the mainland and Republic of China (ROC) moved to Taiwan. In 1950, the Republic of China (ROC) resigned from GATT, and the People's Republic of China (China) denounced GATT for ideological reasons. In 1986, the People's Republic of China applied to renew, or resume membership in GATT.[51] A working party was convened to consider China's request of resumption of its original membership.[52] In 1988, a Chinese delegation indicated that China originally assumed contracting party status by accepting the protocol of provisional acceptance, dated 30 October 1947.[53]

A problem for APEC is the China (P.R.C.) – Chinese Taipei debate. More particularly Chinese Taipei includes the separate customs territory of Taiwan, Penghu, Kinmen and Mastu.[54] Previously, in 1965, Taiwan was granted observer status at sessions of the GATT 1947. Observer status was subsequent removed in 1971 following a decision by the United Nations Assembly (UN) that recognized the People's Republic of China as the legitimate government of China. In September 1992, GATT's Council of Representatives did establish a separate working party that examined request for accession of Chinese Taipei. During consultations of the working party, eventually, all contracting parties acknowledged China's viewpoint that Chinese Taipei, as separate customs territory, should not accede to GATT 1947 before China. Issues of China's accession, or resumption, also involved the territories of Hong Kong, then a British Crown Colony, which China resumed sovereignty over on 1 July 1997, and Macao, then a Portuguese colony, which China resumed sovereignty over on 20 December 1999.[55]

---

49 General Agreement on Tariffs and Trade, Oct. 30, 1947, 61 Stat. A-11, T.I.A.S. 1700, 55 U.N.T.S. 194 [hereinafter GATT].

50 *See* Nicholas R. Lardy, INTEGRATING CHINA INTO THE GLOBAL ECONOMY, 4, 178 M. 25, Brookings Institution Press (2002) 4, 178 n.25.

51 *See* Penelope B. Prime, *China joins the WTO: how, why, and what now? The overall, long-term, effects should be positive, but don't expect too much, too soon,* (Statistical Data Included), Business Economics (April 2002), at Table 1, China and Taiwan Join the WTO: Major Milestones, http://www.findarticles.com/cf_dls/m1094/2_37/86851408/p8/article.jhtml?term=.

52 *See* Wang Yi, (ed.), GATT & WTO – LAW AND RULES FOR WORLD TRADE, Publishing House of Law Beijing (1998), 168-74.

53 *Id.*, at 168-74.

54 WTO News: 2001 Press Releases, WTO Successfully Concludes Negotiations on China's Entry, Press/243 17 September 2001, Notes to Editors, http://www.wto.org/english/news_e/pres01_e/pr243_e.htm.

55 *Id.*

Second APEC Ministerial Meeting (Singapore 1990)

The Joint Statement of the Ministerial Meeting shows that present at this meeting, as observers were the ASEAN Secretariat, the PECC and the South Pacific Forum (SPF).[56] The initial tone of the meetings was delivered by then Prime Minister Lee Kuan Yew in a keynote address. An excerpt from his address follows.

> All countries present today have grown faster because of the GATT-IMF multilateral free trade regime. It is in all our interests to keep open the system of free and fair trade. Indeed APEC countries should set themselves up as examples of good GATT abiding citizens of the world and oppose the formation of trading blocs. In that way we will contribute to world economic growth.

At paragraph 4 of the Joint Statement, ministers while recognizing the need for strong regional economic performance, noted that without economic performance neither democratic institutions, nor social justice can flourish and be promoted. Economic growth was therefore seen as a contingent for promoting security in the Asia-Pacific region. The 1990 agenda fairly conformed to and reflected the first agenda of 1989. The agenda, set forth at paragraph 5 of the Joint Statement, included a broad range of topics such as world and regional economic developments/regional economic outlook, global trade liberalization through the GATT Uruguay trade round, and APEC work projects and future participation. Ministers, at paragraph 12 of the Joint Statement, recognized the opening of the Central and East European economies to the world, and perceived this as possibly leading to an increase flow of goods, technology, capital and investment in the region, and possibly new export markets. However, at paragraph 14, there is some reservation, in that ministers hoped that creation of a single European market would lead to the emergence of a more outward-looking economy, rather than a more restrictive trade bloc.

At the 1989 Canberra meeting, there was a consensus that in order for APEC to eventually lead to tangible benefits, there was a need to progress beyond mere agreement on general principles. For this purpose, ministers reached a consensus on more substantive work projects. At paragraph 20 of the Joint Statement, they identified broad areas of cooperation, which included economic studies, trade liberalization, investment, technology transfer and human resource development, and sectoral cooperation. It was also during this meeting that APEC formed seven working groups, addressing trade and investment data, trade promotion, investment and technology transfer, human resource development, regional energy cooperation, marine resource conservation, and telecommunications. Ministers, at paragraph 27 of the Joint Statement, further reaffirmed their earlier commitment at the 1989 Canberra meeting to seek the participation of the three economies, China, Taiwan and Hong Kong, in future consultative meetings of APEC.

Finally, at paragraph 17 of the Joint Statement, there is consensus continuing from the 1989 meeting that the primary objective of APEC was to ensure a successful conclusion of the GATT Uruguay trade round. Pursuant to this purpose, at paragraph 18, the ministers

---

[56] Joint Statement, Second APEC Ministerial Meeting, Singapore, 29-31 July 1990.
It was also during the 1990 meeting that APEC formed seven working groups, addressing trade and investment data, trade promotion, investment and technology, transfer, human resource development, regional energy cooperation, marine resource conservation, telecommunications.

issued the Singapore APEC Declaration on the Uruguay Round, which is contained at Annex B of the Joint Statement. The Singapore Declaration essentially directed that consultations concerning the trade round between APEC representatives should be intensified.

Third Ministerial Meeting (Seoul, South Korea 1991)

The Joint Statement of Ministers reflects several important changes in the goals, agenda, especially future participation of APEC. The most obvious change is the participation of the three economies, China, Taiwan and Hong Kong, all at the same time. This was a significant accomplish for APEC. Paragraph 3 also recognized a keynote speech by H.E. Roh Tae Woo, President of the Republic of Korea from 1988 to 1993.[57] Former President Woo emphasised that APEC, "whose fifteen economies are producing one half of the global output, has reached a stage where an institutional base should be established in order to represent the common economic interests of the region and to promote intraregional trade and economic cooperation."

There are two important aspects of APEC addressed in Woo's keynote speech. Following the enlarged participation of the three economies, especially that of China, it is reasonable to assume that this enlarged participation resulted in both increase to fifteen member economies and a regional body producing one-half of global output. His speech also addressed a problem remnant of the first meeting concerning the organizational structure of APEC. A consensus-based body, rather then rules-based body, reliant on cooperation and non-form consultations was now encouraged to establish a more formal organizational structure. It is perhaps in light of this concern that ministers, at paragraph 23 of the Joint Statement recognised the need to consider possibility of establishing a mechanism on a permanent basis that would provide support and coordination for APEC activities at various levels such as financing APEC activities, apportionment of expenses, and other organisational matters.

The agenda remained in conformity with agendas from previous years. Except for consolidation of APEC's principles and objectives, at paragraph 6 of the Joint Statement, the general goals correspond with that of earlier meetings. The general announced goals are consolidation of APEC's principles and objectives, regional economic trends and issues, Uruguay trade round and regional trade liberalization, APEC work program, and future steps for APEC. In the Seoul Declaration, at paragraph 4, Mode of Operation, APEC reaffirmed cooperation based on consensus building.

The agenda was also expanded. In terms of the APEC work program, ministers increased the work projects by addition of projects in the areas of fishers, transportation and tourism. As a result, the work projects were increased from the ten established at the 1990 Singapore meeting to fifteen work projects. In addition, during this meeting that the idea of open regionalism, as a core concept of APEC, begins to take shape. Open regionalism is generally defined as a concerted and unilateral trade liberalization that is along the lines of the most-favoured-nations (MFN) status.[58] Because one of the four Seoul Declaration goals reads, "to

57 Country Briefings: South Korea, Political forces, Economist (Economist.com), Mar 26th 2004, at http://www.economist.com/countries/SouthKorea/PrinterFriendly.cfm?Story_ID=2536193.

58 Berger, *supra* note 22, at 24, note 38, *citing* Peter Drysdale, David Vines and Brett House, EUROPE AND EAST ASIA: A SHARED GLOBAL AGENDA? in Peter Drysdale and David Vines, eds., EUROPE, EAST ASIA AND APEC: A SHARED GLOBAL AGENDA?, (Cambridge: Cambridge University Press, 1998), 6-9.

reduce barriers to trade in goods and services and investment among participants in a manner consistent with GATT principles." The Seoul Declaration represented the clearest statement to-date of the goals of APEC. The other three Seoul Declaration goals are: "to enhance the positive gains resulting from increasing economic inter dependence...; to develop and strengthen the open multilateral trading system...; to reduce barriers to trade in goods and services and investment among participants in a manner consistent with GATT principles."[59]

Fourth Ministerial Meeting (Bangkok, Thailand 1992)

During this ministerial meeting, the goals and objectives of APEC remain substantial the same as in earlier years, with only a few noticeable changes. One noticeable change was a move toward greater institutionalization. In terms of future steps of APEC, at paragraph 23 of the Joint Statement, ministers expressed appreciation to senior officials for conducting, pursuant to Joint Statement from Seoul (1992), a study based on the Thai Secretariat Working Paper, being Future Steps of APEC. Recognizing that APEC had evolved to a stage where institutionalization could possibly strengthen APEC and enhance efficiency in promoting regional cooperation, ministers agreed, per recommendations of senior officials, that it was time to set up an APEC Secretariat, as an effective support mechanism. It was agreed to establish an APEC fund for financing APEC activities. Ministers endorsed both the Consolidated Report on the Future Steps for APEC and the Bangkok Declaration on APEC Institutional Arrangements, which is contained in Appendix 3 of the Joint Statement.

The most significant change pursuant to greater institutionalization was the establishment of a permanent Secretariat. It was agreed that the seat of APEC Secretariat would be in Singapore. The members agreed to make annual contributions to the APEC fund on proportional basis for covering administrative and operations costs. However, members still remained committed to a consensus-based organization, especially at paragraph 27 of the Joint Statement, by reaffirming APEC is an open and evolving process, and recalling the criteria for participation earlier set forth in the Seoul APEC Declaration, "[T]hat decisions regarding participation be made on the basis of a consensus of all existing participants, and that participation in APEC be open, in principle, to those economies in the Asia-Pacific region."

In terms of future participation, at paragraph 29 of the Joint Statement, members agreed to examine the case of Mexico's membership in APEC and report these findings to the next ministerial meeting (United States 1993). The impetus for considering Mexico as a new member was the growing integration of a North American economy and growing economic links between the North American economy and the Asia-Pacific region.

During this meeting, an Eminent Persons Group (EPG) was also established, comprising individuals from each member economy. Initially, the concept of EPG was to develop a vision in the Asia-Pacific for year 2000, identify problematic constraints, and report to the next ministerial.[60]

---

59 Janow, *supra* note 37, at 10 n.31.

60 Janow, *supra* note 37, at 11 n. 36.

Fifth Ministerial Meeting (Seattle, Washington 1993)

Many contend that the dynamics of APEC as a ministerial-level organization made an abrupt change after President Clinton's 1993 invitation to leaders to attend a meeting at Blake Island, which is attributed as commencing the annual APEC leaders' meetings. The fifth ministerial meeting was convened with the first leaders' meeting, with leaders calling for continuing reductions in trade and investments barriers.[61]

This meeting constitutes the first ministerial meeting of a more institutionalized APEC. Pursuant to greater institutionalization, an APEC Secretariat is now in attendance. In terms of future participation, at paragraph 37 of the Joint Summary, APEC welcomed the admission of two new economies, Mexico and Papua New Guinea. It was also decided to admit Chile at the next ministerial meeting in 1994. As for other possible participation, APEC deferred consideration of other possible new memberships pending senior officials study on APEC's membership policies. The latter also reflected APEC growing institutionalisation. As a result of growing institutionalisation, the agenda is also expanded, reflecting a more structured organization. The items on the agenda listed at paragraph 5 of the Joint Statement are generally the Report of the EPG, economic trends and issues, trade and investment issues, the APEC work program, participation issues, and organizational issues.

The Report of the EPG bears mention.[62] At this time, C. Fred Bergsten chairs the EGP. This EPG report emphasized a need for APEC to accelerate and expand cooperation in order to respond to three pending threats to the continued vitality of the region, being the erosion of the multilateral global trading system, evolution of inward looking regionalism, and the risk of fragmentation within the Asia-Pacific region. The EPG recommended that APEC undertake initiatives in four key areas, which were regional and global trade liberalization, trade facilitation programs, technical cooperation, and further institutionalising APEC. In response, the ministers agreed to develop a more long term vision for open trade in the APEC region, and further proposed a program of initiatives to implement their vision.

At paragraph 10 of the Joint Statement, ministers instructed senior officials to implement the EGP recommendations by developing pragmatic programs for trade liberalization and facilitation, technical cooperation, and most importantly, the structural development of APEC and its decision-making process. Senior officials were further requested to prepare a strategy and program that would advance regional and global open trade, and identify mechanisms for achieving that goal. Ministers, at paragraph 11, also requested the EPG to present specific proposals on achieving long-terms goals. Ministers, as in earlier years, at paragraph 17, reaffirmed that trade and investment liberalization was the cornerstone of APEC. "Strengthening the multilateral trading system, expanding regional and global trade and improving investment rules and procedures in a GATT-consistent manner are, therefore, central APEC objectives. The Uruguay Round must conclude by December 15."

Notwithstanding the namesake of first annual economic leaders meeting, this meeting also established committees on trade and investment, budget and administration, and shows that the EGP was established for a two-year period.

---

61 White House, Office of the Press Secretary, Highlight of the APEC Leaders' Meetings, November 11, 2000, http://clinton4.nara.gov/WH/new/html/Mon_Nov_13_094715_2000.html.

62 Janow, *supra* note 37, at 12 n.37, Report of the Eminent Persons Group, A Vision for APEC: Towards an Asia Pacific Economic Community, at 8 APEC Doc. No. 93-EP-01 (Oct. 1993).

Bogor Goals Period (1994)

This is the year of the Bogor, Indonesia ministry, which resulted in the Bogor goals, being the Bogor Declaration, or the APEC Economic Leaders' Declaration of Common Resolve.[63] The Bogor Declaration or Declaration of Common Resolve reflected a consensus earlier reached at Blake Island. The Bogor Declaration, at paragraph 2, expressed this declaration as a pledge or vision statement of member economies. This vision statement reads as follows.

> [T]o find cooperative solutions to the challenges of our rapidly changing regional and global economy: to support an expanding world economy and an open multilateral trading system; to continue to reduce barriers to trade and investment to enable goods, services and capital to flow freely among our economies; to ensure that our people share the benefits of economic growth, improve education and training, link our economies through advances in telecommunications and transportation, and use our resources sustainably.

It is a vision statement, at paragraph 3, based on recognition of a growing interdependence of an economically diverse region, comprising developed, industrializing and developing economies. APEC's approach is intended to be coherent and comprehensive, and embracing the pillars of sustainable growth, equitable development and national stability. The statement contained in paragraph 6 of the Bogor Declaration, however, is the most important consequence of the Bogor ministry. In anticipation of the new millennium, or twenty-first century, at paragraph 6, ministers agree to adopt a long-term goal of free and open trade and investment in the region. A goal that will be accomplished by further reductions in barriers to trade and investment, and promoting free flows of goods, services and capital, or what they referred to as being in a GATT-consistent manner. Pursuant to this announced goal, ministers also committed to accomplish this goal by a specific date. In particular, ministers agreed to the following.

> [T]o complete the achievement of our goal of free and open trade and investment in the Asia-Pacific no later than the year 2020. The pace of implementation will take into account differing levels of economic development among APEC economies, with the industrialized economies achieving the goal of free and open trade and investment no later than the year 2010 and developing economies no later than the year 2020.

In pursuance of this goal by a certain date, they emphasized the creation of an outward-looking, rather than inward-looking, trade bloc. A possible drawback to their commitment may be found at paragraph 9, which, while recognizing that APEC economies are ready to implement a cooperative arrangement, still allowed those that are not ready to participate to join at a later date. However, the Bogor Declaration did not specify which member economies fit in the year 2010 category and the year 2020 category. As a result, there has been debate concerning which economies fit in these categories such as the case of China, and even debate

---

63 APEC Economic Leaders' Declaration of Common Resolve, Bogor, Indonesia, 15 November 1994.

concerning whether the Bogor Declaration did bind all member economies such as the case of Malaysia.[64]

Another important development stemming from the Bogor Declaration is a renewed interested in creating a dispute settlement service. Its proposed creation was justified as resolving trade and other economic disputes and their recurrences, which hamper the implementation of agreed cooperation arrangements. Ministers agreed, at paragraph 9, to explore possibility of a voluntary consultative dispute mediation service, which would supposedly supplement the WTO dispute settlement mechanism.

However, in fairness to APEC, especially in terms of setting the Bogor-date-specific-goals, they recognized, at paragraph 10, that this was an ambitious goal. "Our goal entails a multiple year effort. We will start our concerted liberalization process form the very date of this statement." A firm implementation plan had yet to be developed for the accomplishment of this ambitious and seemingly larger than life goal. Ministers and senior officials were directed to immediately begin preparing detailed implementation proposals. The history of APEC reveals that there were several attempts and several plans implemented for the purposes of accomplishing the Bogor goals within the specified periods. To-date, all of the implementation strategies have failed. Nonetheless, a focal point of this meeting was also the elemental concern of how best to advance APEC's ambitious Bogor goals.[65]

Ministers and senior officials were also requested to consider the recommendations contained in the second reports prepared by the EPG and the Pacific Business Forum. The second EPG report is significant because it attempted to explain the concept of open regionalism, mostly in response to notions of the concept of APEC being a regional initiative. Instead, APEC should be outward looking, rather than inward looking, by ensuring that whatever opportunities are available in the APEC context are equally available to both non-member Asiatic nations and the global economy.[66] Another important aspect of this meeting is the establishment of the economic committee and policy-level group on small and medium-sized enterprises.

Finally, during the economic leaders' meeting, Jiang Zemin, then China President, in a keynote speech stressed that trade liberalization should be based on the principle of non-discrimination, and that it should accommodate the diversity of the Asian-Pacific region. He urged APEC members to proceed in a gradual, orderly and phased manner,[67] perhaps reminiscent of China's "gradualist" approach to economic development.

---

64 Janow, *supra* note 37, at 17 n. 57.
Malaysia's Prime Minister initially asserted that he did not consider the timetable binding, since the proposal was delivered to the leaders without proper vetting at the level of senior officials. He later introduced the caveat that it was unclear where Malaysia would fit by 2020. Some trade analysts have questioned whether it is fully appropriate to include all of China in the 2020 timetable. They note that some parts of China, such as Guangzhou and Shanghai, will be industrial areas in 2010.

65 White House, *supra* note 61.

66 Janow, *supra* note 37, at 15.

67 APEC 2001 in China, Role of China in APEC, http://www.china.org.cn/e-apec/china-aspec/2.htm (Discussing China's Participation in APEC's Important Activities and APEC activities sponsored by and held in China.) [hereinafter Role of China].

Post-Bogor Goals Period (1995-Present)

During this period, APEC enlarged the areas of economic and technical cooperation. The milestones of this period are the 1995 Osaka Action Agenda, requiring economic and technical cooperation among APEC members; and the 1996 Manila Action Plan (MAPA 1996) that included a collective action plan and individual action plans from its eighteen members.[68] The post-Bogor goals period include the ministerial meetings and leaders' meetings at Osaka, Japan (1995); Subic, Philippines (1996); Vancouver, Canada (1997) Kuala Lumpur, Malaysia (1998); Auckland, New Zealand (1999); Brunei Darussalam (2000); Shanghai, China (2001); Los Cabos, Mexico (2002); and Bangkok, Thailand (2003), and Santiago, Chile (2004).

1995 APEC - Osaka, Japan Summit

On 16-19 November 1995, the seventh APEC ministerial and the third leader's meeting were hosted in Osaka, Japan. Ministers adopted the Osaka Action Agenda,[69] a blueprint for implementing APEC's commitment to free and open trade and investment, business facilitation and economic and technical cooperation.[70] A significant aspect of this meeting was the creation of individual and collective action plans. At paragraph 5 of the Joint Statement, the ministers recognized that, in response to the decisions made by the economic leaders at the Bogor, Indonesia ministry (1994), APEC activities this year focused on the formulation of the Action Agenda to achieve the Bogor Declaration goals. For this reason, the most significant aspect of this meeting was the Osaka Action Agenda. It was the first strategy implemented by APEC for purpose of accomplishing the Bogor goals.[71]

This new focus required intensive and wide-ranging deliberations in all APEC fora.[72] The ministers also agreed to establish the APEC Business Advisory Council (ABAC) in 1996. This need was deemed based on a recognized need for continued cooperation and active involvement of the business and private sectors in APEC activities. In addition, the EPG recommended a fifty percent rule, in that members should reduce by fifty percent or half the transition period for implementing trade liberalization and rule-making reforms that they had committed to in the Uruguay trade round.[73]

Finally, Jiang, then China President, stressed that the importance of revitalizing developing countries to the prosperity of both the Asian-Pacific region and the world should be recognized from a historical viewpoint. Jiang suggested that APEC should evolve into an economic organization with distinctive characteristics of the Asia-Pacific region.[74] As in the

---

68 APEC FAQ, *supra* note 47.

69 APEC Economic Leaders' Declaration for Action, Osaka, Japan, 19 November 1995.

70 White House, *supra* note 61.

71 *See* C. Fred Bergsten, (speech), *Back to the Future: APEC Looks at Subregional Trade Agreements to Achieve Free Trade Goal*, Institute for International Economics, October 31, 2000, Washington, DC (Institute for International Economics), http://www.iie.com/publications/papers/bergsten1000.htm.

72 APEC, Joint Statement, Seventh Ministerial Meeting, Osaka, Japan, Nov 16-17, 1995.

73 APEC Eminent Persons Group, Implementing the APEC Vision, (1995), http://www.apecsec.org.

74 Role of China, *supra* note 67.

previous year, Jiang's speech arguably contains political rhetorical cultural relativism reflecting Chinese notions of Asian values.

1996 APEC – Philippines, Manila Summit

The President of the Republic of the Philippines, H.E. Fidel V. Ramos, opened the meeting by stating that this year's APEC chair, the Philippines, has set three leadership tasks for itself, carrying out the Manila Action Plan for APEC 1996 (MAPA 1996), strengthening economic and technical cooperation, and further engaging the private sector in the APEC process. Ramos stressed that APEC has moved from the commitment-making phase of setting a vision, goals and agenda to an action phase of carrying out individual initiatives and collective initiatives.[75]

Ministers adopted the Manila Action Plan (MAPA '96) for APEC, which included individual and collective action plans for purposes of achieving the Bogor goals. An important aspect of this meeting was the endorsement of improved individual action plans (IAPs). The first strategy manifest in the Osaka (1995) action agenda was being followed by detail in Manila (1998) with implementation of the IAPs.[76] In addition, the ministers endorsed the Information Technology Agreement, which led to the conclusion of the agreement in the WTO. Ministers further agreed that APEC's economic and technical cooperation activities should focus on six priority areas for cooperation, which were identified as human resources, efficient capital markets, economic infrastructure, technologies of the future, sustainable development, and small and medium-sized enterprises.

Jiang Zemin noted that APEC economic and technical cooperation differs from traditional development. The reciprocity for cooperation is equality, mutual benefit and "complementarity." For Jiang, an APEC-approach encompassed recognition of diversity, flexibility, a "gradualist" approach and openness, mutual respect, equality, mutual benefit, consensus and "voluntarity," and combination of individual and collective action.[77]

1997 APEC – Vancouver, Canada Summit

The ministers agreed that the East Asian financial crisis (1997-1998) reinforced the importance of APEC laying the foundation for realizing their longer-term growth potential, which was expressed as still being exceptionally strong.[78] The most important event of this meeting is adoption of the Early Voluntary Sectoral Liberalization (EVSL) initiative. Ministers endorsed the EVSL initiative, which sought to cut tariffs in key economic sectors. Nine priority sectors were identified for immediate action, being chemicals, fish products, forestry products, energy goods and services, environmental goods and services, gems and jewelry, medical equipment, the Telecommunications Mutual Recognition Agreement and toys. Ministers further endorsed a framework of public-private partnerships in infrastructure

---

75 Joint Statement, Eighth APEC Ministerial Meeting, Manila, Philippines, 22-23 November 1996.

76 Bergsten, *supra* note 71.

77 Role of China, *supra* note 67.

78 Joint Statement, Ninth Ministerial Meeting, Vancouver, Canada, Nov 21-22, 1997.

development that aimed at making more resources available for infrastructure investment in the Asia-Pacific region.[79]

During this meeting, Jiang Zemin emphasized that the APEC approach responds to the reality of the Asia-Pacific region, in that it is conducive to achieving a balance of rights, interests and needs of various member economies, while better enabling member economies to give full play to respective capabilities for common development. Moreover, members should decline financial policies in light of their specific conditions. In terms of trade and investment liberalization, Jiang stressed that APEC members should realize the Bogor goals based on the principles of self-determination, voluntarism and flexibility, and by adopting a pragmatic approach to the Bogor timetable. The point stressed was that APEC members should be allowed adjustments in speed and means, in accordance with individualistic nation-specific characteristics resulting in what was deemed an active and steady way.[80]

The most important event of this meeting was the EVSL initiative. APEC now perceived that the Osaka Action Agenda (1995) was experiencing difficulty toward achieving the Bogor goals. As a result, APEC employed a second strategy of sectoral liberalization, the EVSL initiative. Its initial start is a success that is attributable to the first sectoral liberalization in the Information Technology Agreement (1996), which was ratified by the Europeans and others. Facing a perceived failure with the IAPs, despite MAPA '96, APEC considered sectoral liberalization as a more probable means of achieving the Bogor goals.[81]

1998 APEC - Kuala Lumpur, Malaysia Summit

The ministers expressed concern that the East Asian financial crisis (1997-1998) with its associated contagion effects has had serious socio-economic implications for growth, employment and poverty levels in member economies.[82] The ministers requested senior officials to intensify APEC efforts in addressing the social impact of the crisis. Ministers also endorsed the submission of improved individual action plans (IAPs). In addition, joining the ranks of APEC are three new members, which were Peru, Russia and Vietnam.

Ministers also agreed to place the tariff-cutting elements of the priority sectors of the EVSL initiative into the WTO, intending to obtain an early WTO agreement on these sectors by the time of the 1999 Seattle WTO ministerial. In addition, leaders re-committed to help the Asia-Pacific region emerge from the East Asian financial crisis and return to economic growth. The strategy for doing so was a call for economic reforms and stronger international financial architecture.[83]

1999 APEC – Auckland, Australia Summit

The Joint Statement shows that the APEC agenda was broadened to reflect three themes of APEC 99. The themes are expanding business opportunities in the region, strengthening the

79 White House, Office of the Press Secretary, Highlight of the APEC Leaders' Meetings, November 11, 2000, http://clinton4.nara.gov/WH/new/html/Mon_Nov_13_094715_2000.html [hereinafter White House].

80 Role of China, *supra* note 67.

81 Bergsten, *supra* note 71.

82 Joint Statement, Tenth APEC Ministerial Meeting, Kuala Lumpur, Malaysia, 14-15 November 1998.

83 White House, *supra* note 79.

functioning of markets, and, most importantly, broadening support for APEC.[84] Broadening support for APEC is undoubtedly based upon, as set forth at paragraph 46 of the Joint Statement, building greater understanding of APEC's goals.

The ministers were attempting to maintain the momentum for economic reform as many regional economies emerged from the East Asian financial crisis. Ministers also approved an agenda designed to foster a new dynamic for the region, strengthen and open markets, reform regulatory regimes, enhance competition, and create greater opportunities for businesses. In addition, there were the goals of launching a new round of WTO trade negotiations and ensuring preparations for possible Y2K problems.[85] Finally, in 1999 and beyond potential new members include Russia, India, Sri Lanka, Pakistan, Ecuador, Mongolia, Panama, and Colombia.

This meeting also evidences a third strategy toward accomplishing the Bogor goals, implying the earlier strategies, such as, Osaka Action Agenda (1995), IAPs (MAPA 1996), and the EVSL initiative (1997), are deemed to be failing. It is a strategy built around a greater dependence that is within a broader liberalization through the launch of a new round of trade talks, which focused on the trade talks in Seattle (WTO 1999).[86] As for China's participation, Jiang stressed that APEC can only maintain its vitality and make achievements, by keeping its nature as an economic form, maintaining the APEC approach, and attaching importance to economic and technical cooperation.[87]

2000 APEC - Brunei Darussalam Summit

It was hoped that the APEC leaders' meeting in Bandar Seri Begawan, Brunei Darussalam on November 15-16, 2000, would build on the progress of the seven previous leaders' meetings. In 1994, the ministers had reached a landmark agreement to achieve the goal of free and open trade and investment in the region no later than 2010 for industrialized economies and 2020 for developing economies, the Bogor goals. In 1993, APEC leaders envisioned an Asia-Pacific that harnessed the energy of its diverse economies, strengthened cooperation and promoted prosperity. To that end, ministers called for continued reduction of trade and investment barriers to allow goods, services, capital and investment to flow freely among APEC economies. [88]

In 2000, C. Fred Bergsten, former EGP chairperson, observed that the origins of APEC, in conjunction with the work of the EPG, provided a perspective on where APEC then stood and what needed to be accomplished in the up-coming ministerial meetings.[89] Bergsten perceived APEC to have been functioning on a two-track system. One track was captured in the Seattle (1993) and Bogor (1994) ministerial meetings. The emphasis of the first track is best described by former President Clinton, host of the Seattle summit, in exclaiming, "We want to put together a community of Asia-Pacific economies." The other track characterized the 1994 Bogor goals of achieving free and open trade in the Asia-Pacific region by 2010 or 2020. While the 1993 Seattle summit may have been praiseworthy, the 1994 Bogor summit

---

84 Joint Statement, Eleventh APEC Ministerial Meeting, Auckland, New Zealand, 9-10 September 1999.

85 White House, *supra* note 79.

86 Bergsten, *supra* note 71.

87 Role of China, *supra* note 67.

88 White House, *supra* note 79.

was more spectacular for having set a free-trade goal. The Osaka Summit showed the way to accomplish the Bogor goals, while the 1996 Subic summit is hailed for the Information Technology Agreement.

As for accomplishing the Bogor goals, Bergsten had doubts, perceiving APEC as experiencing an eroding process over the years. The Bogor goals have been extremely difficult to implement. By the year 2000, APEC had attempted three different strategies for achieving the Bogor goals, all of which failed. Bergsten proposed a fourth strategy for APEC. It was a strategy of developing on a *de facto* basis, what economists refer to as revealed preferences. He perceived this strategy in terms of an evolution in regionalism. It is an evolutionary process suggesting the evolution of a large number of subregional trade and financial arrangements. This proposed strategy required that member economies work in smaller groups, and set their own respective timetables with selected partners. In 2000, there was a small occurrence of such agreements at various stages: some agreed upon, some were being negotiated, some were being studied, and others were being considered. Free trade areas represented part of global movement toward subregional and plurilateral trade agreements, for example, the arrangements of Singapore-New Zealand, Japan-Singapore, Japan-Korea, Japan-Mexico, and Korea-Chile.[90]

APEC leaders earlier foresaw this problem during the 1994 Bogor, Indonesia ministry, when setting a goal of free trade by 2010. Later in the Bogor Declaration, leaders raised the issue of the creation of sub regional arrangements. It was an issue of the compatibility of sub regional arrangement with APEC goals and strategies.

2001 APEC – Shanghai, China Summit

The year of 2001 is a challenging year for APEC because of two primary reasons. APEC had to contend with both a near global economic shutdown and the events of September 11, 2001. It is the first APEC meeting following the 9/11 attacks. This also presented the issue of whether APEC as an economic forum was capability of confronting this crisis. In Shanghai, APEC leader maintained a commitment to a traditional economic mission, while also taking a strong stance against the threat of global terrorism. As a result, a counter terrorism program evolved, with initiatives also launched that focused on both advancing APEC's Bogor goals and development of an e-APEC strategy, which was also in response to fear of an economic shutdown.[91]

APEC's 2001 theme was, "Meeting New Challenges in the New Century: Achieving Common Prosperity through Participation and Cooperation." There had been an economic slowdown in the U.S., Japan and Europe, which the ministers perceived as dampening prospects of a global and regional economy. Recent 9/11 terrorists attack in the U.S., posed risk to industries and consumer confidence. Nonetheless, ministers agreed to strengthen

89 Bergsten, *supra* note 71.

90 *Id.*

91 California Chamber of Commerce Home Page, What's Happening in APEC?, Business Briefing, Vol. 12– February 2002, http://www.calchamber.com/documents/apec_happening.htm [hereinafter What's Happening in APEC?].

cooperation in confronting short-term problems, while emphasizing the importance of achieving the Bogor goals within the agreed period.[92]

Ministers also urged that China's accession be finalized at the forthcoming WTO ministerial conference. Ministers reiterated strong support for approval of accession to the WTO by Chinese Taipei at that conference and the advancement of WTO accession by the Russian Federation and Viet Nam. In addition, ministers supported the participation of all acceding economies in the new round of WTO negotiations.

The issue of confronting the threat of global terrorism is of critical importance because APEC had historically, at least explicitly, confined itself to economic issues. APEC, now, when confronting threat of global terrorism, explicitly addressed political issues. As a result, the significance of this first post-9/11 meeting is APEC, as a gathering of world leaders after the attacks, committed to both coordinating a response to terrorism and trying to minimize the economic effects of terrorism. The threat of terrorism had become a global concern, in that it now manifests a risk both to security of nations and economic prosperity, for Asian and non-Asian nations alike.[93]

Finally, in the Shanghai Declaration, leaders endorsed the pathfinder approach for attaining the Bogor goals of free and open trade and investment. "Leaders reaffirm that those economies ready to initiate and implement a cooperative arrangement may proceed to do so, consistent with the Bogor Declaration.... Use of 'pathfinder initiatives' based on a group of members piloting the implementation of the initiatives, will invigorate progress towards the Bogor Goals." A problem of pathfinder approach was the subsequent interpretation of its concept by members. A narrow interpretation would still require a full consensus of members, despite some members desiring to delay implementation. Contrarily, it could be interpreted as being consistent with the spirit of the Shanghai Accord and the principle of voluntarism. The essence of pathfinder approach is that it allowed members to join when they were ready. For instance, the non-binding investment principles can be implemented, in part or in full, in accordance with an agreed timetable that reflects a coalition of the willing. The principles on trade facilitation could also have been readily transformed into an APEC action agenda.[94]

2002 APEC - Los Cabos, Mexico Summit

The 2002 theme for APEC is "Expanding the Benefits of Cooperation for Economic Growth and Development, Implementing the Vision." The keynote speech of Luis Ernesto Derbrez highlighted growth policies for trade and investment, building human capital and micro enterprises, the participation of women and young people, and improving the functioning of APEC.

APEC continued with the theme of TILF. One source, however, argued that APEC should also address the controversial "Singapore issues," which the WTO would not address

---

92 Joint Statement, Thirteenth APEC Ministerial Meeting, Shanghai, People's Republic of China, 17-18 October 20001.

93 What's Happening in APEC?, *supra* note 91.

94 APEC International Assessment Network (APIAN), Remaking APEC as an Institution, The Third APIAN Policy Report, August 2002, at 9, [hereinafter APIAN Assessment].

until 2003.[95] In the following year, the fifth ministerial conference of the WTO in Cancun, 10-14 September 2003, ended without a consensus.[96] In 2003, then WTO Chairperson Luis Ernesto Derbez attributed lack of consensus partly to members remaining entrenched on the "Singapore issues,"[97] which are issues of trade and investment, trade and competition policy, trade facilitation, and transparency of government procurement.[98] It was also suggested that growing regionalism is a major concern, because the WTO rules, Article XXIV of GATT 1947, did not provide an adequate standard ensuring that they are non-discriminatory. The importance of RTAs being consistent with the WTO was a major concern.

In regards to the new and evolving political agenda of APEC, one source observed that the 2001 APEC meeting would probably be recorded in history as the occasion on which Bush, Jiang and Putin realigned the globe. In some viewpoints, especially Bush, the credibility of APEC is becoming dependent on an agenda for counter terrorism. Some, perhaps not so critical of tying APEC's credibility to an agenda for counter terrorism, found that these deliverables were no more than a repackaging of what APEC was already doing in finance and transportation.[99]

This meeting is also heavily influenced by the events of 9/11. The history of APEC lets us know that APEC was formed as an economic consultative group, which allowed leaders of Asian-Pacific economies to get together and discuss trade and the global economy. A distinguishing feature of the Los Cabos meeting was the dominance of security issues. Bush had a priority of issues concerning Saddam Hussein and Iraq. The problem of impending war in Iraq, in conjunction with the meeting being led by Mexico, naturally lent to President Bush's priorities. Because Mexico was one of the rotating seats on the United Nations Security Council, and Bush wanted Mexico's backing on a resolution, or ultimatum, concerning Saddam and Iraq.[100] While APEC had positively expanded to become a useful venue for discussing security and diplomatic issues, the negative consequences were an economic agenda that had largely disappeared, resulting in formal statements that were seemingly vague and lacking in content.[101]

---

95 *See* C. Rammanohar Reddy, *Decision time on Singapore issues at WTO*, THE HINDU, Online Edition of India's National Newspaper, July 28, 2003, http://www.hinduonnet.com/thehindu/2003/07/28/stories/2003072803001200.htm.

96 WTO News, Summary of 14 September 2003, Day 4: Conference ends without consensus, http://www.wto.org/english/thewto_e/minis_e/min03_14sept_e.htm.

97 *Id.*

98 WTO news: 2002 news items, 16 January 2002, International Conference on Financing for Development, Statement by Mr. Ouedraogo, WTO Deputy Director-General to the final Preparatory Committee, 14-25 January 2002, New York, USA, http://www.wto.org/english/news_e/news02_e/ ouedraogo_stat_fin%26 dev_conf_e.htm.

99 Asia Pacific Foundation of Canada, APEC Study Centre in Canada, Report on International Symposium on Perspectives for APEC: 2002 and Beyond December 3 and 4, Mexico City, http://www.asiapacific.ca/about/apec/apec2002.pdf.

100 Bush Meets With Asian Leaders at APEC Summit, CNN Transcript, Aired October 26, 2002, http://edition.cnn.com/TRANSCRIPTS/0210/26/cst.11.html

101 Edward Lincoln, *supra* note 40, at 1.

2003 APEC - Bangkok, Thailand Summit

As one source noted, "APEC 2003 was not a disaster for the U.S. but neither was it a crowning success."[102] In the past thirty years, Indonesia had led ASEAN and Southeast Asia. In 1997, during the East Asian Financial Crisis and stepping down of President Suharto, leadership had passed to Singapore. Because of Singapore Prime Minister Goh Chok Tong and Malaysian Prime Minster Mahthir Mohammed stepping down, Thailand and Thaksin arose as the new leadership.[103]

During 2003, China made state visits to Thailand and Australia. The problem of terrorism seemed not to be a primary concern for China, in that China did not talk much about the problem of terrorism. Rather, China more so talked about the future, China's role in the future, China's intent to become a major player in the region, the need for free trade, and China's intention to increase investment and prosperity for the region via increased trade. Comparatively, the U.S., represented by President Bush appeared more so focused on the past and issues of security and war on terrorism, including war on Iraq.[104] Finally, a Counter Terrorism Task Force and other initiatives related to the problem of growing terrorism were established, eventually producing the APEC Counter Terrorism Action Plan.[105]

2004 APEC- Santiago, Chile Summit

The theme for this year is "One Community, One Future." In 2004, the goal of APEC remains the advancement of free trade. However, in retrospective, when one examines the history of APEC from its 1989 inception to its present body in 2004, one notices discernible, albeit subtle, differences in organization structure, policies, and goals. The leaders' meeting in the Chilean capital of Santiago on 21-22 November 2004 is an organization different in appearance and substance. The most important new ingredient of the APEC agenda is explicit concerns of a political nature, rather than the former APEC promotion of aid and trade in the Asia-Pacific region.

As a reminder of the 2003 summit, U.S. President Bush continued his diplomatic agenda concerning the fight against terrorism. In terms of politics, most problematic for an American populace is that economics, and not politics, dominate the agenda. Conversely, in terms of economics, this meeting is dominated by moves for bilateral free trade agreements.

Initially, APEC, as a forum of only twelve members that met at ministerial-levels, emphasized helping poorer member economies promote economic growth through technical assistance and trade. APEC has grown to now include Japan, the U.S., China, Australia, Southeast Asia and Latin American countries. APEC continues to operate by consensus approach and without legally binding text such as an international treaty. It had experienced some degree of institutionalization, but remained a loose institutional structure by virtue of consensus approach and continuing voluntarism. It is for this reason, membership in APEC is

---

102 Christopher W. Runckel, APEC 2003 and The U.S. Role in Asia, Runckel & Associates, 2003, http://www.business-in-asia.com/apec2003.html.

103 Report on International Symposium on Perspectives for APEC: 2002 and Beyond, December 3 and 4, Mexico City, http://www.business-in-asia.com/apec2003.html.

104 Business-In-Asia.Com, APEC 2003 and The U.S. Role in Asia, http://www.business-in-asia.com/apec2003.html.

105 2004 APEC Outcomes, *supra* note 1.

loosely defined. Membership is a simple criterion of geography, belonging to the Asia-Pacific region. Russia's membership exemplifies the looseness of this criterion for membership.

On the positive side, due to President Clinton's 1993 proposal at Seattle, APEC's economic consultative forum evolved into an annual meeting of top-level presidents and prime ministers. Clinton's 1993 proposal is significant because it represented APEC transition from economic only forum to both economic and, at least implicitly, political forum. What was hailed as an apolitical forum did implicitly commence an evolution to wider agenda embracing economic and political regional concerns. There has always been an implicit and hidden political agenda of APEC. At its inception, it is announced that the nomenclature of economies in reference to members should enjoy a freedom apart from typical political concerns. The reference of economic leaders' meeting, as opposed to, simply, a meeting of Asia-Pacific nations, was arguably done so in pursuance of political objectives.

In Bogor, Indonesia (1994), APEC set a goal for trade and investment liberalization to be accomplished by 2010 for industrialized members and 2020 for developing members. The Bogor goals were to be accomplished by action guidelines adopted at the Osaka ministry (1995). As continuing proof of a commitment to consensus approach and voluntarism, the Bogor goals and pledges of implementation were not to be coerced, and in the absence of a more formally structured enforcement mechanism, implementation was depended on no more than peer pressure.

Initially, APEC pursued a liberalization agenda that supplemented and accelerated the WTO goal of multilateral trade negotiations. However, due to complications and speed in pursuing liberalization within the WTO structure, there evolved a growing preference for FTAs on a bilateral basis. The Chile summit evidenced this growing international trend and saw many opportunities for members to search for new bilateral trade agreements.

Before the WTO and pending Uruguay round trade talks, the prevailing fear of Asian nations was trade blocs dominated by the U.S., Japan and Germany. History now reveals a new growing fear born of a new international political economy concern. In 2004, the new and prevailing fear is being left behind in the region-wide moves for FTAs, with China seen as taking the initiative. Moreover, the scope of these FTAs are directed to agreements to make the flow of investment and manpower resources easier, and not just simply trade liberalization. These agreements are called Economic Partnership Agreements (EPA), which seek to strengthen bilateral economic relations.

The APEC-Chile summit leaves us with the question of the future role of APEC. Because the summit's showing of diplomacy leaves one with no doubt of the growing importance of politics to APEC's agenda. During this summit, the latter is evidenced by Japan's Prime Minister Junichiro Koizumi's attempt to break a diplomatic stalemate between China and Japan, while reaffirming a Japan-U.S. alliance. This presents critical concerns of what happened to the original economic only agenda of APEC for free-world trade, and prospects of APEC playing a leading role in promoting free trade in the new millennium.[106]

[106] Advancing Free Trade Remains Key Goal of the APEC, Foreign Press Center/Japan, November 24, 2004, http://www.fpcj.jp/e/shiryo/jb/0453.html.

APEC: Credibility and Regionalism

APEC has been criticized as being an undemocratic and non-transparent structure, and examining economic issues to the exclusion of social issues. Separating economic issues from social issues denies reality. Consequently, some social issues that manage to make it on the agenda, such as sustainable human development, are seriously truncated.[107] However, there are many criticisms of APEC, ranging from a failure to respond to the East Asian financial crisis (1997-98), to failing to adequately meet challenge of growing regionalism.

APEC failures are partly attributable to the East Asian financial crisis.[108] This crisis brought into question whether the Asian development model after all lacked substance, especially in merely relying on foreign capital. There is also the question of whether in the beginning too much had been expected of Asian industrialization. Debates also ensued concerning how to deal with the Asian financial crisis and whether the International Monetary Fund's (IMF) prescription was correct.[109] There was also the question concerning the problem of an influx of international short-term capital. During this period, the U.S., Europe and Japan were criticized for doing too little, too late. The East Asian financial crisis left the Asia-Pacific region feeling the blunt of uncertainty, especially about the future. The East Asian financial crisis has been described as Asian economies forgetting to steadfastly pursue an industrialization pattern reflective of Asian reality.[110] Asian economies depended on international short-term capital via financial liberalization for combating capital shortages. If Asian economies had developed their soft infrastructures such as human resources, and hard infrastructures such as road, factories and transportation, and then pursued a more orthodox industrial development path of cultivating industries, this problem would have never intensified to the degree that it did.

The severity of the financial crisis varied from economy to economy, as did the IMF's prescription and proposed solutions to the problems of economic globalization that ensued. One source described the theories of origin of the Asian financial crisis as either a failure in Asian capitalism or Western capitalism. A problem of these theories is that both treat Asia as a block, failing to take cognizance of differing economies, cultures, religions and polities. Treating Asia as a block also ignores the fact that Asian economies were hit at different times, in different ways, with some not even being directly hit.[111] Proposing liberalization and facilitating trade without consideration of the particularities of the various economies, and without confirmation of time needed to weather such crisis, or where the greater problems lie, inevitably created the problem of restructuring economies in a vacuum.

APEC is also criticized for losing sight of its original goals. In an increasingly borderless world, industrial development seeks markets generating maximum benefits for investors, that

---

107 Canada and APEC: Perspectives from Civil Society, First Draft, April 22, 1997, Prepared by the Policy Working Group, Canadian Organizing Network for the 1997 People's Summit on APEC.

108 Takeshi Isayama, *supra* note 10.

109 The International Monetary Fund (IMF), http://www.imf.org/, "The IMF is an organization of 184 countries, working to foster global monetary cooperation, secure financial stability, facilitate international trade, promote high employment and sustainable economic growth, and reduce poverty."

110 Takeshi Isayama, *supra* note 10.

111 *See* Susan Glazebrook, *The Role of the Law in the Asian Financial Crisis*, The paper is based on the Presidential address given by Dr. Glazebrook at the Plenary session of the Inter-Pacific Bar Association Ninth Annual Conference, Bangkok, Thailand, May 1, 1999, http://www.ipba.org/membersonly/papers/documents/glazebrook.pdf.

is, a global market where industries choose and reject economies. Economic alignments are necessary, because a single economy in the global economy cannot maintain international competitiveness and growth in all sectors of an economy. There are comparative and absolute advantages in trade, and every economy tends to enjoy a comparative advantage and even comparative disadvantage.[112] Outward-looking directions are necessary, because an economy cannot close its borders indefinitely in today's global economy. An economy must search for means to form economic links with other economies, or suffer the consequences of autarky. For these reasons, some argue that APEC should return to its origins, and redirect its attention to this new environment.

APEC became the leading forum for political and economic collaboration in the Asia-Pacific region. APEC, by its member economies, was granted a broad agenda for promoting trade and economic cooperation. Pursuant to this broad agenda, APEC members signed the 1994 Bogor Declaration. However, the accomplishment of the Bogor goals would experience a serious setback because of the East Asian financial crisis. Many expected that APEC would find solutions to the financial crisis. A problem for APEC is that it was generally perceived as indecisive and ineffective in meeting this challenge. As recession and economic slowdown took its toll on economies in the region, the prestige of APEC suffered. The political economy of the financial crisis found Asian economies looking to other forms of economic cooperation, if not regionalism. A perception of APEC failing to adequately respond to the financial crisis negatively affected its credibility.[113]

A new thinking about Asian regionalism begins to evolve, which is at least partly attributable to the failure of APEC to deal with the financial crisis. The idea of a new East Asian regionalism was embraced by many Asian economies. There was a commonly held view in Asia, especially Korea and the ASEAN countries, that they had been let down by the West, in particular, the United States and Japan, during the crisis. This view was based on a belief that the West, or the G-7 nations, now G-8, made the financial crisis worst by pulling from their region funds from their banking and financing institutions.[114] For this reason, they felt that more assistance should have come from the West. [115]

---

112 *See* Richard N. Block, et al., *Economic Perspectives on International Labor Standards*, 11 MSU-DCL J. INT'L L. 417, 419 (2002):

Traditionally, economist have referenced the "factor cost model" when discussing international trade. Specifically, the theory suggests that countries should specialize in the production of goods in which they can produce at least cost. . . . [T]heorists take into account a country's productive factor endowments, including land, capital, labor and climate. In applying the factor cost model, economists compare the costs of production of each product both within and between countries. When a jurisdiction has the capability to produce a particular product at least cost compared to other jurisdictions, it is said to have an "absolute advantage." Meanwhile, that country is said to have a "comparative advantage" in a certain product if it can produce that output cheaper relative to other products within its boundaries.

113 *See* Shalendra D. Sharma, *Beyond ASEAN and APEC: Towards a New Asia-Pacific Economic Regionalism*, Vol. 14, No. 3 East Asian Review, 37-48 (Autumn 2002).

114 University of Toronto G8 Information Center: What is the G8?, http://www.g7.utoronto.ca/what_is_g8.html, The six countries at the first summit, held at Rambouillet, France in November 1975, were France, the United States, Britain, Germany, Japan and Italy. They were joined by Canada at the San Juan Summit of 1976 in Puerto Rico, and by the European Community at the London Summit of 1977. From then on, membership in the G7 was fixed, although 15 developing countries' leaders met with the G7 leaders on the eve of the 1989 Paris Summit, and the USSR and then Russia participated in a post-summit dialogue with the G7 since 1991. Starting with the 1994 Naples Summit, the G7 met with Russia at each summit (referred to as the P8 or Political 8). The Denver Summit of the Eight was a milestone, marking full Russian participation in all but financial and certain economic discussions; and the 1998 Birmingham Summit saw full Russian participation, giving birth to the G8 (although the G7 continued to function along side the formal summits).

115 Sharma, *supra* note 113.

This feeling of abandonment by the West was intensified in two respects. The G-7 nations either refused to assist, as in the case with the U.S. and Japan concerning Thailand, or when assisting, as through the IMF, imposed seemingly excessive and stringent demands. Despite the merits of these contentions, there was a consensus among Asian economies that they should reduce their dependence on the G-7 nations and multilateral financial institutions such as the IMF and World Bank.[116]

The aftermath of a growing proclivity toward East Asian regionalism is a resulting credibility problem for APEC. It is a credibility problem only attenuated by its failure at the 1997 Vancouver ministerial meeting to support Japan's proposal for an Asian Monetary Fund (AMF), and further, its endorsement of central role of the IMF in resolving the crisis.[117] This event on the part of APEC alienated many Asian economies. However, the growing idea of East Asian regionalism is claimed not to be an explicit rejection of multilateralism, or global economic integration, rather a claimed consensus of Asian economies regarding mostly regional autonomy, especially in economic matters. Asian economies claimed that a more regionally focused institution could better design more appropriate conditionality than the IMF.[118] This was perceived to be mostly due to closer geographical proximity of Asian economies.[119]

During this period of growing global regionalism, APEC seems caught in the midst of the regionalism versus multilateralism debate. There has yet to be resolved the debate contrasting regionalism to multilateralism in trade.[120] Some criticisms focus on APEC as a regional trading agreement. These critiques perceive liberalization as the cause of social and economic problems, rather than as a solution. In this respect, APEC by adopting a neo-liberal agenda had adopted an incorrect model. There are criticisms that simply center on APEC's adoption of economic liberalization or neo-liberalism. This is mostly an issue of state sovereignty that results from models of regionalism embracing both developed and developing economies. Some development theorists, in challenging liberalization as the best option, argue that the retention of state control over strategic economic instruments and sectors provides more options for development. There are simply critiques such as liberal economists that encourage

---

116 The International Bank for Reconstruction and Development (IBRD) or (World Bank) or (The World Bank Group), http://www.worldbank.org/ (Explaining that The World Bank consists of five institutions: International Bank for Reconstruction and Development; International Development Association; International Finance Corporation; Multilateral Investment Guarantees Agency; International Centre for Settlement of Investment Disputes. In the World Bank Group, there are also the regional development banks, such as the Inter-American Development Bank).

117 Edward Lincoln, *supra* note 40, at 5,

A key motive behind the Chiang Mai Initiative on currency swaps has been to insulate Asian nations from the behavior of Western "speculators" and the policy demands of the IMF. This is a scaled back approach from the AMF proposed by the Japanese government in 1997, but the motive remains the same. In fact, talk of an AMF has not disappeared, though the concept is now carefully couched in terms of making it a clear subsidiary or supplement to the IMF— disbursing funds to troubled Asian countries only with IMF approval. Still, there is an underlying desire to gain more independence from IMF or Western demands.

118 Articles of Agreement of the International Monetary Fund, Art. V, sec. 3(a),

"The Fund shall adopt policies on the use of its general resources, including policies on stand-by or similar arrangements, and may adopt special policies for special balance of payments problems, that will assist members to solve their balance of payments problems in a manner consistent with the provisions of this Agreement and that will establish adequate safeguards for the temporary use of the general resources of the Fund."

119 Sharma, *supra* note 113.

120 Bowles, *supra* note 19.

a multilateral approach, rather regional approach, to trade liberalization. Regionalism for these critiques is a second best choice to multilateralism.[121]

There are also criticisms that speak to APEC's vagueness and generalities. APEC is perceived by some as saying much the same every year since its 1989 formation, and suffering a failure in its primary goal of TILF and the Bogor goals. The 2004 APEC-Chile summit has been described as an APEC weekend resulting in with a 9,000-word, 24-page commitment to continue being vague, and as, "a voluntary come-along-to-the-party-if-you-wish organisation."[122] The 2005 APEC-Busan, South Korea summit hardly differed and reflected the same routine, especially formal statements that continue to be seemingly vague and lacking in content.

A growth in FTAs may also have challenged APEC's goal of TILF. While the world witnesses a struggling WTO Doha Development Agenda, there are increasing numbers of FTAs or PTAs.[123] Between 1990-1994, the number of FTAs substantially jumped, in that twenty-nine new FTAs were reported to the WTO. From 1995-1999, the number of FTAs grew by an additional sixty-four agreements with twenty-eight of these FTAs being transition economies. After 2000, South-South agreements accounted for a larger percentage of the new FTAs reported to the WTO. In a three-year period (2000-2002), there was a fifty-five percent growth in the number of new FTAs.[124]

The growing proliferation of FTAs pose a threat to the WTO goal of free trade, in that political considerations for entering FTAs may be overriding economic considerations offered via the avenue of the WTO. The world has witnessed a growth in both FTAs motivated solely by political considerations, and FTAs motivated by a combination of economic and political considerations. If motivations for FTAs are grounded in political considerations, then the WTO may lose its appeal as a feasible alternative.[125] The problem of FTAs motivated by solely political considerations, or even in part by political considerations, is that they can in

---

121 *Id.*, *citing* A. Singh, *Openness and the Market Friendly Approach to Development: Learning the Right lessons from Development Experience*, World Development, Vol. 22, No. 12 (December 1994).

122 *See Red tape chokes Apec, Focus*, November 24, 2004, THE STANDARD, Sing Tao Newspaper Group and Global China Group, http://www.thestandard.com.hk/stdn/std/Focus/FK22Dh02.html.

123 *See* Andrew L. Stoler, *Preferential Trade Agreements and the Role and Goals of the World Trade Organization*, Institute for International Business, Economics & Law, The University of Adelaide, Conference on Free Trade Agreements in the Asia-Pacific Region: Implications for Australia, 4-6 July 2004, Perth, Australia, at 2 n. 3.

In the time since the launch of the Doha Round, Australia – long seen as one of the most ardent backers of the GATT-WTO – has negotiated and agreed PTAs with Singapore, Thailand and the United States. Canberra has embarked on a feasibility study of a PTA with China and has been invited by ASEAN members to consider joining New Zealand in a PTA with the regional grouping. And Australia's pace of PTA activity, while impressive, pales in comparison with that of the United States. As of this writing, Washington is simultaneously negotiating PTA's with the Andean Group, SADC, Bahrain and Thailand and there are signs that a negotiation might be possible with Malaysia. Pending before the Congress are recently negotiated PTAs with Australia, the Central American Common Market, the Dominican Republic and Morocco. And the United States has not given up in its now-stalled effort to negotiate a PTA encompassing nearly all of the countries of the Western Hemisphere. Japan and Mexico have concluded a PTA, as have Korea and Chile. Singapore and Panama are exploring a deal. The European Union is in active negotiations on a PTA with Mercosur.

Id., at 2.

124 WTO: Regional Trade Agreements: Facts and Figures, http://www.wto.org/english/tratop_e/region_e/regfac_e.htm; *see also* Stoler, *Id.*, at 2-3, *citing* World Trade Report 2003, Table IB.9, page 47 (World Trade Organization, Geneva, 2003).

125 *Id.*, at 6. "For example, political considerations drove the negotiations of the U.S.-Israel, U.S.-Jordan or U.S. Morocco PTAs. In addition, the Mercosur agreement linking Brazil, Argentina, Uruguay and Paraguay was also an agreement motivated by political considerations."

terms of economics have a negative effect, both nationally and globally. FTAs have a potential to result in trade diversion, which is welfare reducing.[126] Politically motivated FTAs may potentially undermine the WTO and multilateral trade,[127] if not APEC's primary goal of TILF.

Most problematic for the non-Asian economies with the advent of growing interests in regionalism and a perceived weak APEC, Asian nations began to actively pursue regional dialogues to the exclusion of non-Asian economies. In light of a perceived weak and ineffective APEC, Asian nations started turning to ASEAN, or ASEAN Plus Three, and FTAs between Asian nations,[128] such as, the 2004 ASEAN-China accord. The consequence of a growth in Asian FTAs or PTAs, especially the new potential of Asian regionalism proposed by ASEAN at the 10th ASEAN summit in Vientiane, Laos, may pose a threat to multilateral trade, the WTO and APEC. The ASEAN summit struck an accord between China and ASEAN that could result in the world's largest FTA.

2004 Asean-China Accord

Since 1991, China has been an active participant in APEC.[129] The participation of China during the present reign of China President Hu Jintao reflects the earlier posturing of former President Jiang Zemin. Hu Jintao, not unlike Jiang Zemin, continues to present a positive image of China's active participation in APEC.[130]

A vision and understanding of China's active participation in APEC becomes blurred, if not suspect, however, when one considers China's relation with ASEAN, especially in the year 2004. As previously mentioned, on 29 November 2004, at the 10th ASEAN summit in Vientiane, Laos, China and ASEAN signed a landmark agreement to cut tariffs, resulting in a substantial step towards creating the world's largest FTA by 2010.[131] The most prominent of the series of agreements and mechanisms produced by the summit are the Agreement on Trade in Goods of the Framework Agreement on Comprehensive Economic Cooperation between ASEAN and China, and the Agreement on Dispute Settlement Mechanism.[132] An

126 *Id.*, at 7.
There is a potentially dark side to the economic justification for a PTA. If there is a concern one hears expressed frequently by economists in respect of PTA's it is that they are likely to produce some degree of trade diversion. Trade diversion is welfare reducing, but that does not mean that it cannot be saleable on a sectoral basis. It is not impossible that a government might pursue a PTA as a way to realize economic rents from trade in sectors where its companies might not be competitive internationally. In classic trade diversion scenarios, the most efficient suppliers are shut out of the market when less efficient overseas producers (in the PTA partner) are granted preferential access through discriminatory tariff reductions. Clearly, a PTA grounded in an exclusionary motivation will be neither welfare enhancing nor complementary to the WTO multilateral process as participants in such a PTA will have little interest in seeing progress at the multilateral level.

127 *Id.*, at 11.

128 Edward Lincoln, *supra* note 40, at 1.

129 Role of China, *supra* note 67 (For instance, For instance, President Hu, at the 2003 Bangkok summit made a three-point proposal expressly language similar to Jiang; i.e. " . . . voluntarism and consensus, should be upheld;" " . . . reform and innovation by willingly adapting itself to changing circumstances.").

130 Hu outlines China's ideas on improving APEC process, Embassy of the People's Republic of China in Australia, November 24, 2003, http://www.chinaembassy.org.au/eng/xw/t45610.htm; *see also* Advancing Win-Win Cooperation for Sustainable Development, Speech by President Hu Jintao of China at the APEC CEO Summit, November 19, 2004, http://www.apec2004.cl/imc/economy.asp?id=12.

131 *See* Sun Shangwu, *ASEAN deal hailed as milestone for regional co-operation*, CHINA DAILY, November 30, 2004.

132 *See* Sun Shangwu, *ASEAN links push free trade,* CHINA DAILY, November 29, 2004.

important aspect of this accord is that it requires the two regions to begin building a massive tariff-free market over the next five years in an area comprising nearly two billion people.[133]

The establishment of this FTA will boost the development of this region, which already has about 1.7 billion consumers, about US $1.8 trillion in GDP, and US $1.2 trillion in trade volume. Statistics from the China Ministry of Commerce (MOFCOM) shows that since 1990, ASEAN has been China's fifth largest trade partner for eleven consecutive years. Trade volume in the first ten months of 2004 hit US $84.61 billion, which is up by 35.2 percent over the same period in 2003.[134] The accord between China and ASEAN is expected to build on two-way trade that is expected to surpass US $100 billion in 2004.[135] Notwithstanding a trade deficit with ASEAN, China anticipates that trade will balance out with growth in the region, and as noted by one Chinese source, the agreements are expected to create a win-win situation for economic and trade relations.[136]

Moreover, the significance of 2004 ASEAN-China accord is enhanced by China's increasingly growing global trade volume. In 2005, MOFCOM reported that in 2004 China registered a 34.7 percent surge in foreign trade, with US $1.15 trillion being exchanged. As a result, China became the world's third largest trading power, only lagging behind the U.S. and Germany. Conversely, Chinese sources fearing that some analysts will use these figures for promoting trade protectionism, are insisting that China is not a large trading power or strong trading power. In defense of a large trade volume, and yearly surplus that amounted to US $32 billion, which is up by 25.5 percent year-on-year, Chinese sources are arguing that China's trade accounts for just 5.5 percent of global trade volume, its per capital trade value is only US $850 compared to world average of US $2,400, and that in the first quarter of 2004 it

---

133 10th ASEAN Summit Vientiane, Laos 2004, ASEAN Overview, Paragraphs 10-11, ASEAN Free Trade Area, http://www.10thaseansummit.gov.la/asean_view.htm, [hereinafter 10th ASEAN Summit 2004].

10. In realising the ASEAN Free Trade Area (AFTA), 98.62% of the products in the CEPT Inclusion List (IL) of ASEAN-6 have been brought down to the 0-5% tariff range. As of September 2004, products in the IL, which continue to have tariffs of above 5% are those that have been transferred from the Sensitive Lists (SL) and General Exception Lists (GE) in 2003. Tariffs on 60.89% of the products in the IL of ASEAN-6 have been eliminated. The average tariff for ASEAN-6 under the CEPT Scheme is now down to 1.91% from 12.76% in 1993. For the new ASEAN Member Countries (Cambodia, Laos, Myanmar and Viet Nam), 79.13% of the products traded in the region have been moved into the IL and tariffs on 69.88% of these items have already been brought down within the 0-5% band.

11. Regional financial cooperation has also strengthened. The bilateral swap arrangements network under the Chiang Mai Initiative now comprises 16 agreements with a combined size of US$36.5 billion. The Finance Ministers of ASEAN are also working on a series of promotional activities to attract more funds from developed capital markets outside Southeast Asia to move into ASEAN to strengthen the regional financial markets.

134 Sun Shangwu, *ASEAN links push free trade*, *supra* note 132.

135 *Deal forms free-trade megazone, China, ASEAN sign landmark accord*, *supra* note 9.

136 *See* Sun Shangwu, *ASEAN links push free trade*, *supra* note 132, "Zhai Kun, a researcher on Southeast Asian affairs with the China Institute of Contemporary International Relations." . . . "The agreements have paved the way for building up a China-ASEAN FTA, and are expected to create a win-win situation for economic and trade relations, said Zhai; *see also* 10th ASEAN Summit Vientiane, Laos 2004, ASEAN Overview, *supra* note 133, at Paragraphs 7-9.

7. ASEAN's trade performance grew significantly in 2003. Total ASEAN exports grew by 12.12% from US$ 383.85 billion in 2002 to US$ 430.39 billion in 2003. Total ASEAN imports grew by 9.51% or from US$ 328.11 billion in 2002 to US$ 359.32 billion in 2003.
8. Intra-ASEAN exports grew higher than the total ASEAN exports. The overall growth was 15.4% or in value term it grew from US$ 86.39 billion in 2002 to US$ 99.7 billion in 2003. Intra-ASEAN imports experienced modest growth in 2003, from US$ 72.23 billion in 2002 to US$ 74.49 billion in 2003.
9. The United States, Japan, the European Union, China and the Republic of Korea (ROK) remained ASEAN's largest trading partners. The share of ASEAN's total trade with these countries in overall ASEAN trade in 2003 were 14.1%, 13.7%, 11.5%, 7.0% and 4.1%, respectively.

registered a trade deficit of US $8.4 billion.[137] Admittedly, becoming the world's third largest trader by volume may not necessarily be commensurate with being a strong trading power. However, it is difficult to deny that the economic data, especially potential gross trade volume, enhances the potential and threat of the 2004 ASEAN-China accord.

As for implementing the 2004 ASEAN-China accord, ASEAN plans to accomplish this task by strengthening economic relations and expanding trade through the establishment of FTAs and Closer Economic Partnerships (CEPs).[138] A Vientiane Action Programme, adopted by the 10th ASEAN summit, calls for the ten-member group to develop strategies for attracting the investment required to sustain economic growth.[139] In the past decades, economic growth was largely driven by FDI and exports. Exports have stabilized and show signs of expanding. However, since the East Asian financial crisis (1997-98), ASEAN had experienced a sustained decline in FDI.[140] Therefore, the action program calls for a strategy that will strengthen links and promote agreements with major trade partners such as China, Japan, South Korea, the U.S., Australia, New Zealand, the EU, and emerging India.[141]

ASEAN members also signed an agreement that will move them closer to formation of a EU-style single market. They also linked the pact for reduction of tariffs to Bogor-type target dates. ASEAN economic ministers called for tariffs to be abolished by 2007 for the more developed members such as Brunei, Malaysia, Indonesia, the Philippines, Singapore and Thailand. The other four members, being Cambodia, Myanmar, Laos and Viet Nam will have to abolish tariffs in sectors including autos, textiles and electronics by 2010.[142] In addition, the Agreement on Dispute Settlement Mechanism sets up a three-person panel of independent experts to resolve trade dispute between ASEAN and China.[143]

China and ASEAN present genuine probability of accomplishing what APEC failed to accomplish, more particularly, accomplishing Bogor-type target goals within an earlier period than APEC. China and ASEAN appear to be moving forward in the new millennium, while APEC seems stalled by an inability to accomplish the all-important Bogor goals. Earlier failures in the Osaka Action Agenda, the IAPs, the EVSL initiative, a strategy of greater dependence within a broader global liberalization through launch of the new rounds of trade talks at the WTO, and being seemingly outraced by the ASEAN-China Accord in attempting to form the world's largest FTA, may serve as a harbinger for demise of APEC as the major IGO for TILF in the Asia-Pacific region.[144] However, in the new millennium, factors contributing to the continued relevancy and survivability of APEC may warrant new definitions and meanings. The critical issue of the role that APEC will play in the new

---

137 *See* Zhang Jin, *Nation now No. 3 global trader*, CHINA DAILY, January 12, 2005; *see also* Zhi Ming, *Large trade volume itself not a reason for being content*, CHINA DAILY, January 13, 2005.

138 Sun Shangwu, *ASEAN deal hailed as milestone for regional co-operation, supra* note 131.

139 Association of Southeast Asian Nations, Vientiane Action Programme, http://www.aseansec.org/VAP-10th%20ASEAN%20Summit.pdf.

140 10th ASEAN Summit *supra* note 133.
Despite the unfavourable external outlook and against the backdrop of slowdown in global foreign direct investment (FDI) flows, FDI flows to ASEAN increased by 48%, up from $ 13.7 billion in 2002 to $20.2 billion in 2003, resulting in ASEAN being one of the highest FDI growth regions. The overall improved ASEAN investment environment and strong regional economic growth and integration have increased the attractiveness of ASEAN to foreign investors. The increase in FDI flows in 2003 was the highest since 2000.

141 Sun Shangwu, *ASEAN deal hailed as milestone for regional co-operation, supra* note 131.

142 *See ASEAN Summit stresses integrated region*, CHINA DAILY, November 30, 2004.

143 Sun Shangwu, *ASEAN links push free trade, supra* note 132; *Deal forms free-trade megazone, China, ASEAN sign landmark accord, supra* note 9.

144 Takeshi Isayama, *supra* note 10.

millennium, especially after the ASEAN-China accord, may well warrant the balancing of both economic and political considerations, in gauging APEC's relevancy and survivability.

The New Millennium: APEC and China

China appears to be an active participant in the economic consultative forums of APEC. However, a second glance reveals China more in pursuance of a political agenda rather than economic consultations. Moreover, the issue of a political rather than economic agenda engenders problems for APEC, especially in terms of preserving its relevancy in the new millennium.

APEC experienced an evolution, albeit limited in scope, to encompass both an explicit economic and explicit political agenda. Many attribute APEC's evolution to an explicit political agenda to the 2001 APEC – Shanghai summit. Moreover, the political economy of post-9/11 further heightened the need for an explicit political agenda at both the 2001 APEC – Shanghai summit and 2002 APEC – Mexico summit. As previously mentioned, one suspects that APEC since its 1989 inception has always had a hidden or implicit political agenda. The first evidence of a political agenda was clearly shown at the first ministers meeting, when ministers discussed both the need and means to bring abroad the three economies of China, Taiwan and Hong Kong. Political problems require political solutions. As a result, the solution to the problem implied a political, rather than economic, solution.

In 1989, APEC was presented to the world with both implicit politics and explicit economics as stock of its agenda. The prevailing international political economy, politics intertwined with economics, makes this true. As earlier mentioned, one criticism of APEC is the examination of economic issues to the exclusion of other societal or social issues.[145] Suggesting that solely an economic consultative forum can resolve economic development issues, is an attempt to redress economic issues in a void not only divorced from reality, but, more particularly, political reality. It is the problem of economic modeling and attendant general assumption that economic actors taken individually or *en masse* are rational decision makers. For Alfred Marshall (1842-1924), the father of neoclassicism, a definition of economics had to encompass the terms of political economy and economics.[146] As a result, the term of political economy implied that economics and politics were interrelated, implying value statements and normative judgments. As previously noted, generally, regionali*zation* refers to economic integration process mostly driven by private sector activities, while, conversely, regional*ism* refers to the political process that is driven by state cooperative initiatives.[147]

APEC was commenced during periods of evolving, if not enlarging, international political economy concerns. APEC is a by-product of the international political economy concerns of the Cold War, post-Cold War, East Asian Financial crisis, 9/11 and the economics of terrorism that ensued. However, international political economy concerns are not static, they are dynamic and evolve with changing world trends such as the growth of

---

145 Canada and APEC: Perspectives from Civil Society, First Draft, April 22, 1997, Prepared by the Policy Working Group, Canadian Organizing Network for the 1997 People's Summit on APEC.

146 *See* Harry Landreth, HISTORY OF ECONOMIC THEORY SCOPE, METHOD, AND CONTENT, Houghton Mifflin Company Boston, 1976, at 285.

147 Berger, *supra* note 22.

FTAs or PTAs. A Western world should not be dismayed at both the present posture of APEC and China's geo-political posturing, because the new concept of Asian regionalism was, in part, borrowed from Western models of FTAs such as the EU and NAFTA.[148]

China will eventually demonstrate to a multilateral-inclined, free trade world the difference between traditional and West-centric trade methodologies and the praxis of PTAs with Chinese characteristics. A problem for APEC and the global economy may be a lack of understanding of China's dual participation in APEC and ASEAN. It is a question of the economic, political, or combination of both motivations that influence China in its respective relations with APEC and ASEAN.

Whether perceived as a good or bad consequence, when China began to assume role of world player, the fate of APEC became increasingly intertwined with the economic and political development of China. In the international arena, China in a bid for world player extended growing economic powers into forming a corresponding center, if not region, of international political power. While Western economists and politicians debated the merits and likelihood of success and failure in East Asian regionalism, in terms of ASEAN, and APEC's Bogor goals, China in the interim continued to both engage ASEAN and pursue regional FTAs or PTAs. To the dismay of the Western world and especially Western regional theorists,[149] Asian regionalism now seems a likely probability, despite thematic discourses in doubt such as the following. "There is no Asian regionalism based strictly on regional identity or ideology, except perhaps for the original ASEAN 6. Even that may have diluted as ASEAN 10, comprising six relatively more developed and rich states and four poorer transition economies, was forged by politics and security."[150] Thus, China is demonstrating to a doubting Western world and its West-centric taxonomies of regionalism, the difference between West-centric regional trade taxonomies and the praxis of regionalism with Chinese characteristics. Moreover, because of an increasing connectedness between China and ASEAN, rather than APEC, the fate of APEC became largely intertwined with China's fate.

The combined regional force of China and ASEAN presents a problem for APEC, because the recent ASEAN summit held in Vientiane, Laos on 28-29 November 2004, may have broken new ground in Asian regionalism and community building. Albeit other agreements are effected, this meeting most importantly resulted in the landmark 2004 ASEAN-China accord. In particular, the 2004 ASEAN-China accord also laid the groundwork for the introduction of a new possible rival for APEC. The future of Asian

---

148 *See* Tianshu Liu, *Implication of Trade Creation and Trade Diversion Effect on Trade between RTAs and China and Australia*, Proceedings of the 16th Annual Conference of the Association for Chinese Economics Studies, Australia (ACESA) Brisbane, QLD, 19 - 20 July 2004, (PhD Thesis), at 2, "After fifteen years of the long awaited WTO membership . . it is merely the beginning of China's free trade goal considering that other countries around the world, like European Union (EU), the United States and Canada, have been pursuing economic and trade cooperation within a particular region."

149 *See* Walden Bello, *Viewpoint: Is ASEAN irrelevant?*, PHILIPPINE DAILY INQUIRER (Dec 17, 2004), http://www.bilaterals.org/article.php3?id_article=1060 (Filipino academic and writer Walden Bello discussing problems of ASEAN regionalism.).

150 *See* Linda Low, *East Asian Regionalism: Would that Help Globalisation, Growth and (In) Equality?*, Paper for Globalisation, Growth and (In) Equality, 5th Centre for the Study of Globalisation and Regionalisation Annual Conference, coorganised by University of Warwick, CSGR and Economic &V Social Research Council, University if Warwick, 15-17 March 2002, http://ww.warwick.ac.uk/fac/soc/GSGR/PLow.pdf, *citing* William D. Coleman, and Geoffrey Undershill, (eds.), REGIONALISM AND GLOBAL INTEGRATION: EUROPE, ASIA AND THE AMERICAS, London and New York: Routledge (1998), at 11; Donald Barry and Ronald C. Keith, (eds.), REGIONALISM, MULTILATERALISM, AND THE POLITICS OF GLOBAL TRADE, Vancouver: University of British Columbia Press (1999), 10-13.

regionalism, which garnered some support at the 10th ASEAN summit, may well be what is being dubbed "JACIK," comprising Japan, ASEAN, China, India and the Republic of Korea.[151] As a result, APEC, which had been universally acknowledged as the major IGO for TILF in the Asia-Pacific region,[152] has been relegated to minimum importance. The ASEAN-China accord created the prospect for a free trade mega zone, while a prospective "JACIK" FTA, turned the prospect of a free trade mega zone, more accurately, into the prospect of a free trade super mega zone.

The latter presents critical issues of the significance and role of APEC in the new millennium. One witnesses China actively participating in both APEC and ASEAN, and suspects that China's supposed active participation in APEC is more politically motivated, rather than motivated by economic concerns. The verbiage contained in the speeches of former China President Jiang Zemin and later China President Hu Jintao during earlier APEC summits, when measured against actions undertaken, especially in geopolitical posturing in the Asian region, reflected China's grave doubts about APEC providing an effective mechanism for promoting the political and, especially, economic interests of China. There is a seeming commonality in the postures of Asian leaders, such as Jiang, Hu and former Malaysian Prime Minister Mahathir Mohamad. Because these leaders spoke, and continue to speak, the language of political rhetorical cultural relativism, reflecting a model of East Asian regionalism that views cultural differences as the cause of Asia's path to economic success.[153] Perhaps it is a East Asia-centric fear of Western institutions and models for development that are reminiscent of the international politically economy concerns of the Cold War, post-Cold War, the East Asian financial crisis, and the seemingly rigorous conditionalities of the IMF and World Bank. Moreover, developing countries more often than not perceive that their development agendas are bypassed in the WTO for rules benefiting the rich and powerful, the developed countries. It is a recurrent theme in international law and politics, especially concerning the WTO and other Bretton Woods institutions.[154] In addition, because of the potentiality in the particular development of the East Asian region, rather than more generally described Asian-Pacific region, the Bogor goals became increasingly irrelevant. The issue of accomplishing the Bogor goals pales in comparison to the magnitude of what may now transpire in the new millennium, being a potential ASEAN-China FTA and "JACIK" FTA.

The significance of APEC seems tied to a past period. In the 1990s, it was APEC threatening the relevancy of ASEAN by creating a trans-Pacific free trade area. Nonetheless, the growth of West-centric regionalism in the EU, then NAFTA, may have precipitated the demise of APEC as leader in the Asia-Pacific region. One could argue that regionalism prognosticated APEC's demise, because of the growing trend of regionalism and APEC's seeming incapability to respond to this growing trend. If APEC had shown a capability to accomplish the Bogor goals, or even perhaps better responded to the East Asian financial crisis, then its credibility may have been spared. For now, it is perhaps rightly characterized as a loosely institutionalized, consensus-based organization that appears ineffective and

---

151 *See* Eric Teo Chu Cheow, *Bigger Steps towards Asian Integration*, CHINA DAILY, November 21, 2004.

152 Takeshi Isayama, *supra* note 10.

153 *See* Katharina Pistor & Philip A. Wellons, (eds.), THE ROLE OF LAW AND LEGAL INSTITUTIONS IN ASIAN ECONOMIC DEVELOPMENT 1960-1995, New York, Oxford University Press (1998), 34-35 (Culture theory, such as Asian values, can be associated with the theories of Baron de Montesquieu.).

154 *See* Fatoumata Jawara & Aileen Kaw, BEHIND THE SCENES AT THE WTO: THE REAL WORLD OF INTERNATIONAL TRADE NEGOTIATIONS, (Zed Books, 2003) (Discussing WTO trade negotiations and dominance by the EU and US, and lack of full participation by poor countries.).

inefficient. APEC's agenda turned from implicit politics and explicit economics, to explicit politics and implicit economics, which ran contrary to the changing goals and emphasis on economic cooperation adopted by ASEAN in 1992, when planning to establish an AFTA. From 1989 to 2004, one witnessed the apolitical concerns of APEC evolve to the implicit political concerns, then manifest as the explicit political concerns. In light of this historical evolution, APEC seems to do well in political posturing, especially in its recent leaders' meetings. Conversely, in light of failings in pursuance of the Bogor goals, it seems not to do well as the supposed major forum and IGO for TILF in the Asia-Pacific region.[155]

It is perhaps in terms of international relations (politics) such as promoting regional security and continuing the fight against mega-terrorism, rather than economic cooperation, that APEC will somehow manage to survive and discover new relevancies in the new millennium. Moreover, in the new millennium, the latter political agenda would represent an important role for APEC in the Asia-Pacific, which would lend to substantive relevancy. Admittedly, some that might argue that the refocusing of APEC goals towards political concerns and security measures might further weaken its efficacy as an IGO or regional economic cooperation organization. A problem for APEC is a weakened credibility dating back to the East Asian financial crisis, and most recently, a doubtful ability to accomplish the Bogor goals.

Nonetheless, and most important, APEC remains relevant to China. First, although China is a member of other East Asia sub regional groups, before China acceded to the WTO in 2001, the only international economic organization that China was a member of was APEC. Second, China stands to benefit from APEC's continuing role in promoting trade negotiation rounds in the WTO, especially the Doha Development Agenda. In terms of multilateralism, the promotion of free trade and investment, or TILF, benefits China. Third, APEC, as seen in the 2004 APEC-Chile summit and earlier summits, presents China with an international stage for self-promotion of political and diplomatic interests. APEC summits have allowed China to interchange and interact with major world powers such as the United States, EU, Mercosur (South American Common Market, Mercado Comun del Cono Sur or Southern Cone Common Market)[156] and others. Fourth, although in China the ASEAN Regional Forum (ARF) became the most important official channel for multilateral security dialogue, APEC is still important to China in terms of security in the Asia-Pacific region.[157] In terms of political considerations, many deem China ambitious to dominate the Asian region.[158] One Chinese source described China's maturing diplomacy in 2004 as "omni-directional foreign policy."[159]

---

155 Takeshi Isayama, *supra* note 10.

156 The official site of the Mercosur Secretariat, http://www.mercosur.org.uy/. The EU's Relation with Mercosur – Overview, http://europa.eu.int/comm/external_relations/mercosur/intro/, "Mercosur was created by Argentina, Brazil, Paraguay and Uruguay in March 1991 with the signing of the Treaty of Asuncion. It originally was set up with the ambitious goal of creating a common market/customs union between the participating countries."

157 China's National Defense 2004, White Papers of the Government, China Information Office of the State Council, http://www.china.org.cn/e-white/.

158 *See Potential Chinese dominance of North Korea*, CHINA REFORM MONITOR No. 572, Editor: Al Santoli, American Foreign Policy Council, Washington, DC, December 21, 2004, http://www.afpc.org, (This source notes that China is ambitious to dominate Asia and discussion examples involving North Korea and Taiwan.); *see also* Chen Zhou and Deng Hongzhou, *Paper maps military future*, CHINA DAILY, December 28, 2004. "But the old security problems in the region have not been fundamentally removed while new insecure elements are emerging. The United States is realigning and beefing up its military presence in the region and strengthening military alliances."

159 *See* Hu Xuan, *Maturing diplomacy in 2004*, CHINA DAILY, (January 1-2, 2005).

Notwithstanding a relevancy more couched in political considerations, than economic considerations, APEC remains relevant to China in the new millennium.

In addition, in terms of possible roles that APEC may play in the new millennium, APEC's survival being intertwined with China's economic and political development presents a potential dilemma. The proposed ASEAN-China FTA implies an exclusionary model of regionalism that is primarily based on political considerations, and may pose a threat to TILF, the WTO, multilateral trade, and the APEC.

The latter model of regionalism presents an FTA motivated by exclusionary motivations, which is probably more trade diverting than trade creating. In terms of trade liberalization, trade diversion is the welfare change caused by consumer and producers substituting higher cost imports from an exporting economy for lower cost imports from third economies.[160] Trade creation is the welfare improvement that arises because high-cost domestic production in one economy is replaced by lower-cost production in another economy. Thus, trade creation allows aligned economies to better exploit their comparative advantage. In terms of more liberalized trade, both economies supposedly further specialize their production, hence, serving the markets of aligned economies with products at lower prices. In terms of FTAs, trade creation improves resource allocation and welfare. Whether overall a net static welfare gain in an economy will be the result of aligned economies, is contingent on whether trade creation outweighs trade diversion or vice versa.[161]

Assuming net trade creation, and not diversion, custom unions or regional trade arrangements such as NAFTA should enjoy greater economic efficiency, and further benefits stemming from increased trade and investment.[162] Even the former U.S. Trade Representative, Robert Zoellick, advocated PTAs as triggering "competitive liberalization," and as an alternate route to free trade with economies competing to open markets to each other. A fear of exclusion serves as impetus of non-members to either join the group or accept broader agreements.[163] However, the factor of political motivation engenders a tacit assumption of trade diversion. FTAs or PTAs grounded in exclusionary motivations such as political motivations are neither welfare enhancing, nor complementary to the WTO and

---

160 *See generally* Jacob Viner, THE CUSTOMS UNION ISSUE, New York: Carnegie Endowment for International Peace (1950) (In 1950, Viner introduced the concepts of trade creation and trade diversion.).

161 *See* Viner, *Id; see also* Stefan Szepesi, *Coercion or engagement?, Economics and institutions in ACP-EU trade negotiations*, ECDPM Discussion Paper No. 56, June 2004, at 8.

162 *See* Viner, *Id*; *see also* James E. Meade, THE THEORY OF CUSTOMS UNION (1955); *see also* Kym Anderson, *The Challenge of Reducing Subsidies and Trade Barriers*, University of Adelaide, World Bank and CEPR, World Bank Policy Research Working Paper 3415, September 2004, at 4, *citing* Jagdish N. Bhagwati, THE GENERALIZED THEORY OF DISTORTIONS AND WELFARE, in TRADE, BALANCE OF PAYMENTS AND GROWTH, edited by J.N. Bhagwati et al, Amsterdam: North-Holland (1971), In terms of the general theory of the welfare effect of trade distortion, "The standard comparative static analysis of national gains from international trade emphasizes the economic benefits from production specialization and exchange so as to exploit comparative advantage in situations where a nation's costs of production and/or preferences differ from those in the rest of the world."

163 Soamiely Andriamananjara, *On the Relationship between Preferential Trade Agreements and the Multilateral Trading System*, U.S. International Trade Commission, Remarks prepared for the PECC Trade Forum Meetings at the Institute for International Economics, Washington, DC., April 22, 2003, at 3.
"The term "competitive liberalization" has been widely used in APEC dialogue, and was first coined by Bergsten in 1996 in C. Fred Bergsten, *Competitive Liberalization and Global Free Trade: A Vision for the Early 21st Century*, Working Paper 96-15, Institute for International Economics. He argues for instance that the United States initiated the Kennedy Round in the 1960s and the Tokyo Round in the 1970s to counter the discrimination inherent in the creation and expansion of the European Community."
Id., at 3 n. 4.

multilateralism.[164] Thus, models of regionalism motivated by political considerations threaten multilateral trade and, most important, create trade distortion and are welfare reducing.[165]

Most problematic in terms of the 2004 ASEAN-China accord portending the world's largest FTA is that typical trade areas comprising subsets of nations are not necessarily welfare enhancing for all participating nations.[166] The harm from discrimination in trade affects exports to a PTA market and terms of trade, such as, decreased export prices required to maintain competitiveness in a preferential market.[167] A PTA and its discriminatory nature especially have potential to adversely affect the poorest economies. Due to trade diversion, especially stemming mostly from non-participants in the global economy, the global economy will be adversely affected by impending trade distortion.[168]

Notwithstanding an exception to general theory of the welfare effect of trade distortion,[169] an ASEAN-China FTA constituting the world's largest FTA may pose a serious threat to the global economy.[170] Admittedly, free trade might not be best policy for lesser-developed countries or economies (LDCs) that are facing what economists refer to as a market distortion.[171] Nonetheless, FTAs such as even NAFTA, and the European experiment that was clearly driven by both politics and economics,[172] "inevitably politicize trade more than multilateral trade agreements do."[173] However, China and ASEAN members are developing countries, as opposed to LDCs, thus voiding any arguable exceptions to the general theory prognosticating a welfare reducing effect. The advent of politically motivated ASEAN-China FTA as the world's largest FTA more probable, than not, will produce trade

---

164 Stoler, *supra* note 123, at 7.

165 Edward Lincoln, *supra* note 40, at 6. Conversely, "Despite trade diversion concerns, the United States has clearly moved in the direction of free trade areas itself, creating the North American Free Trade Area with Canada and Mexico, and now discussing a broader Free Trade Area of the Americas."

166 Edward Lincoln, *Id.*, at 6, Conversely, "Despite trade diversion concerns, the United States has clearly moved in the direction of free trade areas itself, creating the North American Free Trade Area with Canada and Mexico, and now discussing a broader Free Trade Area of the Americas."

167 Soamiely, *supra* note 163, On the Relationship between Preferential Trade Agreements and the Multilateral Trading System, U.S. International Trade Commission, Remarks prepared for the PECC Trade Forum Meetings at the Institute for International Economics, Washington, DC., April 22, 2003, at 2.

168 *Id.*, at 8, *citing* R. Pomfret, THE ECONOMICS OF REGIONAL TRADING ARRANGEMENTS, London: Oxford University Press (1997); M. Schiff and L.A. Winters, REGIONAL INTEGRATION AND DEVELOPMENT, London and New York: Oxford University Press for the World Bank (2003).

169 Anderson, *supra* note 162, at 2.

The reluctance to reduce trade distortions is almost never because such policy reform involves government treasury outlays. On the contrary, except in the case of a handful of low-income countries still heavily dependent on trade taxes for government revenue, such reform may well benefit the treasury (by raising income and/or consumption tax revenues more than trade tax revenues fall, not to mention any payments foregone because of cuts to subsidy programs).

170 *Id.*, at 2 n. 1, "Not all subsidies are welfare-reducing, and in some cases a subsidy-cum-tax will be optimal to overcome a gap between private and social costs that cannot be bridged à la Coase (1960);" *see also* Rajiv Sethi & Peter Skott, *Uneven Development and the Dynamics of Distortion*, Department of Economics, Working Papers 1997-23, University of Aarhus, http://ideas.repec.org/p/aah/aarhec/1997-23.html (Discussing trade distortion and instances where distorted industrial policies of LCDs may be welfare enhancing).

171 *See* Jagdish Bhagwati, FREE TRADE TODAY 26-27 Princeton University Press, 2002, "We also realized, as no one had pointedly done earlier, that if a suitable policy was addressed to offset that distortion, then we could get back to endorsing free trade."

172 *See* J. F. Francois and M. Rombout, *Preferential Trade Arrangements, Induced Investment, and National Income in a Heckscher-Ohlin-Ramsey Model*, TI 2000-061/2, Tinbergen Institute Discussion Paper, June 2000, at 2, http:// www.tinbergen.nl/discussionpapers/00061.pdf.

173 Bhagwati, *Id*, at 110.

distortion in the global economy.[174] Assuming *arguendo* trade distortion, the world's largest FTA could produce immeasurable and exponentially growing welfare reducing effects.

The latter presents an issue of the WTO rules governing FTAs, at Article XXIV of GATT 1947,[175] which implicitly tolerates trade diversion. Conversely, an important feature of multilateralism is supposed to be the absence of discrimination among trading partners, because multilateral trade is welfare enhancing.[176] An assumed characteristic of international trade agreements, such as NAFTA and EU, is that by their nature as international agreements, they assumedly frustrate protectionism. Whether these international agreements are in fact welfare enhancing is perhaps another issue, because this conclusion does not necessarily apply in reality to liberalization between selective groups of nations.[177]

As early as APEC's third ministerial meeting (Seoul 1991), the idea of open regionalism as a core concept of APEC begins to take form. As reflected in APEC's Seoul Declaration goals (1991), it would be open regionalism, rather than closed or exclusionary regionalism, generally definable as a concerted and unilateral trade liberalization that is along the lines of the most-favored-nations (MFN) status. For this reason and others, Article XXIV has been referred to as the GATT loophole for FTAs. This clause exempts FTAs and customs unions from the obligation in Article I to accord MFN treatment.[178] This loophole is justified for two historical reasons: First, for encouraging membership in GATT, political reality meant accommodating a long history of custom unions that predated GATT, and second, exceptions were permitted under specific or controlled conditions, intending to avoid ad hoc and partial discrimination practiced during the interwar period.[179] In addition, the WTO Memorandum of Understanding on Article XXIV fails to clear up existing ambiguities and contradictions.[180] As a result, Article XXIV remains a continuing source of debate concerning FTAs. A problem only exasperated by fact that only one working party has ever determined that a FTA or regional trade agreement (RTA) satisfied Article XXIV, while, conversely, no FTAs or RTAs have been found to be incompatible with GATT. A GATT Study Group concerning Article XXIV reads, "They have set a dangerous precedent for further special deals, fragmentation of the trading system, and damage to the trade interests of non-participants... GATT rules on customs unions and free trade areas should be examined, redefined so as to avoid ambiguity, and more strictly applied."[181]

---

174 Liu, *supra* note 148, at 3-4.

Generally speaking, a country will benefit from importing commodities that are once highly protected in domestic market with a lower-cost member, while suffer a loss when diverts her imports from a low-cost third country to a high-cost member country because of tariff deduction within the regional free trade area. The former is known as the trade creation effect in comparison with the trade diversion effect defined by the latter. As a member country and the whole world will decrease their welfare when trade diversion effect occurs, many studies have been done to observe if it is worth to form or participate in a RTA.

175 GATT, Part III, Article XXIV: Territorial Application - Frontier Traffic- Customs Unions and Free-trade Areas, 5, http://www.wto.org/english/docs_e/legal_e/gatt47_02_e.htm.

176 The European Union's Trade Policies and their Economic Effects, OECD 2000, at 8.

177 Szepesi, *supra* note 161, at 8.

178 GATT 1947, Art. I, (Outlining most favored-nation treatment).

179 Srinivasan, *supra* note 9, at 2-3.

180 WTO: Understanding on the Interpretation of Article XXIV of the General Agreement on Tariffs and Trade 1994, http://www.wto.org/english/tratop_e/region_e/regatt_e.htm.

181 *See* Kerry A. Chase, *Multilateralism Compromised: The Origins of GATT Article XXIV*, Tufts University (2004), *citing* WTO: REGIONALISM AND THE GLOBAL TRADING SYSTEM (Geneva: WTO, 1995), 69-70, n. 8.

An additional problem for global trade is that the 2004 ASEAN-China accord came at a time that the WTO agreement on textiles and clothing would conclude, being January 1, 2005, ending the Multi-Fibre Agreement (MFA) of 1974.[182] The MFA was widely acknowledged as trade distorting with distortions having paradoxical effects. The MFA protected developed economy markets, in that it limited clothing imports from developing economies by quotas. At the Uruguay round in 1994, it was agreed that the MFA would be dismantled in phases, ending on January 1, 2005, when developed economies would remove all quota allocations. Developing and less-developed economies agreed, perceiving the removal would benefit them. However, termination of the MFA is producing mixed results.

The effect of removing this trade barrier will mostly accrue to China first, India second. China and India can produce clothing at lower cost than any other developing economies because of labor-intensive industries. As a result, nine developing and lesser-developed economies, being Bangladesh, the Dominican Republic, Fiji, Madagascar, Mauritius, Sri Lanka, Uganda, Jamaica and Nepal, on September 2004, requested the WTO's Council for Trade in Goods to conduct country-specific analyses for measuring the effect of the MFA's termination. They are seeking assistance for large scale restructuring to prevent impending disastrous economic and social consequences that will befall their countries. These nations, not unlike the rest of the world, have had difficulty competing with China. In their particular situation, China clothing imports raised from 11 million units in 1995 to 213 million units in 2003. Estimates indicated that at the termination of the MFA, job losses would be between 27 million and 31 million worldwide.[183] A prospective ASEAN-China FTA, in conjunction with termination of the MFA, further enhances the anticipated welfare reducing effect.

In 2005, both the European Union and the United States entered into Memorandum of Understanding with China regarding the pending global trade crisis of Chinese textile and apparel products. In 2009, the latter Memorandums of Understanding and the WTO safeguards will have ended. The pending global trade crisis in textiles and apparel will present itself as still unresolved in 2009, if not sooner. The Memorandums of Understanding offer at best short-term solutions to a still pending crisis. The latter will eventually present the issue of the need for buffers sanctioning trade distortions such as non-tariff barriers (NTBs) or measures, pursuant to the greater interests of the global economy. It is perhaps a matter of choosing the lesser of two evils, that is, seemingly prospective immeasurable trade distortions from a proposed ASEAN-China FTA versus seemingly more quantitative and measurable trade distortions implicitly tolerated by the WTO rules.

It must be borne in mind that ten years subsequent to the Uruguay Round of multilateral trade negotiations, many subsidies and trade distortions remain. In terms of the implicitly tolerated trade distortions, there is Article XX(b) of the GATT, which does allow an importing country to impose measures necessary to protect human, animal or plant life or health.[184] In addition, the WTO Agreement on Technical Barriers to Trade governs the

---

182 GATT, Multi-fibre Agreement, which was in force from 1974 to 1994; *see* WTO Legal Texts: The Uruguay Round agreements, http://www.wto.org/english/docs_e/legal_e/ursum_e.htm#cAgreement.

183 *See Textiles Trade Reform: Unstitched By China, WTO*, EFU, (October 22, 2004), http://www.efu.com.cn/eng/onllinesales/promotion/allround/2004-10-22/6605.htm.

184 *See* Joel P. Trachtman, *Decisions of the Appellate Body of the World Trade Organization European Communities-Measures Affecting Asbestos and Asbestos-Containing Products*, EJIL-Current Developments, 5 April 2001, http://www.ejil.org/journal/curdevs/sr13.html#TopOfPage (Discussing Article XX(b)).

imposition of technical requirements on products by an importing country.[185] They include trade taxes-cum-subsidies, protection measures such as anti-dumping, regulatory standards and domestic production subsidies. In addition, insufficient or excessive taxation or quantitative regulations also lead to inefficiencies and can be trade distorting.[186] Most important, FTAs or PTAs that are primarily motivated by exclusionary motivations, especially non-economic motivations, which are implicitly tolerated by the WTO rules,[187] produce trade and investment diversion rather than creation. In terms of the WTO rules, the same holds true for FTAs, and proposed buffers such as NTBs to offset trade distortion, both produce implicitly tolerated trade distortion. However, most discerning is that the purported world's largest FTA, the ASEAN-China FTA, taken in conjunction with termination of the MFA, could produce immeasurable and exponentially growing welfare reducing effects.

Notwithstanding employing NTBs as a buffer, which are possibly the only alternatives available following a failed Istanbul Declaration,[188] in the event a proposed ASEAN-China FTA is motivated in part or in entirety by exclusionary motivations, then APEC could conceivably serve as a possible "non-NTB-type" buffer to trade distortions that may ensue. Regardless of likelihood of accomplishing the Bogor goals, there are many reasons to believe APEC can, and will, play an important role in buffering anticipated trade distortions. Because, as observed by one assessment of APEC's continuing and substantive relevancies, "[S]trategically, APEC helps stabilize relations among its diverse membership by providing a unique forum for regular discussions among leaders, ministers, technical experts and corporate executives."[189] No other international economic cooperation organization or other IGO is better suited for this task.

> APEC helps to keep the United States engaged in the region, assists the accommodation of China, and facilitates exchange between the wealthier and poorer nations of the region

---

185 *See* Willy Lin, (speech), *Implications of the end of the WTO Agreement on Textiles and Clothing*, Pacific Economic Cooperation Council's 15th General Meeting held September 1, 2003 in Brunei, http://www.tdctrade.com/shippers/vol26_5/vol26_5_chairman_03.htm.

186 Anderson, *supra* note 162, at 2.

187 GATT, Part III, Article XXIV: Territorial Application - Frontier Traffic- Customs Unions and Free-trade Areas, 5, http://www.wto.org/english/docs_e/legal_e/gatt47_02_e.htm; *see also* John H. Jackson, THE JURISPRUDENCE OF GATT & WTO - INSIGHTS ON TREATY LAW AND ECONOMIC RELATIONS, Higher Education Press, 2002, at 101-102.

188 *See* Seventy-two textile and apparel groups from thirty-six countries made the Istanbul Declaration to the WTO, requesting the WTO extend the MFA quota free deadline from December 31, 2004 to December 31, 2007, but it failed, *Istanbul has no Future, Press Release, Fair Trade Association*, Brussels, June 14, 2004, http://www.fta-eu.org/en/new/pmpdf.php?site=fta&pm_id=79; *see also* Brussels Communiqué by the Istanbul Declaration Partners in the Global Alliance for Fair Trade in Textiles and Clothing Brussels, June 17, 2004, http://www.deik.org.tr/genel/ 20046251416l0brusselscommunique-june2004.pdf, The Istanbul Declaration is a call to their individual governments to undertake the following actions:

1. Request an emergency meeting of the WTO in order to analyze and identify WTO solutions to the pending crisis associated with the expiration of textile and clothing quotas on January 1, 2005. These could include an extension of the current system, the development of a new system or the use of other WTO mechanisms.
2. Implement automatic and seamless transitional safeguard mechanisms in order to prevent massive disruptive surges of trade from a few countries. The damage associated with the removal of a limited number of quotas in 2002 under the third stage of the phase – out must not be repeated. For example, during that removal, almost all the benefits went to a single supplier, which significantly cut prices.
3. Demand expedited and effective remedies to all types of unfair trading practices employed by certain major supplying countries, including currency manipulation, state sponsored subsidies and state provided non – performing loans, among others.

189 APIAN Assessment, *supra* note 94, at 3, Preface.

and between East Asia and nations of North and South America. And while it is difficult to measure its precise contributions, APEC has added its weight to those reformers throughout the Asia Pacific that advocate for more open markets and effective government and, especially in recent years, for more focus on human capacity building and on a more equitable sharing of the fruits of globalization.[190]

The latter presents an additional substantive relevancy of APEC that benefits global trade and all economies participating in global trade. APEC has always been relevant in promoting free trade and new rounds of trade negotiations with the WTO, a relevancy that continues into the new millennium. The latter relevancy is also enhanced by the promotion of regional security and continuing the fight against mega-terrorism. Despite difficulties in implementing the Bogor goals, the original commitment of APEC to TILF continues and bears relevancy in the new millennium. In addition, the latter relevancy of promoting free world trade benefits developed and developing economies, because free trade benefits all participating countries.[191] In this respect and others, APEC remains relevant to all participating economies in global trade, and most important, remains relevant in the new millennium. APEC is not expendable as an international economic cooperation organization.

Admittedly, the 2004 ASEAN-China accord may not establish a trade region that is welfare reducing. It may create a trade region manifesting a net static welfare gain, that is, trade and investment creation, and not diversion. A welfare-enhancing ASEAN-China FTA is based on the existence of three key assumptions. First, most ASEAN economies did in fact make the transition from an emphasis on agriculture to industrial development and export-based growth.[192] Second, ASEAN nations have addressed a post-East Asian financial crisis of declining FDI.[193] Third, an ASEAN-China FTA is primarily motivated by economic concerns or economic cooperation, rather than political concerns. However, it is suggested that most ASEAN economies fail in one or more of these respects, especially transition from food, agriculture and forestry,[194] to industrial development and export-based growth. ASEAN is still a relatively weak economic body,[195] with intra-ASEAN exports in 2001 accounting for

---

190 *Id.*

191 *See* Peter Malanczuk, AKEHURST'S MODERN INTRODUCTION TO INTERNATIONAL LAW 231 (Routledge 7th ed. 1997).

192 Tan Tai Yong, *supra* note 26.

193 10th ASEAN Summit 2004, *supra* note 133.

194 *See* Ching-Cheng Chang and Shih-Hsun Hsu, *A Partial Equilibrium Analysis on the Effects of Trade Liberalization in APEC Food Sector*, APEC Study Centre Consortium-1999 Conference, Auckland, New Zealand, May 31-June 2, 1999, http://www2.auckland.ac.nz/apec/papers/Chang.html, "[M]ost of the ASEAN countries possess comparative advantages in exporting rice, vegetable oils, and sugar;" *see also* Joint Press Statement, The Twenty Sixth Meeting of the ASEAN Ministers on Agriculture and Forestry (26th AMAF), Myanmar, Oct. 7, 2004, http://www.aseansec.org/16432.htm; *see also* Deputy PM highlights co-operation among Asian countries at Boao forum, (Deputy Prime Minister Vu Khoan of Vietnam), Nov. 4, 2003, http://www.nhandan.org.vn/english/20031104/bai-news2.html,

Yet, Asian countries are at different levels of development. Many are still backward agriculture-based economies, thus being in a disadvantageous position in international competition. The service sector, financial and banking systems, science and technology, including information technology, which all are crucial for development in today's world, are still very weak in Asian economies, except for a few.

195 Edgardo S. Santiago, Chapter 4 Economic Development, in ASEAN State of the Environment Report 2000, 24-37, (2000 UNEP RRC.AP), http://www.rrcap.unep.org/sub-region/aseansoe/, "Most AMC economies, although developing rapidly, continue to depend heavily on agriculture and other food-based industries, which are relatively high polluters." *Id.*, at 25; "[A]griculture was the dominant sector for the economies of Cambodia, the Lao PDR and Myanmar, contributing over 50% of GDP in 1997. For other AMCs, agriculture

only twenty percent of ASEAN's total exports, an export figure reflecting the same proportions from the 1970s.[196] Although ASEAN nations have witnessed an increase in FDI, ASEAN nations are still addressing a post-East Asian financial crisis of declining FDI.

In addition, China in anticipation of the termination of the MFA on January 1, 2005, imposed tariffs commencing on January 1, 2005, on six categories of textile exports. On January 1, 2005, many countries removed textile-trading quotas as scheduled, including the U.S., E.U. and Canada. The export tariff was imposed by China's MOFCOM for purpose of addressing concerns of trade partners. On May 20, 2005, China again imposed export duties on another 74 ten-digit tariff lines.[197] In terms of an impending ASEAN-China FTA, the MOFCOM's tariff impositions may or may not exhibit genuine multilateralism on the part of China, and may or may not sufficiently address fears of the global economy.

A problem of regionalism is that it may well constitute the movement of polities in terms of politics, rather than economies in terms of globalization.[198] Assuming *arguendo* the latter is true, then regionalism is compromised in its capacity as a supposed complement to a multilateral trade approach. Conversely, it may be that nations have acted politically, in pursuance of national and regional interests, rather, as a dual approach to development, seeking to both liberalize and define the terms of their liberalization. Nonetheless, and regardless of whether China is pursuing unilateral trade practices, or pursuing a dual approach to development, APEC will continue to be relevant in the new millennium, because of its historical commitment to TILF, and continuing promotion of regional security and the fight against mega-terrorism.

APEC's relevancy and survivability somehow became contingent on accomplishing the all-important Bogor goals. A problem of the Bogor-goals contingency is that it ignores other relevancies, past, present, and perhaps future relevancies of APEC as an international economic cooperation organization, especially its historical commitment to TILF. APEC was essentially meant to be a loosely institutionalized, consensus-governed body serving as an economic consultative forum for Asia-Pacific nations. APEC is the by-product of prevailing international political economy concerns of the 1980s and 1990s, the Cold War and post-Cold War eras. APEC has undergone growth and evolution, mostly due to changing international political economy environments, ranging from the post-Cold War, post-East Asian financial crisis (1997-98), to the events of 9/11 and the economics of terrorism that ensued. APEC experienced a transition from a seemingly apolitical agenda to a combined political and economic agenda. In the new millennium, the role of APEC must necessarily be

---

was a much lower percentage of GDP than industry or services." *Id.*, at 27; "Agriculture absorbs over half of ASEAN's employment." *Id.*, at 28.

196 *See* Bello, *supra* note 149, China's motivation, says Chinese economist Angang Hu is in two parts. One, integrate China into global economy as "center of the world's manufacturing industry." Two, while opening up ASEAN markets to manufactured products, attract investments from ASEAN into China's western region;. *see also* Teofilo C. Daquila, *Asean's Economic Performance Reviewing the Past, Looking to the future,* 6(2) HARV. ASIA Q. 10 (2002), http://www.fas.harvard.edu/~asiactr/haq/200203/daquila.pdf, "[I]n 1999-2000, the region showed some signs of economic recovery but was interrupted by poor export performance and low FDI inflows. The September 11 incident further worsened conditions in the region, by causing economic slowdowns in ASEAN's major trading and investment partners—the US, Japan and the European Union."

197 *See* Dai Yan, *Textile tariff details unveiled,* CHINA DAILY, December 28, 2004; *see also* Dai Yan, *Textile export curbs to remain,* CHINA DAILY, January 5, 2005; *see also* Ministry of Commerce of the People's Republic of China, *Commerce Minister Bo Xilai Attending Press Conference Hosted by the State Council Information Office,* ASIA REPORT, June 1, 2005, http://english.mofcom.gov.cn/aarticle/counselorsreport/ asiareport/ 200506/20050600106396.html.

198 Bowles, *supra* note 19.

understood and defined in terms of changing, dynamic and prevailing international political economy environments, and count as examples the East Asian financial crisis, the proliferation of regional trade agreements such as the impending ASEAN-China FTA, termination of the WTO Multi-Fibre Agreement (MFA) of 1974, and global threats of mega-terrorism. Perhaps more so for this reason than any other, it is unrealistic to expect that APEC can return to its humbler beginnings, that is, a simple economic consultative forum, rather than what it became, an international forum addressing both economic and political concerns in the Asia-Pacific region. Most will agree that APEC enjoys some tacit relevancies and remains relevant in the new millennium, albeit for different reasons, including an emerging China. However, APEC's organizational structure and goals, which were relevant in the 1980s and 1990s, may be insufficient and inadequate for the new millennium challenges.[199] Despite tacit relevancies, for purposes of survival and continuing relevancy in the new millennium, APEC will have to develop more creative and realistic goals, and perhaps commit to reforms and organizational restructuring, in light of China, ASEAN, and especially the prospects of a future "JACIK" FTA.

Conclusion

APEC remains relevant in the new millennium. As for the Bogor goals, they should never been given the prominence attributed by many. APEC members when adopting these seemingly bigger than life goals well knew the road ahead in terms of implementing them. Critiques judged APEC harshly for failings, one seemingly after another, in implementing the Bogor goals, all the while ignoring other relevancies of APEC. A failure to accomplish the Bogor goals will not, and should not, result in the demise of APEC because of the same reasons. In the new millennium, the survival and continuing relevancy of APEC will lie in its historical commitment to trade and investment liberalization and facilitation (TILF), while allowing adjustments reflecting new international political economy concerns, such as, global threats of mega-terrorism, the 2004 ASEAN-China accord, termination of the WTO Multi-Fibre Agreement (MFA) of 1974, new WTO trade negotiation rounds, and what is being dubbed "JACIK." Moreover, survival for APEC in the new millennium means encompassing an explicit economic agenda, in conjunction with an explicit international relations (political) agenda.

---

[199] APIAN Assessment, *supra* note 94, Executive Summary, at 1.

In: New Developments in Macroeconomics Research
Editor: Lawrence Z. Pelzer, pp. 47-72
ISBN: 1-59454-663-0

Chapter 2

THE EFFECTS OF DOLLAR FLUCTUATIONS ON PRIVATE CONSUMPTION IN THE U.S.*

Magda Kandil[†,1] ***and Ida Aghdas Mirzaie***[‡,2]
[1]IMF, 700 19th St. NW, Washington, DC 20431
[2]John Carroll University, 20700 North Park Blvd, University Heights, OH 44118

Abstract

The paper examines the effects of the change in the value of the dollar on private consumption in the United States. The empirical model includes disposable income, an index of consumer sentiment, the interest rate, and the real effective exchange rate. Anticipated movements in these determinants are likely to affect planned consumption, while unanticipated changes determine cyclical consumption. Dollar appreciation (depreciation) decreases (increases) consumption of non-tradables, while increasing (decreasing) consumption of tradables. The former channel appears to be more dominant on total consumption. A few exceptions suggest, however, that currency appreciation may be associated with higher values of consumption. This is particularly evident for durable goods, which are likely to constitute a large share of tradables.

JEL Classification Numbers: E21, E32, E52, E63
Keywords: Consumption, Planned vs. transitory, Stabilization Policies

1 Introduction

Consumption spending is a major component of aggregate demand. The nature of cyclical fluctuations in the United States has highlighted the importance of private consumption to

---

* This Working Paper should not be reported as representing the views of the IMF. The views expressed in this Working Paper are those of the author(s) and do not necessarily represent those of the IMF or IMF policy. Working Papers describe research in progress by the author(s) and are published to elicit comments and to further debate

† E-mail address: mkandil@imf.org
‡ E-mail address: imirzaie@jcu.edu

aggregate demand and, in turn, to the state of the business cycle. During a recession, the focus has-been on indicators of consumers' sentiment and the design of policy packages that target consumers' spending towards stimulating the economy.

In theory, consumption spending varies with disposable income. Rational agents forecast their steady-state income stream overtime. Planned consumption varies with planned income.[1] In addition, consumption varies cyclically in response to random transitory changes in income.[2]

Financial development has necessitated, however, a change in the traditional approach of modeling consumption spending. Consumers in the U.S. have become increasingly dependent on credit spending. In this connection, the cost of credit, i.e., the interest rate has become an important determinant of consumption spending.[3] Higher cost of credit card borrowing is likely to discourage consumption spending.[4] With this increased dependency, the relationship between consumption spending and disposable income has weakened over time. Hence, consumption spending has become increasingly financed by credit.[5]

The state of business cycles has affected, however, agents' confidence level in the state of the economy. Independently of the change in income and the cost of credit, consumers' confidence may be adversely affected during recessions. Uncertainty about economic outlook would further weaken consumers' confidence and, therefore, private consumption.

While the U.S. economy is mostly driven by domestic demand, fluctuations in the exchange rate of the dollar may have been a source of additional fluctuations in private consumption. An appreciation of the dollar would make imports cheaper and divert private consumption away from non-tradables towards tradable goods.[6]

Given recent recessionary conditions in the U.S., attention has focused once again on private consumption and its role in stimulating the economy. More importantly, recent fluctuations in the value of the dollar and the widening current account deficit has raised

---

1 This relationship is pioneered by the seminal work of Friedman (1957) on the permanent income hypothesis.

2 Empirical research has challenged the steady nature of consumption in relation to permanent income. Hall (1978) indicates that consumption follows a random walk, implying only unexpected policy changes can affect consumption. The findings of Falvin (1981), and Hall and Mishkin (1982) indicate that the Rational Expectation Permanent Income Hypothesis does not hold because consumption displays an excess dependence on current income due to capital imperfection and credit rationing. Campbell and Mankiw (1990, 1991) show that for non-durable and services consumption, the elasticity of inter-temporal substitution is basically zero. Leong and Mcaleer(1999) evaluate two seasonal models that are consistent with an extension of the rational expectations life-cycle permanent income hypothesis. They find that models fail to capture adequately the dynamics in Swedish consumption expenditure. Dejuan and Seater(1999) test the permanent income life cycle hypothesis against the alternative hypothesis of rule-of-thumb and liquidity-constrained consumers. They find no evidence that current income movements cause changes in total consumption of non-durable goods and services. Also, their results offer no support to the hypothesis that liquidity constraint affects consumption significantly.

3 Aggregate consumption arises from aggregating over some consumers following the life cycle hypothesis and others who are liquidity constrained (see, e.g., Abel (1990)).

4 For details, see Campbell and Mankiw (1989).

5 For related references, see Canner and Fergus (1987), Zeldes (1989), Mathieson and Rojas-Suarez (1990), Kaynak, Kncukemiroglu and Ozmen (1995), Scott (1996), Hahm (1998), Sarno and Taylor (1998), Benoit, Keita and Samoson (1999), Girardin, Sarno, and Taylor (2000) and Park and Rogrigues (2000).

6 This channel focuses on the relative prices of tradables and non-tradables. Private consumption may not be affected if consumers substitute imported goods for consumption of domestically produced goods. Other researchers have focused, however, on the contractionary effect of currency depreciation on real income and, therefore, private consumption. According to Diaz-Alejandro (1963), devaluation transfers real income from workers to producers of exports and non-tradables. The latter group has a smaller marginal propensity to consume. Along the same lines, Krugman and Taylor (1978) and Barbone and Rivera-Batiz (1987) have formalized several channels of the contractionary effects of devaluation on private consumption.

concerns about the low saving rate in the U.S. economy and its continued dependency on imports and foreign financing. To that end, this paper analyzes determinants of private consumption and its major underlying components: Durable Goods, Non-Durable Goods, and Services. We build on previous research and account for a collection of factors spelled out in theory as important determinants of private consumption. These determinants include disposable income (a proxy for liquidity), an index of consumer sentiment (a proxy for uncertainty), the interest rate (a proxy for the cost of credit), and the real effective exchange rate (a proxy for relative prices).

Using a rational expectation model, we decompose determinants of consumption into anticipated and unanticipated components. This decomposition aims at separating fluctuations in planned consumption in the face of anticipated forecasts from cyclical consumption that varies in the face of unanticipated random shifts. The results indicate that fluctuations in consumption are mostly cyclical. Consumers in the U.S. tend to decrease consumption as the dollar appreciates in value. This is consistent with an increase in the marginal propensity to save in dollar-denominated assets. While appreciation decreases the dollar cost of imports, this channel does not appear to stimulate a large increase of imports for consumption, in general. The only exception is consumption of durable goods, which responds positively to dollar appreciation, indicating a large share of imported durable goods for consumption in the U.S.

The remainder of the paper is organized as follows. Section II provides a theoretical background to model private consumption. Section III outlines the empirical models. Section IV presents empirical results. The summary and conclusions are presented in Section V.

2 Theoretical Background

In the real world, stochastic uncertainty may arise in the macro economy. Economic agents are assumed to be rational. Accordingly, rational expectations distinguish planned behavior from cyclical behavior in the face of random transitory fluctuations. This forecast represents the steady state trend of the macro economy. We assume random fluctuations are realized around this steady state trend.

The demand side of the economy is specified using standard IS-LM equations with a modification for an open economy. The specifications below describe equilibrium conditions in the Goods and Money markets. All coefficients are positive. The subscript t denotes the current value of the variable.

$$c_t = c_0 + c_1 y_{dt} + c_2 csi_t + c_3\, int_t + c_4 reer_t, \quad 0 < c_1 < 1, \quad c_2 > 0, \quad c_3 < 0, \quad c_4? \tag{1}$$

$$int_t = r_t + E_t\left(p_{t+1} - p_t\right) \tag{2}$$

$$y_{dt} = y_t - t_t \tag{3}$$

$$t_t = t_0 + t_1 y_t, \quad t_1 > 0 \tag{4}$$

$$i_t = i_0 - i_1 r_t, \quad i_1 > 0 \tag{5}$$

$$x_t = x_0 - x_1 reer_t, \quad x_1 > 0 \tag{6}$$

$$im_t = g_0 + g_1 y_t + g_2 reer_t, \quad g_1, g_2 > 0 \tag{7}$$

$$y_t^d = c_t + i_t + g_t + x_t - im_t \tag{8}$$

$$m_t - p_t = m_0 - m_1\, int_t + m_2 y_t, \quad m_1, m_2 > 0 \tag{9}$$

$$y_t^s = s_0 + s_1 \left(p_t - E_{t-1} p_t \right) \tag{10}$$

In equation (1), real consumption expenditure, *c*, varies positively with real disposable income, y_d, and a consumer sentiment index, *csi*. Consumption varies negatively with the interest rate, int_t. An increase in *reer* is consistent with currency appreciation. An appreciation of the real effective exchange rate decreases the cost of tradables and, therefore, consumption of non-tradables. The combined effect will depend on the degree of consumers' substitution between tradables and non-tradables. If the reduction in non-tradable consumption dominates the increase in imported consumption, $c_4 < 0$.

In equation (2), the nominal interest rate is the sum of the real interest rate, *r*, and inflationary expectation, $\left(E_t p_{t+1} - p_t\right)$, where p_t is the aggregate price level and E_t is agents' forecast conditional on information available at time *t*.

In equation (3), disposable income is defined to be the net of real income, *y*, minus taxes, *t*. In equation (4), real taxes are specified as a linear function of real income. In equation (5), real investment expenditure, *i*, varies negatively with the real interest rate.

In equation (6), real exports are related to an autonomous element, x_0, which rises when the income level abroad rises, and to relative prices. The negative relationship between *reer* and *x*, in (7), refers to the fact that when the domestic price is higher relative to foreign goods, exports will decrease. In equation (8), real imports, *im*, are assumed to rise with the level of real income and increase with the real exchange rate of the domestic currency.

Equation (9) describes the equilibrium condition in the goods market. Real government spending, *g*, is assumed to be exogenous. The total expenditure by domestic residents in real terms, y^D, is the sum of real consumption expenditure (*c*), real investment (*i*), real government spending (*g*), and net exports (the real value of exports, *x*, minus the real value of imports, *im*).

Substituting all equations into the equilibrium condition for the goods market results in the expression for real income. It is a function of the exchange rate, the domestic price level, the foreign price level, and the domestic interest rate. This expression is the IS equation which describes the negative relationship between real income and the real interest rate.

In equation (9), equilibrium in the money market is obtained by equating the demand and supply of real money balances. The real money supply is determined by nominal balances, *m*, deflated by price, *p*. The demand for real money balances is positively related to real income and inversely related to the nominal interest rate.

The LM equation is determined by the equilibrium condition in the money market. It establishes a positive relationship between real income and the real interest rate. Solving for the interest rate, *r*, from the LM equation and substituting the result into the IS equation results in the equation for aggregate demand.

Aggregate supply in (10) varies with determinants of the output supply in the production function, s_0, and output price surprises, $\left(p_t - E_{t-1}p_t\right)$. Rational agents forecast the aggregate price level conditional on information available at time $t-1, E_{t-1}p_t$. Aggregate demand shifts induce changes in the output price around its forecasted value. These fluctuations create output price surprises that are the domain of random unexpected shocks on the demand and supply sides of the economy. The solution of the model decomposes each of the endogenous variables, output, price, and the interest rate into anticipated and unanticipated components. Anticipated changes are the domain of anticipated shifts in the economy that vary with agents' forecasts of macroeconomic fundamentals. Unanticipated changes are deviations around these forecasts that vary with random shocks impinging on the economic system.

Having solved for disposable income and the interest rate, we solve for private consumption. According to this solution, planned private consumption varies with anticipated changes in policy variables, government spending and the money supply, as well as anticipated changes in the exchange rate and the consumer sentiment index. Cyclical consumption varies unexpectedly with unanticipated changes in these variables.

An increase in government spending increases income and the interest rate. The effects of an increase in government spending on private consumption is likely to depend on the marginal propensity to consume out of income, c_1, and the sensitivity of private consumption to a change in the interest rate, c_3, as well as on the relative effects of government spending on income and the interest rate. If the income channel dominates, an increase in government spending increases disposable income and, hence, private consumption. In contrast, if the interest rate channel dominates, an increase in government spending increases the interest rate and decreases private consumption.

An increase in the money supply increases income and decreases the real interest rate (the liquidity effect). Theoretical developments have established, however, the positive effect of an increase in the money supply on inflationary expectations (the Fisher effect). If the Fisher effect dominates the liquidity effect, the nominal interest rate may be rising following an increase in the money supply. The effect of an increase in the money supply on private consumption will depend, therefore, on the marginal propensity to consume out of income, c_1, the sensitivity of private consumption to a change in the interest rate, c_3, and the relative effects of the money supply on income and the interest rate. An increase in the consumer sentiment index is usually correlated with an improvement in the current state of the economy and the outlook for future economic conditions. Private consumption increases as a result.

An appreciation of the real exchange rate decreases the cost of imports. The increased demand for imports decreases private consumption of non-tradables. The final effect on consumption will depend on the relative increase in tradable consumption compared to the reduction in non-tradable consumption, i.e., the degree of substitution between tradable and non-tradable consumption.

3 Empirical Models

The empirical investigation analyzes quarterly time-series data of private consumption in the United States. Four series of private consumption are under investigation: Total Consumption, Durable Goods, Non-durable Goods, and Services. Based on data availability, we use two measures of the interest rate that are relevant to private consumption: the rate on the 24-month personal loan and the rate on credit cards. All empirical models using the rate on personal loans extend from 1972q1-2002q3, without the exchange rate, and from 1975q1-2002q3, including the exchange rate. All empirical models using the rate on credit cards extend from 1982q3-2003q3. For data definition and sources, see Appendix B.

The analysis will proceed in two steps. In the first step, we estimate a structural equation that replicates equation (1). Private consumption varies with disposable income, the consumer sentiment index, the interest rate, and the effective exchange rate. In the second step, we substitute the money supply and government spending for disposable income and the interest rate. The results will identify the effect of stabilization policies on the biggest component of aggregate demand. Subsequently, correlation coefficients between policy variables and each of disposable income, and the interest rate will determine the channels of interaction between policy variables and private consumption.

3.1 A Structural Representation of Private Consumption

According to the structural representation in (1), private consumption varies with disposable income, the interest rate, consumers' sentiment, and the effective exchange rate. Disposable income is a proxy for liquidity. Consumers' sentiment is a proxy for uncertainty. The interest rate is a proxy for the cost of credit, and the real effective exchange rate is a proxy for relative prices.[7] Assuming rational expectation, each variable can be further decomposed into anticipated and unanticipated components.[8] Having tested for non-stationarity, the empirical model is specified in first-difference form as follows:[9]

$$\begin{aligned} Dc_t = {} & A_0 + A_1 E_{t-1} Dy_{dt} + A_2\left(Dy_{dt} - E_{t-1}Dy_{dt}\right) + A_3 E_{t-1} Dcsi_t + A_4\left(Dcsi_t - E_{t-1}Dsci_t\right) \\ & + A_5 E_{t-1} Dir_t + A_6\left(Dir_t - E_{t-1}Dir_t\right) + A_7 E_{t-1} Dreer_t + A_8\left(Dreer_t - E_{t-1}Dreer_t\right) \\ & + A_9 EC_{t-1} + V_{ct} \end{aligned} \tag{11}$$

7 Omitted from the model specification is a proxy for household resources, i.e., wealth. In the empirical model (12), we introduce the money supply as a proxy for households' holdings of currency and demand deposits.

8 In Appendix A, we describe the procedure to decompose variables into anticipated and unanticipated components. The results are robust to changes in the forecasting procedures.

9 For details, see Kwiatkowski e. al. (1992). To select lags for the KPSS test, we follow the suggestions of Newey and West (1994). Non-stationarity indicates that the series follows a random walk process. Upon first-differencing, the resulting series is stationary. Table A1 in the appendix summarizes the results of non-stationarity.

Here, c_t is the log value of private consumption, where $D(.)$ is the first-difference operator. Four measures of private consumption are under investigation: total consumption, durable goods, non-durable goods, and services.[10]

The log values of disposable income, the interest rate, consumer sentiment index, and the exchange rate are denoted by y_{dt}, ir_t, csi_t, and $reer_t$. The change in each of these variables is decomposed into anticipated and unanticipated components, where E_{t-1} denotes expectations at time $t-1$[11]. Anticipated values are, by construction, function of lagged variables and, therefore, account for persistence in the behavior of consumption.

Since the model is estimated in first-difference form, we should test if the non-stationary dependent variable is jointly cointegrated with all non-stationary right-hand side variables. Given evidence of cointegration (see Table A2), the error correction term is included in the empirical model.[12] The unexplained residual of the model is denoted by v_{ct}

To establish robustness and draw further insights, we estimate three versions of the empirical model in (11), allowing for variation in data measures as follows:[13]

1. Model (11.1) combines real consumption, real disposable income, consumer sentiment index, the nominal interest rate, and the real effective exchange rate.
2. Model (11.2) combines real consumption, real disposable income, consumer sentiment index, the real interest rate, and the real effective exchange rate.
3. Model (11.3) combines nominal consumption, nominal disposable income, consumer sentiment index, the nominal interest rate, and the nominal effective exchange rate.

3.2 A Reduced-Form Representation of Private Consumption

In theory, income and the interest rate are endogenous to policy changes, including monetary and fiscal policies. In the second step of empirical investigation, we substitute government spending and the money supply for disposable income and the interest rate in the empirical model (11). The objective is to test the direct effect of policy changes on private consumption. Accordingly, the following empirical model is estimated:

$$\begin{aligned} Dc_t &= B_0 + B_1E_{t-1}Dg_t + B_2\left(Dg_t - E_{t-1}Dg_t\right) + B_3E_{t-1}Dm_t + B_4\left(Dm_t - E_{t-1}Dm_t\right) \\ &+A_5E_{t-1}Dcsi_t + A_6\left(Dcsi_t - E_{t-1}Dcsi_t\right) + A_7E_{t-1}Dreer_t + A_8\left(Dreer_t - E_{t-1}Dreer_t\right) \\ &+A_7EC_{t-1} + V_{ct} \end{aligned} \quad (12)$$

[10] The decomposition aims at verifying channels of determining planned and cyclical consumption and underlying components.

[11] We test for the endogeneity of the explanatory variables in the model (see Table A3). Given evidence of endogeneity, the forecast equations account for lagged values of other variables proven to be statistically significant.

[12] As long as there exists at least one cointegrating vector, it is necessary to control for this long-run relationship in the empirical model using stationary data. The error correction term captures deviation around the long-run trend, i.e., the lagged value of the residual from regressing the non-stationary dependent variable on the non-stationary variables in the model.

The log values of real government spending and the money supply are denoted by g_t and m_t. The growth of government spending and the money supply are decomposed into anticipated and unanticipated components.

4 Empirical Results

We report the results of the empirical models in (11) and (12) in a sequence. In each case, the empirical model (11) or (12) is estimated jointly with the equations that represent agents' forecasts of proxy variables, as described in Appendix A.

4.1 Structural Representation of Private Consumption

We estimate the empirical models (11.1) through (11.3) using two interest rates that represent the cost of borrowing for consumers: the interest rate on 24-month personal loan and the interest rate on credit cards.

4.1.1 Results Using the Interest Rate on the 24-Month Personal Loan

The results are summarized in Table 1.

<u>Model (11.1)</u>

The first segment of Table 1 summarizes the evidence explaining real consumption in relation to real disposable income, the consumer sentiment index, the nominal interest rate, and the real effective exchange rate.

In contrast to the permanent income hypothesis, real consumption does not vary significantly with anticipated real disposable income.[14] This evidence is robust for total consumption and its underlying components. In contrast, transitory shocks to disposable income have a positive and significant effect on real consumption, specifically nondurable goods.

The combined evidence indicates that consumers do not plan consumption in anticipation of growth in disposable income. In contrast, fluctuations in consumption appear to be cyclical in the face of random unexpected fluctuations in disposable income.

The effects of consumer confidence are only transitory on consumption. Anticipated changes in consumer sentiment do not determine planned consumption significantly. In contrast, all components of consumption vary positively and significantly with unanticipated changes in consumer sentiment. Changes in consumption appear to be cyclical in the face of random unanticipated fluctuations in consumers' sentiment.

The relationship between private consumption and the interest rate is both planned and cyclical. Anticipated increase in the interest rate decreases total consumption and consumption of durable goods significantly. Unanticipated increase in the interest rate

---

[13] In theory, real consumption varies with the nominal interest rate and real disposable income. To establish robustness, we vary the real and nominal measures of variables for estimation.

[14] For a recent treatment of the permanent income hypothesis, see Lettau and Ludvigsan (2004) where only the anticipated evolution of wealth determines consumption. As further detailed in Campbell (1987) and Attanasio (1999), one challenge of the permanent income hypothesis is that only surprises should affect the change in consumption.

decreases private consumption significantly. This evidence applies to total consumption and consumption of durable and non-durable goods.

In the model specification that includes the real effective exchange rate, the evidence remains robust regarding the significant positive effect of transitory income on consumption, both durable and non-durable goods. The positive effect of consumer sentiment does not appear to be robust, however, in this model. The negative significant effect of transitory changes in the interest rate is pervasive across various components of consumption. Anticipated currency appreciation does not determine planned private consumption, or its underlying components, significantly. In contrast, random unexpected appreciation induces a significant decrease in cyclical consumption. Currency appreciation decreases the cost of imported goods and, therefore, consumption of non-tradables. The latter channel appears more dominant.[15] Nonetheless, there is evidence of an increase in cyclical consumption of durable goods in response to currency appreciation.[16] Since imported goods become cheaper, consumers favor tradable goods, which are mostly durables.

Model (11.2)

The second segment of Table 1 summarizes the evidence explaining real consumption in relation to real disposable income, the consumer sentiment index, the real interest rate, and the real effective exchange rate.

The evidence remains robust concerning the positive effect of unanticipated disposable income on private consumption, particularly non-durable goods. The effect of unanticipated increase in consumer confidence is even more pervasive across total consumption and underlying components, both goods and services. In contrast to the evidence using the nominal interest rate in Model (11.1), the effects of the real interest rate, in Model (11.2), appear transitory.[17] Unanticipated increase in the real interest rate has a negative and significant effect on consumption, particularly durable and non-durable goods.

In the model specification that includes the real effective exchange rate, the negative significant effect of unanticipated appreciation is robust on total consumption. A reduction in the cost of imported goods decreases non-tradable consumption, which appears to be dominant.

Model (11.3)

The last segment of Table 1 summarizes the evidence that explains nominal consumption in relation to nominal disposable income, the consumer sentiment index, and the nominal effective exchange rate.

---

15 It is possible, however, that there is a lag in the relation between currency appreciation (depreciation) and consumption. Factors, such as recognition, order, production or delivery, may prevent a contemporaneous increase (decrease) in imported consumption, following a currency appreciation (depreciation). As Krugman (1987) explains, the J-curve describes the lagged response of the quantity adjustment to a change in the currency price.

16 Currency appreciation may be associated with an increase in wealth attributed to a higher value of savings in U.S. dollars. Through this channel, currency appreciation appears to have a positive effect on consumption of durable goods, which is significant at the ten percent level.

17 The nominal interest rate rises with anticipated inflation. Hence, planned consumption decreases with the increase in expected inflation affecting the nominal cost of borrowing.

The results of estimating this model indicate a positive and significant effect of anticipated disposable income on consumption, particularly services.[18] Unanticipated disposable income remains positive and significant on total consumption, as well as on consumption of non-durable goods and services. An unexpected increase in consumer confidence increases total consumption, particularly of durable goods and services. A rise in the interest rate, either anticipated or unanticipated, has a statistically significant negative effect on total consumption and consumption of durable goods.

The results are robust in the model specification that includes the change in the nominal effective exchange rate. Anticipated appreciation decreases total consumption and consumption of durable goods significantly. Unanticipated appreciation decreases consumption of durable goods significantly, which is consistent with a reduction in non-tradable consumption following currency appreciation. In contrast, both anticipated and unanticipated nominal appreciation, have positive significant effects on consumption of services, which is consistent with an increase in tradable consumption following currency appreciation.

4.1.2 Results Using the Interest Rate on Credit Cards

Table 2 presents the evidence of estimating models (11.1) through (11.3) using the interest rate on credit cards charged by banks.

Across the three models, disposable income, both anticipated and unanticipated, has some significant positive effects on private consumption. The effects of unanticipated changes in disposable income on cyclical consumption are particularly evident on non-durable goods. Unanticipated changes in consumer sentiment appear also to have a robust positive significant effect on private consumption.

The interesting difference, compared to previous results, is in the effect of the interest rate on private consumption. Anticipated and unanticipated changes in the interest rate have negative and significant effects on real consumption of durable goods. Nonetheless, the effect of the nominal interest rate is positive on nominal consumption in model (11.3).[19]

The effect of currency appreciation, both anticipated and unanticipated, is insignificant on private consumption and underlying components in the model specifications that incorporate the interest rate on credit cards.

4.2 Reduced Form Representation of Private Consumption

We present the results of estimating the empirical model in (11), substituting monetary growth and the growth of real government spending for the growth of disposable income and the change in the interest rate. The results are summarized in Table 3.

Anticipated growth in government spending is not significant to stimulate planned private consumption. It is interesting to note, however, the positive effect of unanticipated growth in real government spending on total private consumption, and consumption of durable goods. This positive effect is attributed to the effect of government spending on income, which

18 This may be attributed to the correlation between anticipated inflation affecting the nominal values of both disposable income and consumption.

19 Expected inflation has a large positive effect on the nominal interest rate on credit cards charged by banks, which correlates positively with the nominal value of private consumption.

stimulates private consumption. This channel dominates the reduction in private consumption attributed to the increase in the interest rate in the face of a higher growth of government spending.

In contrast, monetary growth is insignificant on private consumption and its underlying components. This evidence is robust for both anticipated and unanticipated monetary growth. Monetary growth stimulates income growth. Concurrently, the nominal interest rate may be increasing if monetary growth stimulates inflationary expectations. The effects of both channels appear to cancel out on private consumption.[20]

The evidence remains robust concerning the contractionary effect of currency appreciation on private consumption. Unanticipated appreciation of the dollar decreases the cost of tradable goods and, therefore, consumption of non-tradables. The latter channel appears more dominant on total private consumption.

5 Conclusion

We have analyzed determinants of private consumption and its major underlying components. Theory has distinguished between cyclical and planned fluctuations in private consumption. Recent recessionary conditions in the U.S. have brought to the forefront concerns about the impact of cyclical downturns on private consumption, which further exacerbates the severity of business cycles and prolongs downturns.

Our model specification is based on a structural representation in which private consumption varies with disposable income, an index of consumer sentiment, the interest rate, and the effective exchange rate. Private consumption is expected to vary positively with disposable income. In addition, many analysts have been tracking the consumer sentiment index as an important indicator of private spending. Private consumption is likely to increase as consumers' confidence increases in the current state of the economy and its future outlook. The interest rate in the model specification approximates the cost of borrowing to finance consumption. Private consumption in the U.S. has been increasingly dependent on credit financing. Higher interest rate increases the cost of borrowing and decreases private consumption. Dollar appreciation decreases the cost of imports and, therefore, consumption of non-tradables.

Using rational expectation, we decompose determinants of consumption: disposable income, consumers' sentiment index, the interest rate and the effective exchange rate into anticipated and unanticipated components. The results, in general, discount the relevance of the permanent income hypothesis. Private consumption appears to be cyclical in the face of transitory fluctuations in disposable income, increasing during a boom and decreasing during a recession. It is interesting to note, however, that cyclicality is more evident for non-durable consumption, compared to durable consumption.

Consumer sentiment is a major factor in determining private consumption and appears to be more important, compared to disposable income, in determining durable consumption. The relationship between consumption and consumer sentiment is cyclical, however, in nature.

---

20 Along the same line, Fuhrer (2000) explores a monetary policy model in which consumers' utility depends, in part, on current consumption relative to past consumption. He rejects the hypothesis of no habit formation.

Changes in the interest rate, both anticipated and unanticipated, determine private consumption. This evidence indicates that anticipated increase (decrease) in the cost of borrowing has a long-lasting negative (positive) effect on private consumption. In addition, random unexpected fluctuations in the interest rate determine cyclical consumption negatively. This evidence is robust to different measures of the interest rate, both nominal and real.

The real effective exchange rate sheds additional light on the behavior of consumption spending. Exchange rate appreciation (depreciation) decreases (increases) consumption of nontradables, while increasing (decreasing) consumption of tradables. The former channel appears more dominant on total consumption. A few exceptions suggest, however, that currency appreciation may be associated with higher values of consumption. This is particularly evident for durable goods, which are likely to constitute a large share of tradables.

In the last step of empirical investigation, we estimate a reduced-form equation of private consumption. The growth of government spending and the money supply replace disposable income and the interest rate in the empirical model. The evidence indicates that cyclical consumption varies positively and significantly with unanticipated random fluctuations in the growth of real government spending. The effect of government spending in stimulating disposable income and private consumption dominates the crowding out channel via the increase in the interest rate. In contrast, monetary growth, both anticipated and unanticipated, is insignificant in determining private consumption. The effects of monetary growth are not directly transmitted to private consumption.

Overall, the evidence sheds new light on the determinants of private consumption and distinguishes between planned and cyclical consumption. Cyclicality of private consumption and its significant fluctuations in the face of government spending and the interest rate provides support to recent directions of monetary and fiscal policies towards stimulating private consumption and positioning the U.S. economy on a steady growth path.

More importantly, the recent trend of dollar depreciation does not bode well to the ability of the U.S. economy to stimulate domestic savings and reduce dependency on foreign financing. Dollar depreciation is likely to decrease the marginal propensity to save and increase consumption, with the exception of consumption of durable goods. As the U.S. economy imports a large share of durable goods, dollar depreciation increases the cost of imports and decreases consumption. Nonetheless, domestic policies remain a key component of stimulating private savings and addressing the need to finance domestic investment. The widening current account deficit in the U.S. may not be sustainable over time as foreign investors diversify away of dollar-denominated assets given the recent trend of dollar depreciation.

Table 1: Nonlinear 3SLS Parameter Estimates, interest rate on 24 month personal loans charged by banks

Model 11-1. Real Consumption as a function of Real Disposable Income, Consumer Sentiment Index, and Nominal Interest Rate. The sample period is 1975q1-2002q3.

	A0	A1	A2	A3	A4	A5	A6	A7	A8	A9	RHO
Total Consumption											
	0.02**	-1.14	0.27**	-0.37	-0.001	-0.40	-0.15**	0.29	-0.05**	-0.04	0.002
	(2.16)	(-1.21)	(3.05)	(-1.01)	(-0.10)	(-1.06)	(-5.21)	(0.97)	(-2.17)	(-0.62)	(0.02)
	R-square: 0.36										
Durable Goods											
	0.01	-0.10	1.32**	0.10	-0.05	0.49	-0.50**	-0.71	0.17*		-0.45**
	(0.71)	(-0.04)	(3.41)	(0.17)	(-0.72)	(0.56)	(-3.97)	(-0.92)	(1.71)		(-4.73)
	R-square: 0.26										
Nondurable Goods											
	0.01**	-0.44	0.38**	-0.01	0.02	0.04	-0.11**	-0.08	-0.03		0.03
	(2.00)	(-0.70)	(4.48)	(-0.12)	(1.54)	(0.25)	(-4.16)	(-0.63)	(-1.27)		(0.25)
	R-square: 0.09										
Services											
	0.01**	-0.37	0.10	-0.06	-0.002	-0.07	-0.04**	0.09	-0.01	-0.08	0.17
	(3.08)	(-0.83)	(1.48)	(-0.63)	(-0.18)	(-0.59)	(-2.00)	(0.85)	(-0.78)	(-1.20)	(1.42)
	R-square: 0.16										

A0 Intercept
A1 Anticipated Disposable Income
A2 Unanticipated Disposable Income
A3 Anticipated Consumer Sentiment Index
A4 Unanticipated Consumer Sentiment Index
A5 Anticipated Interest Rate
A6 Unanticipated Interest Rate
A7 Anticipated Change in Real Exchange Rate
A8 Unanticipated Change in Real Exchange Rate
A9 Error Correction
RHO Serial correlation
** Significant at 5%.
* Significant at 10%.
t-ratios are in parenthesis

Model 11-2. Real Consumption as a function of Real Disposable Income, Consumer Sentiment Index, and Real Interest Rate. The sample period is 1975q1-2002q3 for the models with the exchange rate.

	A0	A1	A2	A3	A4	A5	A6	A7	A8	A9	RHO
Total Consumption											
	0.04	-5.81	0.25**	-0.59	0.01	-0.70	-0.16**	0.49	-0.06*	-0.03	0.03
	(0.52)	(-0.44)	(2.73)	(-0.51)	(0.43)	(-0.48)	(-5.05)	(0.45)	(-2.88)	(-0.52)	(0.28)
	R-square: 0.33										
Durable Goods											
	0.02	-2.09	1.56**	-0.52	-0.05	-0.47	-0.66**	-0.01	-0.01	-0.07	-0.30**
	(0.65)	(-0.38)	(3.63)	(-0.85)	(-0.71)	(-0.70)	(-4.12)	(-0.01)	(-0.07)	(-1.37)	(-2.78)
	R-square: 0.24										
Nondurable Goods											
	0.03	-3.68	0.34**	-0.36	0.003	-0.47	-0.08**	0.29	-0.01		0.03
	(0.66)	(-0.54)	(3.85)	(-0.65)	(0.24)	(-0.64)	(-2.35)	(0.52)	(-0.64)		(0.66)
	R-square: 0.20										
Services											
	0.02	-1.60	0.11	-0.15	0.002	-0.19	-0.04*	0.17	-0.01	-0.07	0.13
	(0.86)	(-0.50)	(1.52)	(-0.57)	(0.18)	(-0.56)	(-1.80)	(0.67)	(-0.82)	(-1.20)	(1.03)
	R-square: 0.20										

A0 Intercept
A1 Anticipated Disposable Income
A2 Unanticipated Disposable Income
A3 Anticipated Consumer Sentiment Index
A4 Unanticipated Consumer Sentiment Index
A5 Anticipated Interest Rate
A6 Unanticipated Interest Rate
A7 Anticipated Change in Real Exchange Rate
A8 Unanticipated Change in Real Exchange Rate
A9 Error Correction
RHO Serial correlation
** Significant at 5%.
* Significant at 10%.
t-ratios are in parenthesis

Table 1: Nonlinear 3SLS Parameter Estimates, interest rate on 24 month personal loans charged by banks (continued)

Model 11-3: Nominal Consumption as a function of Nominal Disposable Income, Consumer Sentiment Index, and Nominal Interest Rate. The sample period is 1975q1-2002q3.

	A0	A1	A2	A3	A4	A5	A6	A7	A8	A9	RHO
Total Consumption											
	0.01*	0.69*	0.49**	0.002	-0.03	0.10	-0.08**	-0.17**	-0.01		-0.02
	(1.84)	(3.98)	(5.02)	(0.03)	(-1.30)	(1.58)	(-2.13)	(-1.97)	(-0.22)		(-0.20)
	R-square: 0.36										
Durable Goods											
	-0.004	1.25**	1.20**	-0.05	-0.04	-0.09	-0.52**	-0.51*	-0.14**	-0.27**	-0.27**
	(-0.42)	(2.04)	(2.93)	(-0.19)	(-0.65)	(-0.37)	(-1.71)	(-1.00)	(-3.35)	(-2.33)	(-2.33)
	R-square: 0.29										
Nondurable Goods											
	0.002	0.70**	0.50**	0.02	-0.03	0.14**	-0.04	-0.25**	-0.05	-0.05	0.34**
	(0.59)	(3.13)	(4.81)	(0.43)	(-1.31)	(1.96)	(-0.92)	(-2.12)	(-1.27)	(-0.61)	(2.25)
	R-square: 0.38										
Services											
	0.03**	-0.49**	-0.11	-0.09	0.01	-0.10	-0.0002	0.33**	0.08**		0.77**
	(6.07)	(-2.24)	(-1.50)	(-1.27)	(0.49)	(-1.61)	(-0.01)	(2.85)	(3.57)		(12.57)
	R-square: 0.44										

A0 Intercept
A1 Anticipated Disposable Income
A2 Unanticipated Disposable Income
A3 Anticipated Consumer Sentiment Index
A4 Unanticipated Consumer Sentiment Index
A5 Anticipated Interest Rate
A6 Unanticipated Interest Rate
A7 Anticipated Change in Real Exchange Rate
A8 Unanticipated Change in Real Exchange Rate
A9 Error Correction
RHO Serial correlation
** Significant at 5%.
* Significant at 10%.
t-ratios are in parenthesis

Table 2: Nonlinear 3SLS Parameter Estimates, interest rate on credit cards charged by banks

Model 11-1: Real Consumption as a function of real disposable income, consumer Sentiment Index, and nominal interest rate, sample period: 1982q1-2002q3

	A0	A1	A2	A3	A4	A5	A6	A7	A8	A9	RHO
Total Consumption											
	0.01**	-1.38	0.14*	-0.06	0.02	-0.12	-0.02	-0.03	0.02		-0.09
	(4.80)	(-1.56)	(1.76)	(-1.45)	(1.41)	(-1.09)	(-0.32)	(-0.47)	(0.78)		(-0.65)
	R-square: 0.25										
Durable Goods											
	0.03**	-2.36*	-0.16	-0.29	0.09	-1.02**	-0.24	0.12	0.01		-0.34**
	(2.45)	(-1.84)	(-0.41)	(-1.39)	(1.33)	(-2.00)	(-0.99)	(0.51)	(0.06)		(-2.64)
	R-square: 0.22										
Nondurable Goods											
	0.01**	0.08	0.18**	-0.03	0.04**	-0.08	-0.03	0.01	0.004		-0.17
	(3.24)	(0.35)	(2.08)	(-0.65)	(2.74)	(-0.74)	(-0.53)	(0.22)	(0.17)		(-1.23)
	R-square: 0.26										
Services											
	0.01**	0.12	0.14**	-0.02	0.001	0.06	-0.05	0.04	0.03**	-0.19**	0.32**
	(5.73)	(0.92)	(2.57)	(-0.94)	(0.10)	(0.64)	(-1.35)	(0.83)	(2.09)	(-2.46)	(2.03)
	R-square: 0.32										

A0 Intercept
A1 Anticipated Disposable Income
A2 Unanticipated Disposable Income
A3 Anticipated Consumer Sentiment Index
A4 Unanticipated Consumer Sentiment Index
A5 Anticipated Interest Rate
A6 Unanticipated Interest Rate
A7 Anticipated Change in Real Exchange Rate
A8 Unanticipated Change in Real Exchange Rate
A9 Error Correction
RHO Serial correlation
** Significant at 5%.
* Significant at 10%.
t-ratios are in parenthesis

Table 2: Nonlinear 3SLS Parameter Estimates, interest rate on credit cards charged by banks (continued)

Model 11-2: Real Consumption as a function of real disposable income, consumer Sentiment Index, and real interest rate, sample period: 1982q1-2002q3

	A0	A1	A2	A3	A4	A5	A6	A7	A8	A9	RHO
Total Consumption											
	0.01**	0.09	0.17**	-0.04	0.01	-0.08	-0.003	-0.05	0.06	-0.23**	0.16
	(2.22)	(0.46)	(2.07)	(-1.05)	(0.92)	(-0.50)	(-0.07)	(0.87)	(1.13)	(-2.30)	(0.89)
	R-square: 0.28										
Durable Goods											
	0.01	-1.37	0.10	-0.26	0.08	-1.33	-0.02	-0.19	0.03	-0.18**	-0.20
	(0.38)	(-1.19)	(0.26)	(-1.28)	(1.15)	(-1.48)	(-0.08)	(-0.66)	(0.27)	(-2.27)	(-1.37)
	R-square: 0.25										
Nondurable Goods											
	0.01	0.17	0.20**	-0.01	0.03**	0.01	-0.01	0.001	0.02	-0.10	-0.10
	(2.07)	(0.79)	(2.28)	(-0.29)	(2.05)	(0.04)	(-0.14)	(0.01)	(0.74)	(-1.45)	(-0.67)
	R-square: 0.27										
Services											
	0.01**	0.13	0.15**	-0.01	0.0003	0.19	-0.04	0.02	0.03**	-0.24**	0.33*
	(3.94)	(1.01)	(2.66)	(-0.63)	(0.04)	(1.15)	(-1.29)	(0.50)	(2.07)	(-2.49)	(1.91)
	R-square: 0.34										

A0 Intercept
A1 Anticipated Disposable Income
A2 Unanticipated Disposable Income
A3 Anticipated Consumer Sentiment Index
A4 Unanticipated Consumer Sentiment Index
A5 Anticipated Interest Rate
A6 Unanticipated Interest Rate
A7 Anticipated Change in Real Exchange Rate
A8 Unanticipated Change in Real Exchange Rate
A9 Error Correction
RHO Serial correlation
** Significant at 5%.
* Significant at 10%.
t-ratios are in parenthesis

Model 11-3: Nominal Consumption as a function of nominal disposable income, consumer Sentiment, and nominal interest rate, sample period: 1982q1-2002q3

	A0	A1	A2	A3	A4	A5	A6	A7	A8	A9	RHO
Total Consumption											
	0.01**	0.04	0.15*	-0.05	0.01	0.19*	-0.02	-0.09	-0.03		-0.07
	(4.61)	(0.17)	(1.88)	(-1.19)	(1.01)	(1.85)	(-0.34)	(-1.21)	(-1.53)		(-0.54)
	R-square: 0.13										
Durable Goods											
	0.03	-1.34	-0.28	-0.37	0.10	-0.53	-0.28	-0.51	0.17		-0.30**
	(1.49)	(-1.01)	(-0.63)	(-1.48)	(1.32)	(-1.07)	(-0.91)	(-1.08)	(1.30)		(-2.35)
	R-square: 0.12										
Nondurable Goods											
	0.01**	0.17	0.33**	0.01	-0.01	0.10	-0.07	-0.06	-0.02		0.23*
	(2.77)	(0.70)	(3.25)	(0.13)	(-0.80)	(0.64)	(-1.05)	(-0.57)	(-0.58)		(1.71)
	R-square: 0.19										
Service											
	0.01**	0.15	0.19**	-0.03	0.003	0.05	-0.05	-0.04	0.01	-0.20*	0.46**
	(5.71)	(0.88)	(2.77)	(-0.93)	(0.30)	(0.42)	(-1.31)	(-0.53)	(0.66)	(-1.90)	(2.58)
	R-square: 0.36										

A0 Intercept
A1 Anticipated Disposable Income
A2 Unanticipated Disposable Income
A3 Anticipated Consumer Sentiment Index
A4 Unanticipated Consumer Sentiment Index
A5 Anticipated Interest Rate
A6 Unanticipated Interest Rate
A7 Anticipated Change in Real Exchange Rate
A8 Unanticipated Change in Real Exchange Rate
A9 Error Correction
RHO Serial correlation
** Significant at 5%.
* Significant at 10%.
t-ratios are in parenthesis

Table 3: Nonlinear 3SLS Parameter Estimates,

Model 12-1: Real consumption as a Function of Consumer Sentiment Index, Real Government Spending, Nominal Money and Real exchange rate, Sample Period: 1975q1-2002q3

	C0	C1	C2	C3	C4	C5	C6	C7	C8	C9	RH0
Total Consumption											
	0.02	-0.35	0.03**	-4.63	0.39**	0.95	0.03	0.84	-0.07**		0.09
	(0.78)	(-0.88)	(2.00)	(-0.80)	(4.66)	(0.63)	(0.23)	(0.69)	(-2.65)		(0.76)
	R-square: 0.31										
Durable Goods											
	0.04	-1.16	0.11*	-13.58	2.23**	3.07	0.21	2.26	-0.31**		-0.25**
	(0.64)	(-1.12)	(1.81)	(-1.01)	(5.74)	(0.74)	(0.40)	(0.90)	(-2.34)		(-2.34)
	R-square: 0.24										
Nondurable Goods											
	0.01	-0.12	0.02	-0.60	0.22**	0.19	-0.07	-0.03	-0.06**		0.01
	(1.53)	(-1.32)	(1.10)	(-0.79)	(2.43)	(0.67)	(-0.58)	(-0.29)	(-2.03)		(0.10)
	R-square: 0.11										
Services											
	0.01**	-0.01	0.02	-0.03	0.10*	0.11	-0.03	- 0.07	-0.03		0.12
	(3.02)	(-0.28)	(1.49)	(-0.06)	(1.64)	(0.62)	(-0.30)	(-0.96)	(-1.51)		(1.08)
	R-square: 0.09										

Model 12-2: Nominal consumption as a Function of Consumer Sentiment Index, Nominal Government Spending, Nominal Money and Real Exchange Rate, Sample Period: 1975q1-2002q3

Total Consumption										
	0.004	-0.05	-0.01	0.37*	0.20**	0.47**	0.22	-0.57	-0.04	0.25**
	(0.89)	(-1.12)	(-0.79)	(1.87)	(3.27)	(2.47)	(1.77)	(-0.74)	(-1.28)	(2.20)
	R-square: 0.30									
Durable Goods										
	0.01	-0.53	0.10	-0.55	0.14	1.02	2.12**	0.01	-0.12	-0.34**
	(0.55)	(-1.58)	(1.52)	(-0.92)	(0.48)	(1.27)	(3.77)	(0.02)	(-0.88)	(-3.16)
	R-square: 0.24									
Nondurable Goods										
	-0.001	-0.12*	-0.03	0.19	0.30**	0.65*	-0.11	-0.74	-0.07	0.57**
	(-0.09)	(-1.78)	(-1.67)	(0.60)	(3.67)	(1.68)	(-0.53)	(-1.19)	(-1.59)	(5.30)
	R-square: 0.35									
Services										
	0.01*	0.01	0.01	0.39*	0.08*	0.43**	0.39**	-0.09	-0.001	0.47**
	(1.79)	(0.24)	(0.61)	(1.89)	(1.68)	(2.55)	(4.20)	(-0.62)	(-0.05)	(4.67)
	R-square: 0.50									

C0 Intercept
C1 Anticipated Consumer Sentiment Index
C2 Unanticipated Consumer Sentiment Index
C3 Anticipated Real Government Spending
C4 Unanticipated Real Government Spending
C5 Anticipated money
C6 Unanticipated Money
C7 Anticipated Real Exchange Rate
C8 Unanticipated Real Exchange Rate
C9 Error Correction
RH0 Serial correlation ** Significant at 5%. * Significant at 10%. t-ratios are in parenthesis

Table A1 The KPSS Statistics for Null of Level Stationary.
(The 5% critical value is 0.463)

	LM Statistic (Bandwidth)+
Real Consumption	
Total Consumption	1.33 (9)
Durable Goods	1.29 (9)
Nondurable Goods	1.31 (9)
Service	1.33 (9)
Nominal Consumption	
Total Consumption	1.32 (9)
Durable Goods	1.30 (9)
Nondurable Goods	1.31 (9)
Service	1.32 (9)

Test description:

The KPSS (Kwiatowski, Phillips, Schmidt, and Shin) stationarity test procedure examines the null hypothesis of stationarity of a univariate time series. The KPSS test assumes that a time series variable X_t could be decomposed into the sum of a deterministic trend, a random walk, and a stationary error. Then the random walk term is assumed to have two components: an anticipated component and an error term. The stationarity of the error term is established by testing if the variance of the error is zero.

If the calculated lag truncation variable is greater than 0.463, we reject the null hypothesis of stationarity.

\+ Bandwidth is specified using Newey-West using Bartlett Kernel. For detail see Newey-West (1994).

Table A2 Cointegration Test Results

ADF test statistics for the null hypothesis of non-stationary residuals.
Critical value at 10% = -2.58

Interest Rate on Personal Loan

Model 11-1, without exchange rate: Cointegration regression includes Real Consumption, Real Disposable Income, Consumer Sentiment Index, and Nominal Interest Rate.

	t-Statistic (# of Lags)+
Real Consumption	
Total	-1.83 (0)
Durable Goods	-1.84 (2)
Nondurable Goods	-2.28 (1)
Service	-1.85 (0)

Model 11-1, with exchange rate: Cointegration regression includes Real Consumption, Real Disposable Income, Consumer Sentiment Index, Nominal Interest Rate, and Real Exchange Rate.

	t-Statistic (# of Lags)+
Real Consumption	
Total	-2.62* (0)
Durable Goods	-2.26 (0)
Nondurable Goods	-1.59 (1)
Service	-3.31* (0)

Table A2 Cointegration Test Results (continued)

ADF test statistics for the null hypothesis of non-stationary residuals.
Critical value at 10% = -2.58

Model 11-2, without exchange rate: Cointegration regression includes Real Consumption, Real Disposable Income, Consumer Sentiment Index, and Real Interest Rate.

	t-Statistic (# of Lags)+
Real Consumption	
Total	-3.88* (0)
Durable Goods	-1.03 (1)
Nondurable Goods	-1.49 (1)
Service	-2.89* (1)

Model 11-2, with exchange rate: Cointegration regression includes Real Consumption, Real Disposable Income, Consumer Sentiment Index, Real Interest Rate, and Real Exchange Rate.

	t-Statistic (# of Lags)+
Real Consumption	
Total	-4.37* (0)
Durable Goods	-1.08 (1)
Nondurable Goods	-0.76 (1)
Service	-3.96* (1)

Model 11-3, without exchange rate: Cointegration regression includes Nominal Consumption, Nominal Disposable Income, Consumer Sentiment Index, and Nominal Interest Rate.

	t-Statistic (# of Lags)+
Nominal Consumption	
Total	-2.15 (0)
Durable Goods	-1.81 (1)
Nondurable Goods	-2.17 (0)
Service	-1.43 (0)

Model 11-3, with exchange rate: Cointegration regression includes Nominal Consumption, Nominal Disposable Income, Consumer Sentiment Index, Nominal Interest Rate, and Nominal Exchange Rate.

	t-Statistic (# of Lags)+
Nominal Consumption	
Total	-3.44* (3)
Durable Goods	-3.51* (0)
Nondurable Goods	-2.38 (0)
Service	-2.60* (2)

Interest Rate on Credit cards

Model 11-1, without exchange rate: Cointegration regression includes Real Consumption, Real Disposable Income, Consumer Sentiment Index, and Nominal Interest Rate.

	t-Statistic (# of Lags)+
Real Consumption	
Total	-2.83* (0)
Durable Goods	-1.93 (1)
Nondurable Goods	-2.88* (0)
Service	-1.37 (1)

Table A2 Cointegration Test Results (continued)

ADF test statistics for the null hypothesis of non-stationary residuals.
Critical value at 10% = -2.58

Model 11-1, with exchange rate: Cointegration regression includes Real Consumption, Real Disposable Income, Consumer Sentiment Index, Nominal Interest Rate, and Real Exchange Rate.

	t-Statistic (# of Lags)
Real Consumption	
Total	-1.45 (0)
Durable Goods	-1.47 (0)
Nondurable Goods	-2.15 (2)
Service	-3.48* (0)

Model 11-2, without exchange rate: Cointegration regression includes Real Consumption, Real Disposable Income, Consumer Sentiment Index, and Real Interest Rate.

	t-Statistic (# of Lags)
Real Consumption	
Total	-2.65* (1)
Durable Goods	-1.97 (7)
Nondurable Goods	-3.05* (1)
Service	-2.07 (1)

Model 11-2, with exchange rate: Cointegration regression includes Real Consumption, Real Disposable Income, Consumer Sentiment Index, Real Interest Rate, and Real Exchange Rate.

	t-Statistic (# of Lags)
Real Consumption	
Total	-2.68* (1)
Durable Goods	-2.77* (7)
Nondurable Goods	-2.36* (0)
Service	-3.63* (0)

Model 11-3, without exchange rate: Cointegration regression includes Nominal Consumption, Nominal Disposable Income, Consumer Sentiment Index, and Nominal Interest Rate.

	t-Statistic (# of Lags)
Nominal Consumption	
Total Consumption	-0.46 (1)
Durable Goods	-3.38* (0)
Nondurable Goods	-2.36 (2)
Service	-1.11 (0)

Model 11-3, with exchange rate: Cointegration regression includes Nominal Consumption, Nominal Disposable Income, Consumer Sentiment Index, Nominal Interest Rate, and Nominal Exchange Rate.

	t-Statistic (# of Lags)
Nominal Consumption	
Total	-2.46 (0)
Durable Goods	-2.14 (2)
Nondurable Goods	-2.48 (0)
Service	-3.60* (0)

Table A2: Cointegration Test Results (Continued)

ADF test statistics for the null hypothesis of non-stationary residuals.
Critical value at 10% = -2.58
Model 12-1: Cointegration regression includes Real Consumption, Consumer Sentiment Index, Real Government Spending, Nominal Money, and Real Exchange Rage

	t-Statistic (# of Lags)[+]
Real Consumption	
Total	-1.90 (0)
Durable Goods	-0.37 (0)
Nondurable Goods	-0.44 (0)
Service	-1.25 (0)

Model 12-2: Cointegration regression includes Nominal Consumption, Consumer Sentiment Index, Nominal Government Spending, Nominal Money, and Real Exchange Rage

	t-Statistic (# of Lags)[+]
Real Consumption	
Total	-1.89 (0)
Durable Goods	-1.99 (0)
Nondurable Goods	-1.54 (0)
Service	-0.91 (0)

Test Description:

If we have n endogenous variables, each of which is first-order integrated (that is, each has a unit root or stochastic trend or random walk element), there can be from zero to n-1 linearly independent cointegrating vectors. If there is one cointegrating equation, the regression models of the text include a lag of error correction term.

To check for cointegration, we apply the ADF unit root test to the residual from the cointegration regression in which the non-stationary level of real and nominal consumption are regressed on the level of variables that enter the model.

* The results reject the null hypothesis of non-stationarity at the 10% level.

+ The numbers in parentheses represent the lag lengths. The lag length is selected based on Schwartz Information Criteria (SCI) out of max lag of 12)

Table A3: The Results of Endogeneity Tests.

Interest rate on 24-month personal loans provided by banks

	Forecasted Variables			
	Ddy	Dcsi	Dr	
Model 11-1, without exchange rate				
Real Disposable Income (Ddy)		0.40	2.12	
Consumer Sentiment Index (Dcsi)	3.21*		0.38	
Nominal Interest Rate (Dr)	5.95*	2.20		
	Ddy	Dcsi	Dr	Drex
Model 11-1, with exchange rate				
Real Disposable Income (Ddy)		0.70	1.65	8.31*
Consumer Sentiment Index (Dcsi)	2.10		0.30	0.82
Nominal Interest Rate (Dr)	0.80	2.49*		1.55
Real Exchange Rate (Drex)	0.36	0.39	2.59*	
	Ddy	Dcsi	Dr	
Model 11-2, without exchange rate				
Real Disposable Income (Ddy)		0.61	1.09	
Consumer Sentiment Index (Dcsi)	3.26*		0.07	
Real Interest Rate (Dr)	6.28*	2.93*		
	Ddy	Dcsi	Dr	Drex
Model 11-2, with exchange rate				
Real Disposable Income (Ddy)		1.11	2.30	0.46
Consumer Sentiment Index (Dcsi)	2.29		0.12	0.79
Real Interest Rate (Dr)	10.97*	4.57*		3.96*
Real Exchange Rate (Drex)	1.24	0.10	4.79*	
	Ddy	Dcsi	Dr	
Model 11-3, without exchange rate				
Nominal Disposable Income (Ddy)		0.03	1.99	
Consumer Sentiment Index (Dcsi)	2.88*		0.02	
Nominal Interest Rate (Dr)	11.35*	1.83		
	Ddy	Dcsi	Dr	Dnex
Model 11-3, with exchange rate				
Nominal Disposable Income (Ddy)		0.74	3.83*	0.64
Consumer Sentiment Index (Dcsi)	1.85		0.01	0.41
Nominal Interest Rate (Dr)	15.48*	3.25*		4.01*
Nominal Exchange Rate (Dnex)	0.03	0.19	3.72*	

* F-value is greater than the critical value of F at 10%.

Table A3: The Results of Endogeneity Tests. (Continued)

Interest rate on credit cards provided by banks	Forecasted Variables			
	Ddy	Dcsi	Dr	
Model 11-1, without exchange rate				
Real Disposable Income (Ddy)		0.96	0.51	
Consumer Sentiment Index (Dcsi)	0.08		0.17	
Nominal Interest Rate (Dr)	1.50	0.41		
	Ddy	Dcsi	Dr	Drex
Model 11-1, with exchange rate				
Real Disposable Income (Ddy)		1.15	0.62	0.85
Consumer Sentiment Index (Dcsi)	0.03		0.14	1.59
Nominal Interest Rate (Dr)	1.68	0.54		0.56
Real Exchange Rate (Drex)	0.33	0.14	0.89	
	Ddy	Dcsi	Dr	
Model 11-2, without exchange rate				
Real Disposable Income (Ddy)		1.02	0.44	
Consumer Sentiment Index (Dcsi)	0.12		0.02	
Real Interest Rate (Dr)	1.50	0.29		
	Ddy	Dcsi	Dr	Drex
Model 11-2, with exchange rate				
Real Disposable Income (Ddy)		1.20	0.52	0.82
Consumer Sentiment Index (Dcsi)	0.05		0.01	1.61
Real Interest Rate (Dr)	1.61	0.35		0.34
Real Exchange Rate (Drex)	0.30	0.19	0.98	
	Ddy	Dcsi	Dr	
Model 11-3, without exchange rate				
Nominal Disposable Income (Ddy)		0.84	0.84	
Consumer Sentiment Index (Dcsi)	2.29		0.81	
Nominal Interest Rate (Dr)	0.23	0.28		
	Ddy	Dcsi	Dr	Dnex
Model 11-3, with exchange rate				
Nominal Disposable Income (Ddy)		1.63	0.36	1.00
Consumer Sentiment Index (Dcsi)	0.06		0.11	0.91
Nominal Interest Rate (Dr)	2.46*	0.79		0.47
Nominal Exchange Rate (Dnex)	0.01	0.22	0.83	

* F-value is greater than the critical value of F at 10%.

Table A3: The Results of Endogeneity Tests. (Continued)

	Forecasted Variables			
	Dcsi	Dg	Dm	Drex
Model 12-1				
Consumer Sentiment Index (Dcsi)		0.36	3.46*	1.11
Real Government Spending (Dg)	0.79		3.05*	0.67
Nominal Money (Dm)	1.17	0.05		3.15*
Real Exchange Rate (Drex)	0.56	3.51*	2.94*	
	Dcsi	Dg	Dm	Drex
Model 12-2				
Consumer Sentiment Index (Dcsi)		0.42	3.85*	0.93
Real Government Spending (Dg)	0.32		0.82	1.17
Nominal Money (Dm)	1.28	0.84		2.86*
Real Exchange Rate (Drex)	0.10	0.25	2.07	

* F-value is greater than the critical value of F at 10%.

Appendix A

Econometric Methodology

The surprise terms that enter models (11) and (12) are unobservable, necessitating the construction of empirical proxies before estimation takes place. Thus, the empirical models include equations describing agents' forecast of the change in the log values of disposable income, the interest rate, the index of consumer sentiment index, the effective exchange rate, the money supply and government spending. All variables are first-differenced to render the series stationary, as described in Table A1.

To decide on variables in the forecast equations, we follow a formal causality test. We regress each variable on four of its lags as well as four lags of all variables that enter the model: the change in the log value of disposable income, the consumer sentiment index, the interest rate, and the effective exchange rate, in model (11), or the change in the log value of government spending, the money supply, and the exchange rate, in model (12). The joint significance of the lags is tested for each variable (see Table A3). Accordingly, the forecast equations account for the lags of variables proven to be statistically significant. Variables are considered exogenous if none of the lags of other variables are proven to be statistically significant.

Subtracting the above forecasts from the actual change in the variable results in surprises that enter the empirical model. In order to obtain efficient estimates and ensure correct inferences (i.e., to obtain consistent variance estimates), we estimate the empirical models for forecasted variables *jointly* with a forecast equation for each anticipated regressor, following the suggestions of Pagan (1984 and 1986). The joint estimation requires substituting the parameters of the forecast equations into the empirical models for consumption, which renders the estimation technique non-linear.

To account for endogenous variables, we use instrumental variables in the estimation of the empirical models. The instrument list includes five lags of all variables specified in theory as possible determinants of endogenous variables: the growth rate of real GDP, nominal personal income, real disposable income, real and nominal consumption, interest rate, consumer price index, real and nominal government spending, money supply, consumer sentiment index, and the nominal and real effective exchange rate. In a few cases, we modify the number of lags until the estimation did converge. The paper's evidence remains robust with respect to modifications that alter variables or the lag length in the forecast equations and/or the instruments list.

Following the suggestions of Engle (1982), the results of the test for serial correlation in simultaneous equation models are consistent with the presence of first-order autoregressive errors. To maintain comparability, it is assumed in all models that the error term follows an AR(1) process. The estimated models are transformed, therefore, to eliminate any possibility for serial correlation. The estimated residuals from the transformed models have zero means and are serially independent.

Appendix B

Data Sources

The sample period for investigation is 1972q1-2002q3 for models with the interest rate on 24-month personal loan and is 1982q3-2002q3 for models with the interest rate on credit cards. Annual data for the above countries are described as follows:

1. Real and effective exchange rates are taken from *International Financial Statistics*.
2. Interest rate on personal loans is obtained from the Federal Reserve Board.
3. Interest rate on credit cards is obtained from the Federal Reserve Board.
4. Real interest rates are the nominal interest rate divided by the price index.
5. The discount rate, the Federal Fund rate, the consumer price index, and the money supply are obtained from the Federal Reserve Bank of St. Louis.
6. Real GDP, nominal personal income, real disposable income, real and nominal consumption, and real and nominal government are from the Commerce Department, Bureau of Economic Analysis.
7. Consumer sentiment index is from surveys of consumers conducted by the Survey Research Center at the University of Michigan.

References

Abel, Andrew (1990) "Consumption and Investment," in *Handbook of Monetary Economics*, B. Friedman and F. Hahn, eds., Volume 2, Chapter 14.

Andrews, Donald W. K. (1993) "Tests for Parameter Instability and Structural Change with Unknown Change Point," *Econometrica,* Volume 61, Issue 4, pp. 821-856.

Barbone, Luca and Francisco Rivera-Batiz, (1987) "Foreign Capital and the Contractionary Impact of Currency Devaluation, with an Application to Jamaica," *Journal of Development Economics*, (Amsterdam), (June), Vol. 26, pp. 1-15.

Benoit, Carmichael, Sikoro Keita, and Lucie Samoson, (1999) "Liquidity Constraints and Business Cycles in Developing Countries," *Review of Economic Dynamics*, **2**, pp. 370-402.

Attanasio, Orazio, (1999) "Consumption," in *Handbook of Macroeconomics,* J. Taylor and M. Woodford, eds., Volume 1b, Chapter 11.

Campbell, John Y., (1987) "Does Saving Anticipate Declining Labor Income? An Alternate Test of the Permanent Income Hypothesis," *Econometrica,* November, 55(6), pp. 1249-73.

Campbell, J. Y. and Mankiw, N. G., (1989) "Consumption and Interest Rates: Reinterpreting the Time-Series Evidence," *NBER Macroeconomics Annual*, (eds) O. J. Blanchard and S. Fisher, MIT Press: Cambridge.

Campbell, J. Y. and Mankiw, N. G., (1990) "Permanent Income, Current Income, and Consumption," *Journal of Business and Economic Statistics*, **8**(3), pp. 265-279.

Campbell, J. Y. and Mankiw, N. G., (1991) "The Response of Consumption to Income, A Cross-Country Investigation," *European Economic Review*, **35**, pp. 723-767.

Canner, G. B. and Fergus, J. T. (1987) "The Economic Effects of Proposed Ceilings on Credit Card Interest Rates," *Federal Reserve Bulletin*,**73**, pp. 1-13.

Dejuan, Joseph P. and John J. Seater, (1999) "The Permanent Income Hypothesis: Evidence from the Consumer Expenditure Survey," *Journal of Monetary Economics*, **43**, pp. 351-376.

Diaz-Alejandro, Carlos F., (1963) "A Note on the Impact of Devaluation and Redistributive Effects," *Journal of Political Economy*, (August), Vol. 71, pp. 577-580.

Engle, R. R. (1982) "A General Approach to Lagrange Multiplier Model Diagnostics," *Journal of Econometrics*, **20**, 83-104.

Falvin, M. A. (1981) "The Adjustment of Consumption to Changing Expectations about Future Income," *Journal of Political Economy*, **89,** pp. 974-1009.

Friedman, M. *A Theory of the Consumption Function*, (1957), Princeton, NJ: Princeton University Press for National Bureau of Economic Research.

Fuhrer, Jeffrey, C. (2000) "Habit Formation in Consumption and Its Implications for Monetary Policy Models," *American Economic Review*, June.

Girardin, Eric, Lucio Sarno, and Mark P. Taylor, (2000) "Private Consumption Behavior, Liquidity Constraints and Financial Deregulation in France: A non-Linear Analysis," *Empirical Economics*, Vol. 25, pp. 351-368.

Hahm, Joon-Ho "Consumption Adjustment to Real Interest Rates: Intertemporal substitution Revisited," *Journal of Economic Dynamics and Control*, pp. 293-320.

Hall, R. E. (1978) "The Stochastic Implication of the Life-Cycle Permanent Income Hypothesis: Theory and Evidence," *Journal of Political Economy*, **96**, pp. 971-87.

Hall, R. E. and Mishkin, F. S. (1982) "The Sensitivity of Consumption to Transitory Income: Estimates from Panel Data on Households," *Econometrica*, **50**, pp. 461-81.

Heller, W. P. and Starr, R. M. (1979) "Capital Market Imperfection, the Consumption Function, and the Effect of Fiscal Policy," *Quarterly Journal of Economics*, CXIII, pp. 455-463.

Hussein, Khaled A. and DeMello, Luiz R. Jr. (1999)"International Capital Mobility in Developing Countries: Theory and Evidence," *Journal of International Money and Finance*, **18**, pp. 367-381.

Kaynak, Erdener, Orsay Kucukemiroglu and Ahmet Ozmen, (1995) "Correlates of Credit Card Acceptance and Usage in an Advanced Developing Middle Eastern Country," *Journal of Services Marketing*, Vol. 9, No. 4, pp. 52-63.

Krugman, Paul R. and Richard E. Baldwin, "The Persistence of the U.S. Trade Deficit," *Brookings Papers on Economic Activity*, No. **1**, pp. 1-43.

Krugman and Taylor, (1978) "Contractionary Effects of Devaluation," *Journal of International Economics*, **8**, pp. 445-456.

Kwiatkowski, Denis, Peter C. B. Phillips, Peter Schmidt, and Yongcheol Shin, (1992) "Testing the Null Hypothesis of Stationarity Against the Alternative of a Unit Root: How Sure Are We That Economic Time Series Have a Unit Root?" *Journal of Econometrics*, **54**, pp. 159-78.

Leong, Kenneth and Michael AcAleer, (1999) "Testing the Life-Cycle Permanent Income Hypothesis Using Intra-Year Data for Sweden," *Mathematics and Computers in Simulation*, **48**, pp. 551-560.

Lettau, Martin and Sydney C. Ludvigsan (2004) "Understanding Trend and Cycle in Asset Values: Reevaluating the Wealth Effect on Consumption," *American Economic Review*, March, pp. 276-299.

Mathieson, Donald J. and Liliana Rojas-Suarez, (1990) "Financial Market Integration and Exchange Rate Policy," *IMF Working Paper*, WP/90/02, Washington D.C.

Newey, Whitney and Kenneth West, "Automatic Lag Selection in Covariance Matrix Estimation," *Review of Economic Studies*, **61**, pp. 631-653.

Pagan, Adrian, (1984) "Econometric Issues in the Analysis of Regressions with Generated Regressor," *International Economic Review*, **25**, 221-47.

Pagan, Adrian, (1986) "Two Stage and Related Estimators and Their Applications," *Review of Economic Studies*, **53**, 517-38.

Palumbo, Michael, Jeremy Rudd and Karl Whelan (2002) "On the Relationships between Real Consumption, Income, and Wealth," *Finance and Economics Discussion Series*, no. **2002-38**, Board of Governors of the Federal Reserve System.

Park, Sangkyun and Anthony P. Rodrigues, (2000) "Is Aggregate Consumer Borrowing Consistent with the Permanent Income Hypothesis?" *The Manchester School*, Vol. 68, No. 3, pp. 301-320.

Reinhart, Carmen M. and Carlos A. Vegh, (1995) "Nominal Interest Rates, Consumption Booms, and Lack of Credibility: A Quantitative Examination," *Journal of Development Economics*, Vol. 46. pp. 357-378.

Sarno, Lucio and Mark P. Taylor, (1998) "Real Interest Rates, Liquidity Constraints, and Financial Deregulation: Private Consumption Behavior in the U.K.," *Journal of Macroeconomics*, Vol. 20, pp. 221-242.

Scott, A. (1996) "Consumption, 'Credit Crunches' and Financial Deregulation," *CEPR Discussion Paper*, no. **1389**, London, Centre for Economic Policy Research.

Yin, Zhang and Guang Hua Wan (2002) "Household Consumption and Monetary Policy in China," *China Economic Review*, **13**, pp. 27-52.

Zeldes, Stephen P. (1989) "Consumption and Liquidity Constraints: An Empirical Investigation," *Journal of Political Economy*, **97**, pp. 305-346.

In: New Developments in Macroeconomics Research
Editor: Lawrence Z. Pelzer, pp. 73-100
ISBN: 1-59454-663-0

Chapter 3

RESPONSIVENESS TO EXTERNAL DEVELOPMENTS THROUGH THE TRADE CHANNEL: NEW ESTIMATES FOR THE EURO AREA

Daniele Antonucci [*]
Centro Studi Confindustria – Confederation of Italian Industries,
Research Department, Viale dell'Astronomia, 30
00144 Rome, Italy
Alessandro Girardi [**]
University of Rome "Tor Vergata", Department of
Economics and Institutions, Via Columbia, 2
00133 Rome, Italy

Abstract

This work aims at assessing the impact of various external shocks on trade exchanges between the euro area and the rest of the world using cointegration techniques for simulation purposes. The main results are: *i*) non-price competitiveness factors and the real exchange rate affect the euro area trade balance in the long-run. Furthermore, the Marshall-Lerner conditions is strongly rejected; *ii*) extending the sample span over the post-EMU period, i.e. accounting for the introduction of the single currency, the results are qualitatively similar in terms of statistical significance and feedback mechanisms; *iii*) changes in foreign demand and in the price of oil do not exert a statistically significant impact on the trade balance; *iv*) domestic demand and price competitiveness play the main role in explaining trade fluctuations. Moreover, the share of volatility attributable to the former increases over time, while the contribution of the latter remains stable and accounts for the biggest proportion.

JEL Classification: C32, C51, E32, F17.
Keywords: Euro area, trade flows, external shocks, cointegration, forecast error variance decomposition.

---

[*] E-mail address: d.antonucci@confindustria.it
[**] E-mail address: alessandro.girardi@uniroma2.it

1. Introduction

This paper aims at assessing how external factors may affect import and export performances in the euro area. Treating the latter as a single economy is a relatively recent approach focusing on area-wide economic relationships in view of the increasing integration among the Economic and Monetary Union (EMU) member countries. It should be noted that not only there exist very few traditional econometric applications, such as estimated structural or reduced-form specifications as well as calibrated general equilibrium-type models, expressly considering the euro area as a whole (see, for example, Fagan et al., 2001; Smets and Wouters, 2003), but there is also a limited number of time series analyses concentrating on a restricted subset of the variables included in those models, such as trade flows and their main determinants (see, for example, Anderton and Skudelny, 2001; Anderton et al., 2002). In this respect, this paper aims at extending econometric modeling of international trade flows to the euro area in order to contribute to the comprehension of its functioning as a single economic entity.

The current work builds on previous results by Antonucci and Girardi (2005). They estimate a number of vector error correction (VEC) models for the euro area using different specifications and frequencies of data. In particular, they test three alternative long-run determination mechanisms of the trade balance, namely the elasticity, absorption and monetary approaches, using monthly and quarterly observations. On the one hand, they find that real exchange rate changes do not positively affect the trade balance in the long-run. In other words, their empirical work suggests that price elasticities are very low in the case under examination, i.e. the Marshall-Lerner (ML) condition for a devaluation to improve the trade balance is violated. On the other hand, non-price competitiveness factors, such as quality and innovation, exert a relevant influence on the trade balance in accordance with the absorption approach. In the short-run, moreover, a devaluation leads to a deterioration of the trade balance, as it is generally believed assuming the validity of the J-curve theory. However, using the Sequential Elimination of the Regressors Testing Procedure (SER/TP) in order to account for the statistical significance of parameters (Brüggemann and Lütkepohl, 2001) rather than an unrestricted specification, results in terms of shape and time length of trade balance adjustments to a currency shock vary according to the employed time frequency. In more details, estimates based on quarterly data differ considerably, while estimates based on monthly data exhibit only marginal differences. Moreover, the interpretative power of the theoretical J-curve does not prove enough to describe the complexities of interaction among the involved variables arising in the convergence process towards equilibrium. The empirical trajectory describing the evolution over time of the trade balance in response to an exchange rate change recalls more closely the S-shaped pattern mentioned in Backus et al. (1994) and in Roberts (1995) rather than the J-shaped path typically reported in standard textbooks. Finally, in order to check the stability of the estimated system over the possible structural change represented by the adoption of the euro, the authors perform CUSUM and CUSUMSQ tests. Looking at the results for the trade balance dynamic equation, they infer that the changeover has marginally affected the elasticity of extra-EMU trade flows.

Further developing the above-mentioned analytical framework, this paper aims at providing additional evidence on the likely response of euro area merchandise exports and imports to external shocks.

First, even though traditional trade models place considerable emphasis on the consequences on trade flows of changes in the exchange rate as well as in aggregate demand, additional variables may play a relevant role and lead to different trade elasticities over time or according to circumstances (Anderton et al., 2004). For instance, the sharp increase in oil price from the end of 1998 might help to explain the weaker than expected response of the euro area trade balance owing to the depreciation of the single currency during the period 1999-2000. Provided that imports of oil are relatively inelastic, part of such increase may have almost automatically translated into a lower trade surplus. Thus, the price of oil is explicitly introduced as an *ex-post* exogenous factor affecting the dynamics of trade exchanges between the EMU and the rest of the world.

Second, as previous comparisons between estimates based on quarterly and monthly data suggest that different time scales may lead to very diverse conclusions in terms of evolution over time of the variable taken into consideration, the highest frequency of data is employed. In this specific case, the choice to use monthly observations is motivated by the primary objective of this paper. While the length of the period between one observation and the following does not deeply alter the overall picture of structural phenomena changing slowly in a usually very long time span, a correct assessment of the short- and long-run responsiveness of a certain macroeconomic aggregate to an external shock requires an appropriate time unit. For instance, it may apparently seem that imports and exports react to a devaluation of the exchange rate as it is conventionally assumed, i.e. exports should increase and imports should decrease over time, just because looking at two consecutive quarters the trade balance shows an improvement. Looking at each of the corresponding six months, however, this pattern may hide some more articulate dynamics and reveal a worsening of the trade balance for the following four observations which is more than compensated by a considerable improvement in the last month of the sample. For this reason, both estimation and simulation are based on monthly-observed time series.

Third, in order to check whether the adoption of the euro has represented a structural change, the following approach is proposed. Antonucci and Girardi (2005) estimate the model over a sample span including both pre- and post-EMU observations and assess the stability of coefficients employing appropriate statistical tests. In this paper, instead, the impact of the changeover is inferred analyzing the correlation between the cointegration residuals of the models estimated over the pre-EMU period and the whole sample, respectively.

Besides the above-mentioned refinements, we also present an application of recent econometric tools to the analysis of trade flows fluctuations. In particular, forecast error variance decomposition and bootstrapping techniques are employed to quantify the contribution of each shock to the volatility of the trade balance.

The rest of the paper is structured as follows. Section 2 briefly presents an overview of the likely sensitiveness to changes in external conditions for large advanced countries. The patterns of the euro area imports and exports, as well as of the variables usually identified as their main determinants, are described in the following Section. The empirical strategies and the main estimation results are illustrated in Sections 4 and 5, respectively. Final remarks and an appendix presenting data sources and definitions conclude.

2. Relevance of External Trade Exchanges in a Comparative Perspective

Even though its members are relatively small and open, the euro area as a whole is one the biggest world economies in many respects and its structural characteristics are somewhat more comparable with those of the U.S. or, to some extent, Japan rather that with those of the individual countries which are part of the EMU. Accounting for 5% of world population in 2003, in terms of demographic size the euro area is the major advanced economy, roughly comparable with the U.S. (4.7%) and more than twice bigger than Japan (2.1%). In terms of economic size, the euro area can be considered the second largest market in the world. It accounts for approximately 16% of global GDP expressed in purchasing power parity, while the U.S. and Japanese share is around 21% and 7%, respectively.

Concerning international trade relations, however, those three large economies differ considerably (Tab. 1). Looking at the relative position in trade exchanges, the slight increase in export market share for the euro area during the pre-EMU period corresponds to a contraction of one percentage point in Japan. Subsequently, the introduction of the single currency marks an exponential growth of euro area exports, which account for the highest proportion of world exports (19.4%) in the subsample 1999-2003, and a further decline of the importance of Japan in international markets, while the U.S. export share remains substantially stable for the entire period of observation. The pattern of import market shares, on the other hand, shows different peculiarities. Even though there still is an overall acceleration of the increasing weight in world imports of the euro area, the latter exhibits a minor trend reversal during the years 1994-1998. Moreover, U.S. exports not only exhibit a similar tendency, i.e. a growing weight over time, but represent the highest share in global imports during the whole period under examination.

The remaining indicators in Table A.1 provide a measure of the importance of the trade channel for the three economies. While in the euro area the five-year average of the sum of exports and imports represents 28.8% of its GDP during the period 1999-2003, the degree of trade openness in the U.S. (18.8%) and in Japan (18.2%) is similar and significantly lower. In other words, external trade developments affect the euro area to a larger extent with respect to the two countries taken as a benchmark. Moreover, in these economies the indicator under examination exhibits a very diverse pattern over time. On the one hand, not only the EMU has become increasingly more open, but the pace of such process has recorded a substantial acceleration, particularly after the adoption of the single currency, when the sum of exports and imports as a proportion of GDP increased by more than eight percentage points from 20.2% at the beginning of the period of observation. In addition, looking at the simultaneous evolution of the weight of international exchanges as compared to GDP, during the years 1989-1993 both the U.S. and Japan show a higher reliance to external trade with respect to the euro area. In the subsequent periods, however, as a consequence of the divergence of individual trends, i.e. trade openness increases steadily in the euro area, reaches a peak during the years 1994-1998 and lately declines in the U.S., decreases continuously in Japan, trade openness in the EMU exceeds that of the two other economies by at least ten percentage points.

Table 1 – International trade indicators (percentage values)

	EMU	USA	JAP
Export market share			
1989-1993	12.5	13.7	10.3
1994-1998	13.0	13.8	9.3
1999-2003	19.4	13.6	8.2
Import market share			
1989-1993	12.3	16.9	7.3
1994-1998	11.6	17.9	6.9
1999-2003	17.5	21.2	6.2
Trade openness			
1989-1993	20.2	23.7	23.6
1994-1998	23.2	25.9	22.4
1999-2003	28.8	18.8	18.2
Export propensity			
1989-1993	9.9	10.4	13.6
1994-1998	12.1	11.1	12.7
1999-2003	14.7	7.1	10.1
Import penetration			
1989-1993	10.3	13.2	10.2
1994-1998	11.3	14.6	9.9
1999-2003	14.3	11.3	8.2

Other measures of relevance of the trade channel show a substantially similar picture and suggest that the extent of interaction of the euro area with the rest of the world is similar from both the export and import side. Conversely, the U.S. (Japanese) economy is much closer from the export (import) side, partly reflecting trade policy interventions. In more details, export propensity has increased considerably in the euro area, passing from 9.9% in 1994 to 14.7% in 2003 and indicating that more and more output produced within the euro area is exported abroad. By contrast, in both the U.S. and Japan such indicator is smaller, showing a lower dependency from external demand developments. Moreover, import penetration is much higher in the euro area than in the two other major economies, showing that in the former the share of domestic demand satisfied by foreign markets is more relevant.

Hence, given the same trade elasticities, a shock of equal magnitude may have far more severe consequences on EMU international exchanges and deeply affect the overall performance through this channel.

Looking at the trend of the merchandise trade balance and of its components during the fifteen-year period 1989-2003, indeed, the EMU is the only economy experiencing various reversals (Fig. 1). While exports and imports in both the U.S. and Japan seem to follow a rather definite pattern, resulting in an increasing deficit in the former and in an alternating high-and-low surplus in the latter, after small oscillations in the late Eighties and early Nineties the euro area experiences a protracted and more consistent trade surplus for eight consecutive years, a slight deficit in 2000 and a considerable recovery afterwards.

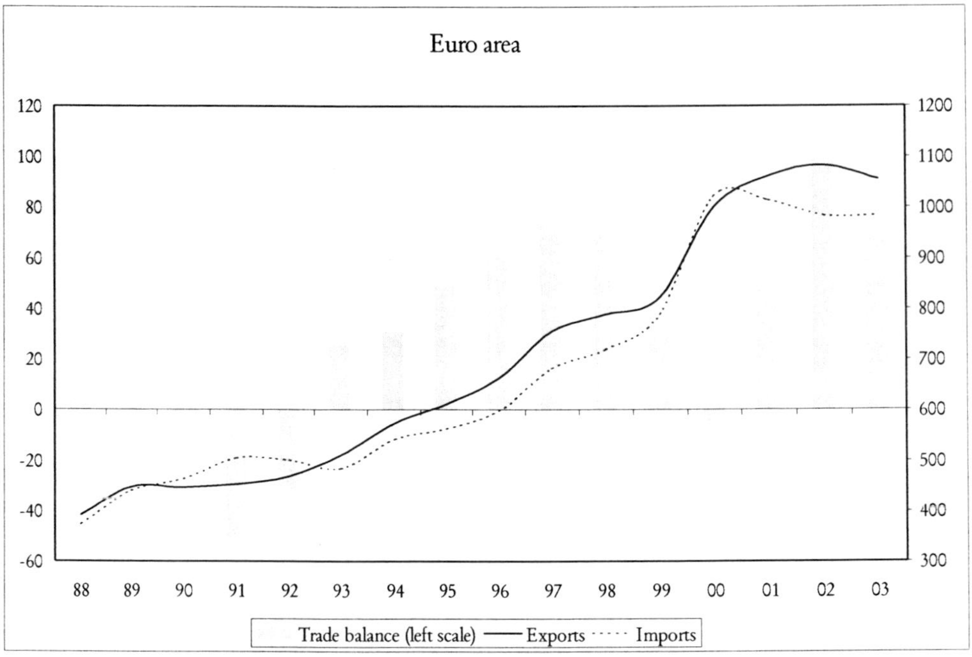

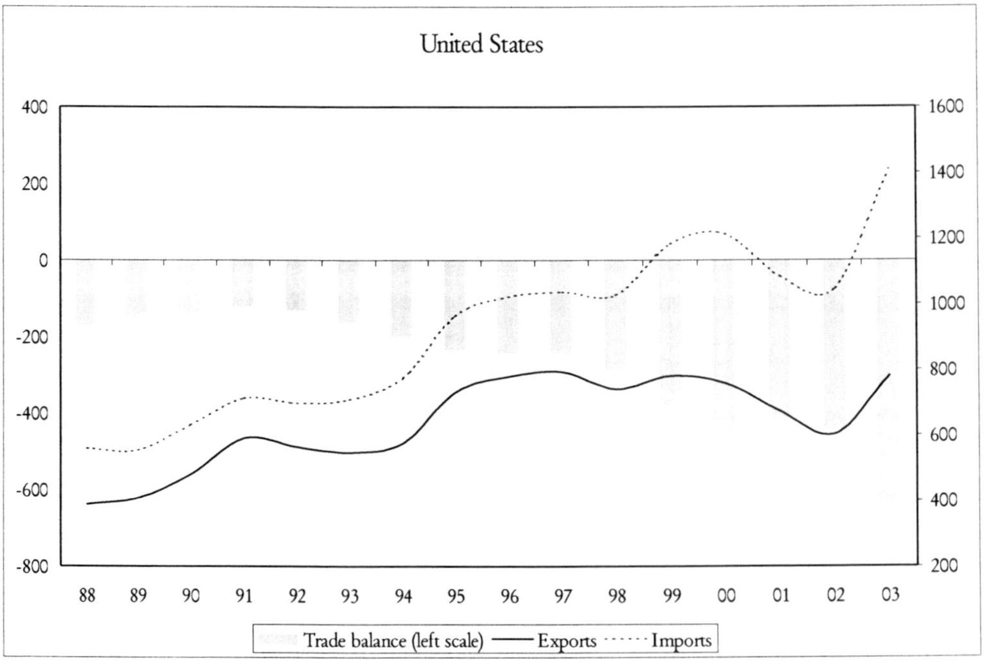

Figure 1 – Merchandise trade balance, exports and imports (EUR billions)

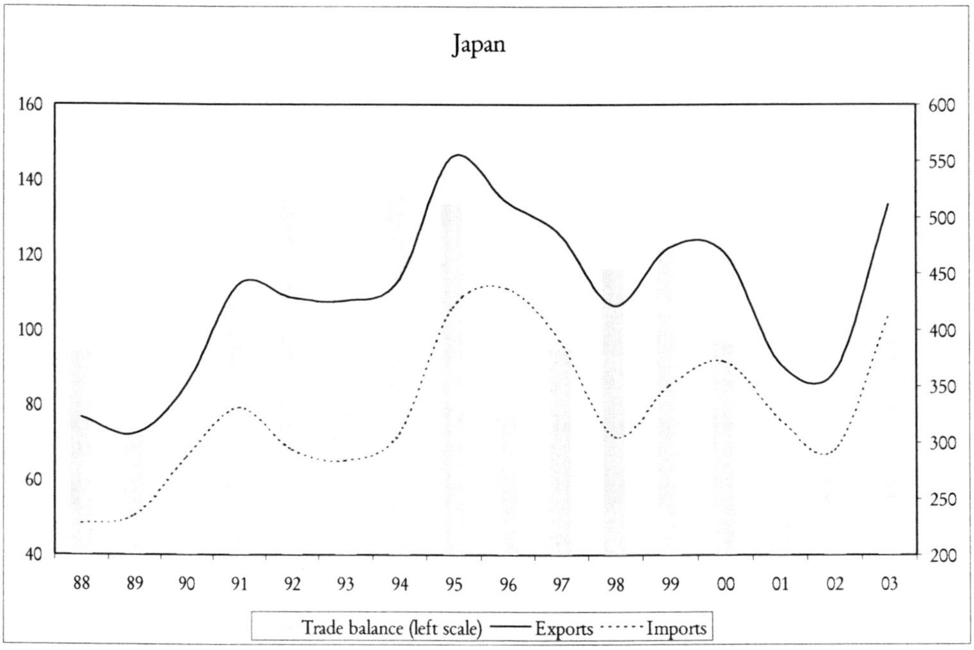

Figure 1 – Merchandise trade balance, exports and imports (EUR billions) (continued)

These different macroeconomic behaviors may have resulted from the preponderance of stable foreign and domestic determinants of trade flows in the U.S. and Japan, such as robust consumption patterns in the former and a sequence of tentative recoveries in the latter. Conversely, the variegated behavior of EMU exports and imports may suggest the presence of more determinants of different nature at work, exerting an influence of changing intensity over time and contributing to an otherwise partial understanding of the behavior of exports and imports in the euro area. In other words, analyzing what drives trade balance fluctuations in the latter may require an analytical framework encompassing a wider set of variables, both foreign and domestic, that may possibly exert an influence on this channel.

3. Puzzling Relationships between Real Exchange Rates and International Trade Developments. Is this the Whole Story?

Before analyzing the relationship between the real exchange rate and the trade balance, an appropriate definition of the real exchange rate must be adopted. This selection is extremely important, because it may lead to different conclusions according to which deflator is chosen for the real exchange rate. Figure 2 shows that the fluctuations of real exchange rates computed using as weights either the consumer price index (CPI) or the unit labor cost (ULC) for the manufacturing sector are very different in magnitude. For instance, the strengthening of the euro area real effective exchange rate during the second half of the Eighties is more evident comparing consumer prices in the same currency rather than unit labor costs. Moreover, the depreciation from 1996 to 2000 is higher employing a ULC-based rather than a CPI-based measure. The subsequent appreciation, on the other hand, brings the latter indicator to the same level observed in 1996, while the former indicator shows only a partial recovery and remains to a higher level.[1] Thus, deciding which price or cost deflator to use is a key issue and has to be carefully considered. Even though there is no single real exchange rate appropriate in any circumstance, the CPI-based measure is usually considered a bad indicator of international price competitiveness because it is distorted by the inclusion of indirect taxes and non-tradeables. Generally, most analysts employ a relative normalized ULC-based measure for the manufacturing sector, because euro area statistics do not provide detailed sectoral data also for the service sector. Thus, in what follows such definition for the real exchange rate is employed.

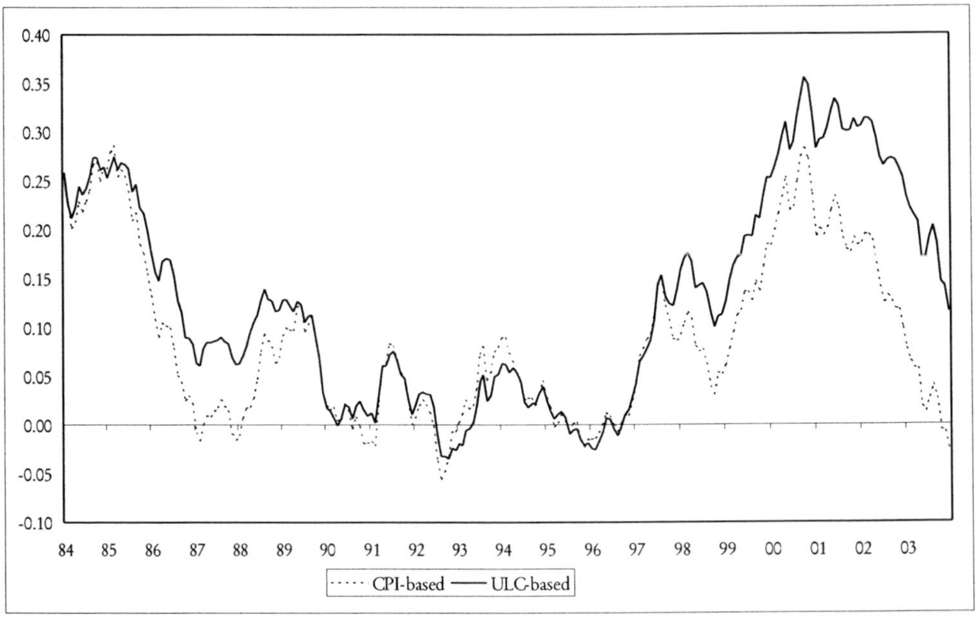

Figure 2 – Real effective exchange rates

The behavior of euro area imports and exports over the last twenty years clearly shows that the real exchange rate is just one of their main determinants and that they respond also to a number of other variables that make the overall picture rather difficult to interpret (Fig. 3).

The real appreciation from the second half of the Eighties to the first half of the Nineties is not coupled with a coherent behavior of the trade balance, which first deteriorates until 1991 and then appreciates considerably. After this recovery, the trade balance seems loosely affected by the subsequent real exchange rate developments. Thus, a depreciation (appreciation) leads to a trade balance improvement (deterioration) only in some instances and usually after a number of adjustments has taken place. The reason for these apparently

[1] Another possible definition of the real exchange rate is the ratio of relative export prices in the same currency. Even though such indicator may seem the most appropriate measure of international price competitiveness, it may not convey important information if firms, for instance, absorb an increase in costs through a reduction in profit margins.

irregular patterns is that many other variables interact with the trade balance and affect or are affected by the latter to an extent that changes over time and across space.

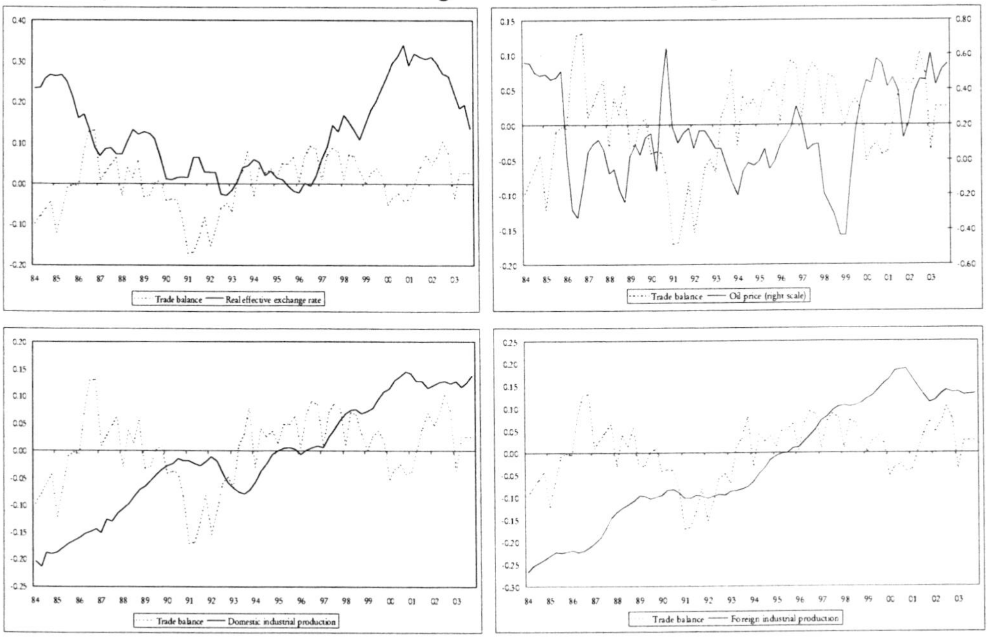

Figure 3 – Determinants of trade balance fluctuations in the euro area

For instance, both economic theory and empirical evidence suggests that domestic and foreign activity influences expenditure behaviors, thus modifying import and export flows, respectively. The relative growth rate of industrial production in the euro area and in the rest of the world may contribute to explain why the EMU trade balance does not follow a clear trend during the mid Nineties in the context of the elasticity-absorption approach. The latter, however, does not seem enough to account for the whole variability of trade flows. Indeed, the behavior of the euro area trade balance during the period 1998-2002 seems partly attributable to the sharp increase in the price of oil in 1999, ultimately resulting in a higher than expected trade deficit. However, besides few anecdotal episodes, the impact of the huge swings in the price of oil on trade exchanges has rarely been taken into account using quantitative techniques. Indirectly, the magnitude of such impact can be inferred looking at the works on the effects of an oil shock on GDP growth by a number of scholars (Jiménez-Rodríguez and Sánchez, 2004; Hamilton, 2003). In general, these studies suggest that oil price fluctuations have considerable consequences on economic activity. For instance, almost every postwar global recession has been anticipated by substantial increases in oil price. Even though the latter may not have induced the downturn in each occurrence, the high correlation between the two variables suggests that households, firms and policy-makers react to rising inflation attributable to changes in the price of this key commodity.

The transmission mechanism of an oil shock includes both supply and demand channels (Rotember and Woodford, 1996; Kim and Lougani, 1992). From the supply-side, it should be taken into account that imports of oil are relatively inelastic because the latter is a fundamental input either directly or indirectly for virtually every industry. From the demand-side, it should be taken into account that both consumption and investment are adversely affected not only by a higher oil price, but also by an excessive volatility of the latter. In terms of magnitude, the first effect is stronger the more the shock is perceived to be permanent, while the second effect is more relevant the smaller than required is the degree of financial sophistication for hedging purposes.[2]

4. An Integrated Framework to Assess the Impact of External Shocks on Trade Flows

4.1. Economic Foundations

The background for the analysis of trade flows can be derived from the traditional consumption and production theory. In this context, the main issue is whether imports and exports are assumed as perfect substitutes for domestically produced goods or as complementary and differentiated products. According to which underlying hypothesis is considered, the perfect or imperfect substitutes model can be employed (Goldstein and Khan, 1985). Within the first framework, traded goods are not only homogeneous, but also exchanged in frictionless international markets. These assumptions imply that there are no separate import demand or export supply functions, but rather excess demand and supply functions of domestic goods. However, since two-way exchanges are usually observed, i.e. imports, exports, domestic production and intra-industry trade, the perfect substitutes model is based on too unrealistic hypotheses and its predictions on aggregate trade flows are not supported on empirical grounds. Conversely, the second framework postulates that imported goods are imperfect substitutes for domestically produced goods and that exported goods are imperfect substitutes for goods produced elsewhere. The demand functions can be derived from the usual utility maximization problem. In this context, variations of the trade balance are typically explained by changes in domestic and foreign income and in relative prices expressed in the same currency, i.e. the real exchange rate.

In general, in most of the empirical work supply equations are not explicitly modeled, assuming that the country under examination adopts a price-taker behavior and that the supply price elasticities for imports and exports are infinite. However, these conditions are more appropriate for small open economies and do not adequately fit the euro area in terms of economic size. Indeed, given the relevance of the EMU, domestic developments within its boundaries may influence what happens in the rest of the world. Even though such international repercussions can be analyzed through a global vector autoregressive (GVAR) approach (Pesaran et al., 2004) or a system of simultaneous equations (Bagnai, 2004), the aim of this work is to evaluate the consequences through the trade channel of shocks in the rest of the world on the euro area and not *vice versa*.

2 Besides the above-mentioned considerations, a number of additional channels should be taken into account because they exert in turn an important impact. For instance, in a general equilibrium perspective an increase in the price of oil and (as a consequence) other energy sources may generate not only direct inflation, but also second-round effects related to the response of wages to higher consumer prices. In more details, if wage earners accept a reduction of their purchasing power in real terms, the labor market is likely to be marginally affected and inflation is expected to converge towards its original path after the absorption of the initial impact. Alternatively, if higher nominal wages are demanded to make up for the decline in real wages, an inflationary spiral may take place and eventually lead to persistent lower growth and higher inflation.

In the context of the outlined framework, long-run demand functions for exports and imports are defined in log-linear terms as

$$x_t = \varphi_1 \cdot z_t^* + \varphi_2 \cdot q_t + \varphi_3 \cdot t$$
$$m_t = \varphi_1^* \cdot z_t + \varphi_2^* \cdot q_t + \varphi_3^* \cdot t \qquad (1)$$

where z_t (z_t^*) indicates the logarithm of domestic (foreign) output, q_t is the real exchange rate, and the linear trend is aimed at capturing the impact of supply-side factors without increasing excessively the number of parameters that have to be estimated (Boyd et al., 2001). Parameters φ_1 (φ_1^*) and φ_2 (φ_2^*) measure export (import) elasticity to changes in output and in the real exchange rate, respectively, and aim at capturing product (technological sophistication, brand reputation, customer services and payment conditions) as well as price competitiveness factors. Expected signs are

$$\varphi_1, \varphi_2, \varphi_3, \varphi_1^*, \varphi_3^* \geq 0,\ \varphi_2^* \leq 0$$

The logarithm of trade balance at time t, tb_t, is conventionally defined as

$$tb_t = x_t - m_t - q_t \qquad (2)$$

Substituting (1) into (2) and adding a stochastic residual, ε_t, the following equilibrium relationship can be written

$$tb_t = \beta_1 \cdot z_t^* + \beta_2 \cdot z_t + \beta_3 \cdot q_t + \beta_4 \cdot t + \varepsilon_t \qquad (3)$$

where $\beta_1 = \varphi_1 \geq 0$, $\beta_2 = -\varphi_1^* \leq 0$, $\beta_3 = (\varphi_2 - \varphi_2^* - 1) \geq 0$ and $\beta_4 = (\varphi_3 - \varphi_3^*) \gtreqless 0$.

4.2. Econometric Methodology

In order to study euro area trade flows, a VEC model (Johansen, 1995) is estimated and used for dynamic simulation purposes. This class of models allows to describe the statistical variation of the data, associating the economic concept of long-run with the statistical concept of stationarity. In particular, the VEC model has been designed to analyze non-stationary time series, focusing on the identification of stationary linear combinations of such series, known as cointegration vectors. Ideally, these vectors describe the long-run equilibrium, which the data tend to converge, even if short-run deviations from the steady-state may eventually take place. Number and structure of these combinations are identified on the basis of appropriate statistical tests.

The empirical investigation is based on a VEC model of dimension $k = 5$

$$\begin{bmatrix} \Delta tb_t \\ \Delta q_t \\ \Delta z_t \\ \Delta z_t^* \\ \Delta p_t \end{bmatrix} = \mathbf{a} + \sum_{j=1}^{m-1} \boldsymbol{\Gamma}_j \cdot \begin{bmatrix} \Delta tb_{t-j} \\ \Delta q_{t-j} \\ \Delta z_{t-j} \\ \Delta z_{t-j}^* \\ \Delta p_{t-j} \end{bmatrix} + \boldsymbol{\Pi} \cdot \begin{bmatrix} tb_{t-1} \\ q_{t-1} \\ z_{t-1} \\ z_{t-1}^* \\ p_{t-1} \end{bmatrix} + \boldsymbol{\Xi} \cdot \mathbf{d}_t + \mathbf{u}_t \tag{4}$$

$$\mathbf{u}_t \sim N\left(\mathbf{0}, \boldsymbol{\Sigma}_u\right) \tag{5}$$

Variables contained in vector $\mathbf{y}_t = \left[tb_t \quad q_t \quad z_t \quad z_t^* \quad p_t \right]'$ are *a priori* endogenous and their possible weak exogeneity is verified *ex-post* in order to avoid the imposition of arbitrary distinctions among them (Sims, 1980).[3]

In system (4), $\boldsymbol{\Gamma}_j$'s are matrices of autoregression coefficients, while vectors $\mathbf{a}$, $\mathbf{d}_t$ and $\mathbf{u}_t$ contain constants, dummy variables with associated parameters collected in matrix $\boldsymbol{\Xi}$ and residuals distributed according to (5), respectively. The number of cointegration vectors is equal to the (reduced) rank of matrix $\boldsymbol{\Pi}$ and is determined on the basis of the trace and the maximum eigenvalue tests (Johansen, 1995). Since $\boldsymbol{\Pi}$ turns out of reduced rank, it can be partitioned as $\mathbf{A} \cdot \mathbf{B}'$. Matrix $\mathbf{B}$ contains the $r < k$ cointegration vectors. Matrix $\mathbf{A}$ contains the feedback coefficients (loadings). According to the theoretical model previously illustrated, a unidimensional cointegration space is expected, hence

$$\left[1 \; -\beta_1 \; -\beta_2 \; -\beta_3 \; -\beta_0 \right] \cdot \begin{bmatrix} tb_{t-1} \\ q_{t-1} \\ z_{t-1} \\ z_{t-1}^* \\ p_{t-1} \end{bmatrix} = \varepsilon_t \tag{6}$$

where β_i 's, $i = 1,...,3$, ε_t is derived from the equilibrium relationship (3) and β_0 captures the long-run effects of the price of oil. It should be noted that the above-specified cointegration space slightly differ from equation (3). In particular, instead of including a linear trend to account for the effects of supply-side factors as in Antonucci and Girardi (2005), the latter are subsumed in the price of oil, p_t. Since our goal is to provide an interpretative framework that goes beyond the traditional elasticity-absorption approach, testing the statistical significance of this commodity as a long-run determinant of trade developments in the euro area, which is a net oil consumer, represents an important economic hypothesis to investigate. Moreover, in all the tentative specifications of the preliminary

[3] From the statistical point of view, the introduction of such distinction may result in non-efficient estimates.

econometric analysis (not reported) the linear trend turns out always statistically negligible when it is included in the long-run relationship together with the oil price. Thus, the former is dropped from the final specification and leaves the role to convey relevant information to the latter.

One of the most important features of the VEC methodology is that it allows to take jointly into account long-run determinants, collected in the vector of residuals of the cointegrating relationship, and short-run dynamics, collected in the k–dimensional vector $\mathbf{y}_t$ of first differences. More specifically, short-run dynamics are modeled on the basis of the statistical significance of parameters collected in matrices $\mathbf{A}$, $\mathbf{\Gamma}_j$ and $\mathbf{\Xi}$, resulting in a parsimonious (Subset) VEC model. Parameters associated to p-values lower than a certain threshold are deleted from the model, according to the SER/TP. A careful modeling of short-run dynamic adjustments is required for several reasons. First, parameters statistically different from zero contribute to explain the fluctuations of the economy around the steady-state. Second, the matrix of adjustment coefficients allows to identify possible weakly exogenous variables (or forcing variables), when some rows in matrix $\mathbf{A}$ contain only zeros. Third, such reduction process has important implications on the dynamic properties of the model because an unrestricted specification, rather than a parsimonious one, implies very different impulse response functions and related confidence intervals (Brüggemann and Lütkepohl, 2001).

The estimated model is used to assess the relative contribution of structural factors in explaining dynamics and fluctuations of trade flows. Following King et al. (1991), the cointegration properties of the VEC model can be used to discriminate between impulses with permanent rather than transitory effects employing a suitable re-parameterization of system (4). Structural shocks, v's, can be retrieved form reduced-form shocks, u's, through proper identifying restrictions. The MA representation associated to model (5) is

$$\begin{bmatrix} p_t \\ y_t^* \\ y_t \\ q_t \\ tb_t \end{bmatrix} = \mathbf{C} \cdot \sum_{i=1}^{t} \begin{bmatrix} u_{p,i} \\ u_{y^*,i} \\ u_{y,i} \\ u_{q,i} \\ u_{tb,i} \end{bmatrix} + \mathbf{C}^*(L) \cdot \begin{bmatrix} u_{p,t} \\ u_{y^*,t} \\ u_{y,t} \\ u_{q,t} \\ u_{tb,t} \end{bmatrix} + \begin{bmatrix} p_0 \\ y_0^* \\ y_0 \\ q_0 \\ tb_0 \end{bmatrix} \tag{7}$$

where $\mathbf{C} = \boldsymbol{\beta}_\perp \cdot (\boldsymbol{\alpha}'_\perp \cdot \mathbf{\Gamma} \cdot \boldsymbol{\beta}_\perp)^{-1} \cdot \boldsymbol{\alpha}'_\perp$, $\mathbf{\Gamma} = \mathbf{I}_k - \sum_{i=1}^{p-1} \mathbf{\Pi}_i$ and $\mathbf{C}^*(L) = \mathbf{I}_k + \sum_{i=1}^{\infty} \mathbf{C}_i^*$.

The relationship between reduced-form and structural shocks can be written as

$$\begin{bmatrix} u_{p,t} \\ u_{y^*,t} \\ u_{y,t} \\ u_{q,t} \\ u_{tb,t} \end{bmatrix} = \mathbf{F} \cdot \begin{bmatrix} v_{p,t} \\ v_{y^*,t} \\ v_{y,t} \\ v_{q,t} \\ v_{tb,t} \end{bmatrix} \tag{8}$$

Taking into account (8), model (7) becomes

$$\begin{bmatrix} p_t \\ y_t^* \\ y_t \\ q_t \\ tb_t \end{bmatrix} = \mathbf{\Phi} \cdot \sum_{i=1}^{t} \begin{bmatrix} v_{p,i} \\ v_{y^*,i} \\ v_{y,i} \\ v_{q,i} \\ v_{tb,i} \end{bmatrix} + \mathbf{\Phi}^*(L) \cdot \begin{bmatrix} v_{p,t} \\ v_{y^*,t} \\ v_{y,t} \\ v_{q,t} \\ v_{tb,t} \end{bmatrix} + \begin{bmatrix} p_0 \\ y_0^* \\ y_0 \\ q_0 \\ tb_0 \end{bmatrix} \tag{9}$$

where $\mathbf{\Phi} = \mathbf{C} \cdot \mathbf{F}$ ($\mathbf{\Phi}^*(L) = \mathbf{C}^*(L) \cdot \mathbf{F}$) captures the impact of cumulated (non-cumulated) structural shocks, i.e. the permanent (cyclical) component of the data.

Matrix $\mathbf{F}$ has $k^2 = 25$ elements. Therefore, its exact identification involves the imposition of as many restrictions. Once the model is structurally identified, impulse response and forecast error variance decomposition analyses can be performed.

Assuming that the structural shocks are orthonormal allows to place $k \cdot (k+1)/2 = 15$ (non-linear) restrictions. As pointed out in Monti (2003), the $k(k-1)/2$ remaining restrictions can be identified through three sources: *i*) the choice of the cointegration rank, which allows to distinguish transitory shocks from permanent innovations, thus producing $r \cdot (k - r) = 4$ restrictions; *ii*) the instantaneous impact of transitory shocks, implying $r \cdot (r-1)/2$ constraints. As the cointegration rank is assumed equal to one, no additional restrictions have to be imposed to identify the transitory subsystem; *iii*) the identification of the four permanent components requires the imposition of at least $(k-r) \cdot (k-r-1)/2 = 6$ additional restrictions, which are obtained through additional constraints aiming at imposing the following causal order of the structural shocks: $v_{p,t} \rightarrow v_{y^*,t} \rightarrow v_{y,t} \rightarrow v_{q,t}$. The chosen recursive structure implies that the euro area economy is affected by two foreign shocks. The first shock has a supply-side nature and can be labeled as energy shock ($v_{p,t}$). The overall exogeneity of such shock relies on the idea that it reflects both economic and meta-economic (for example, geopolitical and long-term strategic) factors having worldwide influence ($v_{p,t} \rightarrow v_{y^*,t}$). In turn, foreign output affects the domestic one ($v_{p,t} \rightarrow v_{y^*,t} \rightarrow v_{y,t}$). Usually, this condition is appropriate to describe a small open economy and it does not apply to the euro area. However, even if the latter is a large entity, it cannot drive alone global trade flows. This two shocks have a demand-side nature and can be interpreted as (foreign and domestic) real demand shocks. Finally, the price competitiveness shock, i.e. an exchange rate change, is assumed to be affected by the two real demand shocks, even though it does not affect domestic and foreign income ($v_{p,t} \rightarrow v_{y*,t} \rightarrow v_{y,t} \rightarrow v_{q,t}$).

5. Empirical Results

The empirical investigation focuses on four main issues. First, an analysis of income and price (including oil) elasticities of EMU trade flows is performed. Second, a comparison of the estimates over the periods 1984-1998 and 1998-2004 is presented in order to assess the effects on euro area exports and imports of the third stage of the EMU. Third, a specification appropriately balancing an economically meaningful and statistically rigorous interpretation of facts is derived. Fourth, the estimated model is used to simulate the effects of structural (unanticipated) shocks on euro area trade flows.

5.1. Model Specification and Long-Run Structure

The econometric analysis presented in this Section follows a broadly established approach in the literature.[4] A cointegrating vector autoregressive (VAR) model is estimated with monthly data over the pre-EMU period 1984M1-1998M12. The sample ends on the basis of the latest observation before the beginning of the third stage of the EMU and does not include the first few years of the European Monetary System (EMS) because of the initial instability of such new foreign exchange platform. From the economic point of view, the time horizon refers to an environment characterized not only by the progressive normalization of the impact of oil shocks, but also by the strengthening of the integration process within the EMU. Form the econometric point of view, the monthly frequency of data seems the most appropriate choice to properly investigate the dynamics of trade flows both in the short- and long-run, as pointed out in Antonucci and Girardi (2005).

The deterministic component of the baseline VAR model is composed by a constant, linear trend and seasonal dummies. Furthermore, five impulse dummies are introduced in order to obtain spherical residuals. The number of lags is chosen according to the general to specific criterion.

Table 2 shows the significance test for each lag included in the vector autoregression, as well as a number of diagnostic tests. Overall, the chosen specification seems to adequately fit the data and does not exhibit signs of misspecification. Normality and heteroschedasticity tests are passed for all equations and residuals do not present autocorrelation, supporting the chosen number of lags. Concerning the system as a whole, the estimated residuals satisfactorily match the multinormal distribution. The Chow tests (not reported) do not indicate the presence of significant parametric instability.

Table 3 presents eigenvalues statistically different from zero (in bold) on the basis of the trace and maximum eigenvalue tests (both corrected, DFC, and non-corrected, NDFC, for the degrees of freedom) at the 1% significance level. In case of contrasting results, the trace test is preferred because the maximum eigenvalue test may produce a non-coherent testing strategy (Johansen, 1992).

[4] For recent works on this topic see, among others, Gupta-Kapoor and Ramakrishnan (1999) and Onafowora, (2003).

Table 2 – Model specification: 1984-1998

Lag Significance Test F(25,532)					
Lag 3 = 1.38 [0.10]					
Lag 2 = 3.32 [0.00]					
Lag 1 = 28.40 [0.00]					
Impulse Dummies Significance Test F(5,143)					
di8607 = 8.61 [0.00]					
d9008 = 7.80 [0.00]					
d9103 = 2.50 [0.03]					
d9212 = 1.99 [0.08]					
d9501 = 3.24 [0.01]					
Univariate Misspecification Tests					
	tb	*q*	*z*	z^*	*p*
AR(1-7), F(7,140)	1.36 [0.23]	0.73 [0.64]	1.21 [0.30]	2.03 [0.06]	0.46 [0.86]
Normality, $\chi^2(2)$	0.80 [0.67]	0.07 [0.97]	5.21 [0.07]	0.26 [0.88]	1.59 [0.45]
ARCH(1-7), F(7,133)	0.51 [0.82]	0.62 [0.74]	0.31 [0.95]	0.80 [0.59]	1.73 [0.11]
Hetero, F(32,114)	0.87 [0.67]	1.06 [0.39]	1.66 [0.03]	0.68 [0.89]	0.79 [0.77]
Hetero-X, $\chi^2(152)$	151.3 [0.50]	160.8 [0.30]	169.6 [0.16]	155.7 [0.40]	158.1 [0.35]
Multivariate Misspecification Tests					
Vector AR(1-7) Test, F(175,540) = 1.10 [0.22]					
Vector Normality Test, $\chi^2(10)$ = 6.39 [0.79]					
Vector Hetero Test, F(480,1421) = 0.88 [0.95]					
Vector Hetero-X Test, $\chi^2(2280)$ = 2341.2 [0.18]					

Table 3 – Determination of cointegration rank: 1984-1998

Eigenvalues							
0.2631	0.1152	0.0647	0.0351	0.0168			
Trace Test				**Max Eigenvalue Test**			
H_0:	H_1:	NDFC	DFC	H_0:	H_1:	NDFC	DFC
$r = 0$	$r \geq 1$	98.49	90.29	$r = 0$	$r = 1$	54.95	50.37
$r \leq 1$	$r \geq 2$	43.54	39.91	$r \leq 1$	$r = 2$	22.02	20.19
$r \leq 2$	$r \geq 3$	21.52	19.73	$r \leq 2$	$r = 3$	12.05	11.04
$r \leq 3$	$r \geq 4$	9.47	8.68	$r \leq 3$	$r = 4$	6.43	5.89
r ≤ 4	$r = 5$	3.05	2.79	r ≤ 4	$r = 5$	3.05	2.79

Since both tests suggests the existence of a single long-run relationship at the 5% significance level, the cointegration rank, r, is set equal to one. Routine (stationarity, weakly exogeneity and exclusion) tests are reported in the upper part of Table 4. They clearly depict the main properties of the unidimensional cointegration space: *i*) all variables of the system are $I(1)$; *ii*) both foreign industrial production and oil price are weakly exogenous, suggesting that they may be the common trends driving the system; *iii*) there is clear evidence of the statistical irrelevance of the oil price in the long-run relationship. The lower part of Table 4 presents the final specification of the cointegration vector and the associated matrix of feedback coefficients.

Table 4 – Properties of the long-run matrix: 1984-1998

		Routine Tests			
	tb	*q*	*z*	z^*	*p*
Stationarity, $\chi^2(4)$	50.11 [0.00]	46.23 [0.00]	50.11 [0.00]	49.49 [0.00]	42.48 [0.00]
Exclusion, $\chi^2(1)$	15.89 [0.00]	25.81 [0.00]	29.41 [0.00]	31.88 [0.00]	**2.70** [0.10]
Weakly Exogeneity, $\chi^2(1)$	6.12 [0.01]	26.40 [0.00]	5.66 [0.02]	**0.48** [0.49]	*3.12* [0.07]
		Long-run Structure			
	tb	*q*	*z*	z^*	*p*
Long-run relationship	1	0.5267	2.8731	-2.1312	-
	.	(0.0933)	(0.3025)	(0.2020)	.
Loading coefficients	-0.1204	-0.1118	-0.0509	-0.0107	0.1416
	(0.0472)	(0.0206)	(0.0172)	(0.0090)	(0.1300)
		LR over-identifying test $\chi^2(2) = 2.70$ [0.10]			

The long-run structure of the model indicates that euro area trade flows are explained by a mix of price and non-price factors. Looking at sign and value of the long-run coefficients, two main features can be highlighted: *i*) the ML condition is violated, providing further evidence of low real exchange rate elasticities in the trade balance equilibrium condition. More specifically, the sign of the coefficient indicates that the sum of elasticities in the import and export demand functions is significantly less than unity; *ii*) the oil price does not exert significant long-run effects on EMU trade flows.

The structure of the adjustment matrix is coherent with the indications of the weakly exogeneity test. External variables (foreign output and oil price) are unaffected by a disequilibrium in the cointegrating relationship. Conversely, trade flows, as well as domestic output and the real exchange rate, exhibit a significant adjustment behavior.

In order to control for the stability of long-run properties of the model, system (5) is estimated over the period 1984M1-2004M4 (Tab. 5).[5] Even though the results are qualitatively similar in terms of statistical significance and feedback mechanisms to those

[5] In order to get spherical residuals, the deterministic part of the extended model includes several additional dummies (d0006; d0012; di0307; d0402; d0404). The cointegration properties seem not to be affected by these variables: the eigenvalues of the long-run matrix (0.2098; 0.1234; 0.0615; 0.039; 0.0109) are almost identical to those reported in Table 3.

obtained using the pre-EMU sample, the magnitude of the coefficient of the real exchange rate is roughly half the previous estimate, suggesting a lower departure from the conditions for a devaluation to improve the trade balance. In more details, even though the ML condition is still violated, trade elasticities seem to exert a somewhat more positive influence on the euro area trade balance, even though market forces that should provide an incentive to improve net exports over time continue to remain too weak for the exploitation of changes in international competitiveness.

Table 5 – Properties of the long-run matrix: 1984-2004

Long-run Structure					
	tb	*q*	*z*	z^*	*p*
Long-run relationship	1	0.2809	2.2731	-1.8460	-
	.	(0.0530)	(0.2485)	(0.1867)	.
Loading coefficients	-0.1115	-0.1178	-0.0470	-0.0034	0.0692
	(0.0421)	(0.0194)	(0.0144)	(0.0085)	(0.1313)
LR over-identifying test $\chi^2(2) = 0.38$ [0.54]					

Figure 4 plots the cointegration residuals of both models. The graph shows a significant overlapping of the deviations from the equilibrium condition (correlation is equal to 0.96), over the period 1984-1998. Furthermore, in the most recent years a clear departure from the historical pattern of the cointegration residuals cannot be detected.

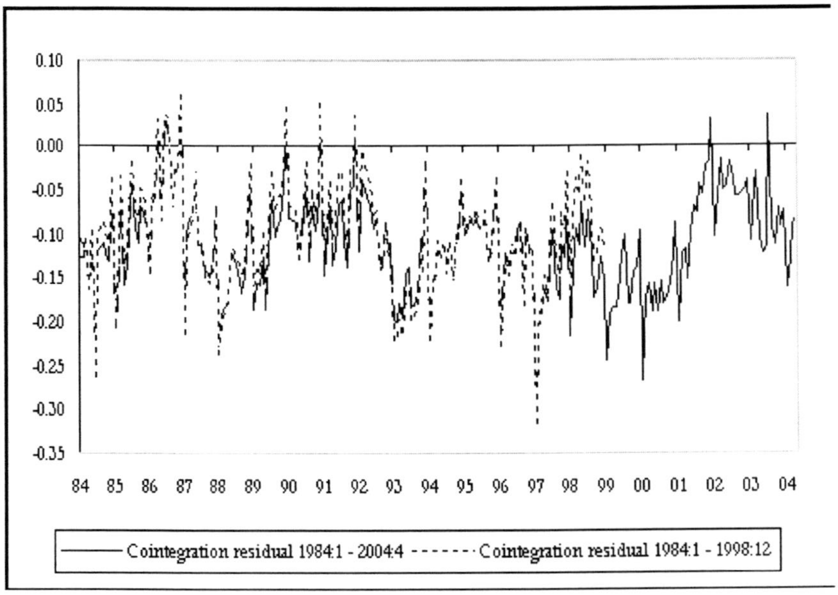

Figure 4 – Cointegration residuals: 1984-1998 and 1984-2004

Thus, the third stage of the EMU seems to have left unchanged the functional form of import and export demand functions, as suggested by the stability of the long-run elasticities (Fig. 5). In other words, the adoption of the single currency does not seem to have significantly modified the responsiveness to external shocks of the euro area trade balance, which seems determined by the same macroeconomic factors of the pre-EMU period.

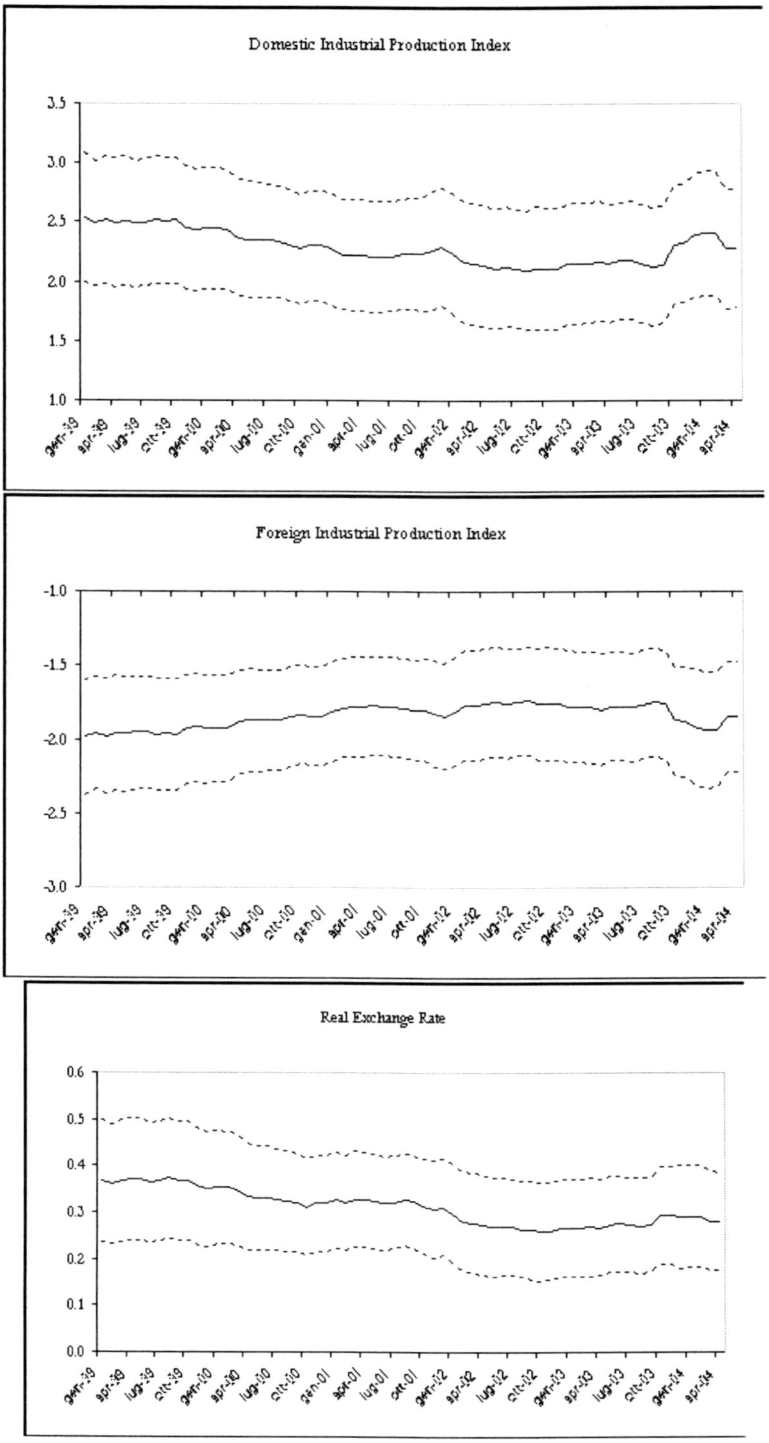

Figure 5 – Recursive estimation of the long-run elasticities: 1999-2004

5.2. Short-Run Structure

Table 6 shows the specification of the Subset VEC model using the three-stage least squares (3SLS) estimation method.[6] Statistically irrelevant parameters are deleted through the SER/TP, employing the BIC criterion and the significance threshold $t = 1.60$. This conservative choice in the reduction process of the model is motivated by the preference to maintain, rather than to delete, coefficients with uncertain significance.

Table 6 – Subset VEC model : estimated coefficients 1984-2004

	Δp	Δz^*	Δz	Δq	Δtb
Constant	.	0.001 (0.000)	.	-0.012 (0.002)	0.047 (0.007)
Coint. Res.(-1)	.	.	-0.023 (0.005)	-0.103 (0.016)	-0.096 (0.035)
Δp(-1)	0.222 (0.054)	0.008 (0.003)	.	.	.
Δz^*(-1)	.	.	.	-0.226 (0.115)	.
Δz(-1)	.	.	-0.465 (0.057)	.	.
Δq(-1)	.	0.062 (0.022)	.	0.391 (0.056)	-0.382 (0.117)
Δtb(-1)	.	-0.014 (0.006)	.	0.070 (0.019)	-0.425 (0.062)
Δp(-1)	.	.	.	.	.
Δz^*(-2)	1.604 (0.765)	0.185 (0.050)	0.169 (0.085)	.	.
Δz(-2)	-0.829 -0.514	.	-0.194 (0.057)	.	.
Δq(-2)	0.643 (0.356)	.	.	-0.192 (0.058)	.
Δtb(-2)		.	.	0.076 (0.022)	-0.136 (0.058)
*di*8607	-0.316 (0.055)	.	.	.	.
*d*9008	0.420 (0.076)	.	.	.	-0.053 (0.024)
*d*9103	.	.	.	0.041 (0.011)	.
*d*9212	.	.	-0.031 (0.008)	.	.
*d*9501	.	.	.	.	0.100 (0.024)

[6] Coefficients for seasonal dummies are not reported.

	Δp	Δz^*	Δz	Δq	Δtb
*d*0006	.	.	.	-0.035 (0.011)	.
*d*0012	-0.271 (0.076)	.	0.013 (0.008)	-0.027 (0.011)	.
*di*0307	.	-0.038 (0.003)	.	.	.
*d*0402	.	0.021 (0.005)	.	.	.
*d*0404	-0.126 (0.077)	-0.023 (0.005)	.	.	.
R^2adj.	0.26	0.40	0.26	0.23	0.79
σ_u	0.0782	0.0050	0.0084	0.0122	0.0248
DW	1.96	2.11	2.01	1.69	1.93

The reduction process involves 132 zero restrictions. Out of these constraints, two concern the loading coefficients, thirty one the lagged endogenous variables and the remaining the elements of the matrix of the deterministic components. It is worthwhile to note that each regressor enters in one or more equations of the system, supporting the adopted specification.

The explicative power of the dynamic equations is high for the trade balance ($\overline{R}^2$ equal to 79%) and satisfactory for foreign and domestic output (40% and 26%, respectively), oil price (26%) and the real exchange rate (23%).

Analyzing the feedback linkages from the long-run structure to the dynamic part of the system, the former results statistically significant in three out of five cases, i.e. the choice of a multi-equation framework is appropriate. Moreover, external variables are not affected by the lagged cointegration residual and can be identified as two of the stochastic trends driving the system. Domestic variables, on the other hand, show considerable adjustment patterns with respect to deviations from the estimated equilibrium condition.

5.3. Dynamic Properties

The dynamic properties of the model are investigated paying particular attention to the euro area trade balance, tb_t. Two simulation exercises are implemented: the first concerns the consequences of an unanticipated innovation on tb_t; the second measures the relative contribution of each shock on the fluctuations of EMU trade flows. As pointed out in Antonucci and Girardi (2005), the use of high frequency data and the reduction process previously illustrated guarantee a greater degree of reliability in the simulation results.

Table 7 presents the correlation structure of the estimated residuals.

Table 7 – Subset VEC model: correlation structure of estimated residuals

	Δp	Δz^*	Δz	Δq	Δtb
Δp	1.0000				
Δz^*	*0.1087*	1.0000			
Δz	0.0460	**0.1999**	1.0000		
Δq	0.0383	0.0686	**0.1367**	1.0000	
Δtb	0.0902	0.0669	0.0664	*-0.1225*	1.0000

Statistically significant co-movements at the 5% (10%) level are reported in bold (italics). In order to compute the critical thresholds, the standard (approximated) formula $\pm 2.00/T^{1/2}$ ($\pm 1.60/T^{1/2}$) is used, where T indicates the length of the sample span.

The structure of the contemporaneous correlations reveals that the estimated Subset VEC model has a non-diagonal variance/covariance matrix. Thus, the Cholesky decomposition is not appropriate, because in this case the simulation exercises (impulse response and forecast error variance decomposition analyses) may be affected by permutations in the ordering of variables collected in $\mathbf{y}_t$. Conversely, generalized impulse response functions (GIRFs) proposed by Pesaran and Shin (1998) allow to overcome the identification problems and to assess the effects of a shock on a specific variable (or on a cointegrating relationship) of the system taking into account the correlative structure of the estimated residuals. Thus, this methodology provides a plausible characterization of the dynamic responses to typically observable shocks, even though it prevents the possibility to give a structural interpretation to the impulses.

In this Section, an explicit structuralization of the VEC model is proposed. The possibility to retrieve mutually orthogonal and economically meaningful shocks calls the problem of structural identification into question. Under the assumption that structural shocks are mutually orthogonal, the exact identification of the model requires ten additional restrictions. The cointegration rank indicates that only one shock can have temporary effects. It implies four linearly independent constraints and it can be expressed by a zero column in the matrix $\mathbf{\Phi}$ of long-run effects of structural shocks

$$\mathbf{\Phi} = \left[\begin{array}{cccc|c} * & * & * & * & 0 \\ * & * & * & * & 0 \\ * & * & * & * & 0 \\ * & * & * & * & 0 \\ * & * & * & * & 0 \end{array}\right]$$

The recursive sequence of permanent shocks can be embedded into $\mathbf{\Phi}$ through the imposition of the following restrictions

$$\mathbf{\Phi} = \left[\begin{array}{cccc|c} * & 0 & 0 & 0 & 0 \\ * & * & 0 & 0 & 0 \\ * & * & * & 0 & 0 \\ * & * & * & * & 0 \\ * & * & * & * & 0 \end{array}\right]$$

Table 8 presents the estimated values for asterisks. Standard errors for each point estimate are derived from 1000 bootstrap replications of the model. Coefficients in bold (italics) are statistically significant at the 5% (10%) level. The columns show the long-run impact of structural shocks on the variables reported in each row.

Table 8 – Subset VEC model: long-run impact matrix

	$v_{p,t}$	$v_{y^*,t}$	$v_{y,t}$	$v_{q,t}$	$v_{tb,t}$
p	0.1088	0	0	0	0
	(0.0126)	.	.	.	.
y^*	0.0038	0.0067	0	0	0
	(0.0013)	(0.0009)	.	.	.
y	*0.0011*	0.0028	0.0038	0	0
	(0.0007)	(0.0006)	(0.0003)	.	.
q	0.0135	0.0183	-0.0023	0.0268	0
	(0.008)	(0.0078)	(0.0045)	(0.0053)	.
tb	0.0006	0.0008	-0.0081	-0.0075	0
	(0.0020)	(0.0023)	(0.0012)	(0.0015)	.

Only a few coefficients are significantly non-different from zero, indicating a substantial estimation accuracy. Focusing on the trade balance, the structure of the fifth row suggests that in the long-run patterns of euro area trade flows are mainly affected by real domestic demand and by price competitiveness.

Figure 6 shows the responses of the trade balance to the structural impulses described above, over a simulation horizon equal to 30 months. The graphs report also 95% confidence intervals (dashed lines), computed holding fixed the estimated cointegrating relationship. As recommended by Benkwitz et al. (2000), this calculation is obtained using a bootstrap method (Hall, 1992) with 1000 replications.

On impact, an energy shock, i.e. an increase in the price of oil, causes a temporary deterioration of the trade balance. Subsequently, the latter follows an increasing trajectory leading to the restoration of the pre-shock level within eighteen months. However, the confidence bounds indicate that the deviation from the baseline path is not statistically significant. Similarly, a positive foreign demand shock produces an instantaneous drop in external trade as well as an increasing trajectory over time, even though the response is statistically irrelevant also in this case.

The responses to an unanticipated domestic demand or competitiveness shock, instead, are statistically significant. The former negatively affects the trade balance for the whole simulation horizon. After one year, the deterioration is 0.8% below the pre-shock level. A competitiveness shock generates an initial -1.2% drop in the level of the trade balance followed by a slow improvement over time, although the pre-shock level, represented by the horizontal axis, is not reached anymore. This result seems to be influenced by the value of the long-run price elasticities, which is lower than the critical threshold indicated by the ML condition to exert a positive effect on the trade balance.

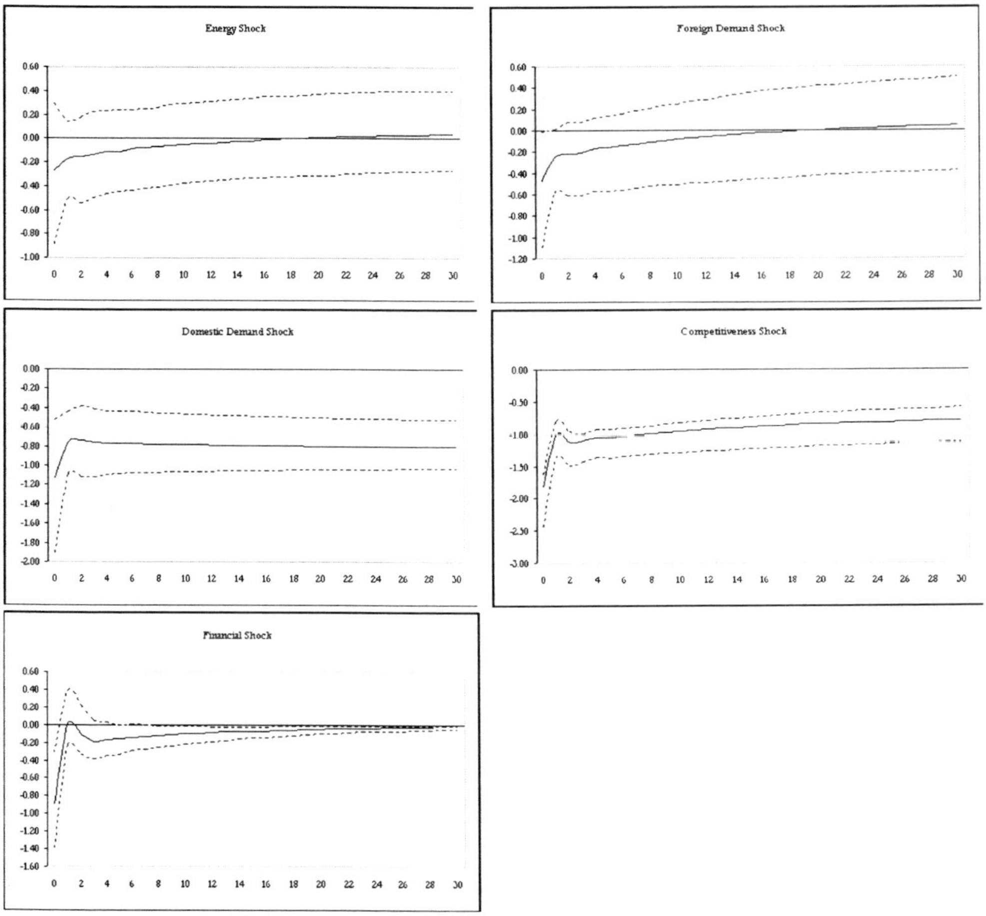

Figure 6 – Response of the trade balance to structural shocks

Finally, the last graph presents the response to a negative shock on the trade balance itself. It can be interpreted as a positive (transitory) financial shock under the assumption that from an accounting point of view capital flows are the counterpart of transactions in goods (and services). Unanticipated capital inflows produce a temporary deterioration of the trade balance, which is absorbed within a quarter.

Table 9 presents the forecast error variance decomposition of the euro area trade balance (consistent with the structure of the long-run impact matrix and the impulse response analysis discussed above) over selected time horizons (1-48 months). The μ-column indicates the average contribution of the shocks over the entire simulation period.

Table 9 – Forecast error variance decomposition

Months	1	3	6	9	12	24	36	48	μ
$v_{p,t}$	0.01	0.01	0.01	0.01	0.01	0.01	0.00	0.00	0.01
$v_{y^*,t}$	0.04	0.04	0.03	0.02	0.02	0.01	0.01	0.01	0.02
$v_{z,t}$	0.22	0.26	0.28	0.3	0.32	0.37	0.41	0.43	0.36
$v_{q,t}$	0.58	0.61	0.62	0.62	0.61	0.58	0.56	0.54	0.58
$v_{tb,t}$	0.14	0.09	0.06	0.05	0.04	0.03	0.02	0.01	0.04

The results suggest that the main sources of trade flows fluctuations are related to real domestic demand and competitiveness shocks. The contribution of the former increases over time from 22% on impact, to 43% after four years, whereas the contribution of the latter, accounting for almost 60% of trade fluctuations, remains roughly stable over the simulation span. The financial shock contributes to explain the volatility of the trade balance only in the very short-run. Finally, foreign demand and energy shocks seem to have negligible effects.

6. Conclusion

This work presents an application of recent econometric techniques to international trade issues. In particular, VEC models are employed to assess the likely short- and long-run response of the euro area trade balance to changes in its main determinants. The latter include not only the traditional variables taken into account in the elasticity-approach framework, i.e. the real exchange rate as well as domestic and foreign income, but also additional factors such as the oil price.

The key finding is that the main drivers of the euro area trade balance are domestic demand and the real exchange rate. In more details, on impact the negative effect on trade flows of the former is one third lower than the negative effect of the latter. In addition, these results suggest the lack or weakness of restoration mechanisms aiming at improving the trade balance over time. In other words, not only the ML condition is violated, but there is also a sort of income effect such that the responsiveness of EMU imports to domestic GDP developments exceeds the responsiveness of EMU exports to foreign GDP developments (this empirical regularity has been documented also for the U.S. by Houthakker and Magee, 1969).

Estimates performed using samples excluding and including observations for the third stage of the EMU, respectively, do not exhibit major differences, i.e. euro area trade flows react to domestic demand and competitiveness shocks, while the impact of foreign demand and energy shocks is negligible. Overall, this result suggests that the adoption of the single currency has not affected significantly the behavior of extra-EMU trade flows during the considered time horizon.

Appendix – Data Sources and Definitions

Elaborations have been performed using J-Multi 3.03 (model reduction and simulation analyses) and Pc-Fiml 10.3 (model specification and estimates) econometric packages, using non-deseasonalized monthly data from OECD and IMF databases.

The euro area trade balance, tb_t, is measured by the logarithm of the ratio between merchandise exports and imports (IMF DOTS *via* Datastream) net of intra-area trade exchanges. z_t (z_t^*) is the logarithm of the industrial production index (IMF IFS) for the euro area (Rest of the World), which is constructed as weighted average of the j (i) EMU (eight of the most important trading partners) countries' indexes of industrial production

$$z_t = \sum_{j=1}^{12} w_j \cdot z_{jt}, \quad z_t^* = \sum_{i=1}^{8} w_i \cdot z_{it}$$

Intra-area weights w_j (w_i) represent the share of national real GDP in PPP of the euro area (Rest of the World) in the base-year (1995) and are reported in the upper (lower) part of Table A.1.

Table A.1 – Country weights

AUT	BEL	FIN	FRA	GER	GRE	IRE	ITA	LUX	NET	POR	SPA
0.0294	0.0379	0.0165	0.2047	0.2979	0.0229	0.0111	0.1965	0.0023	0.0560	0.0232	0.1017

CAN	DEN	JAP	NOR	SWE	SWI	UK	USA
0.0539	0.0094	0.2310	0.0081	0.0143	0.0142	0.0866	0.5824

Note. Weights sum to unity by rows. Source: OECD.

q_t is the logarithm of the real exchange rate based on the relative normalized unit labor cost in manufacturing (IMF IFS). Finally, oil price, p_t, is constructed as logarithm of the oil price index (IMF IFS).

References

Anderton R., Skudelny F. (2001), Exchange Rate Volatility and Euro Area Imports, *ECB Working Paper* **64**, Frankfurt, European Central Bank.

Anderton R., Baltagi B., Skudelny F., Sousa N. (2002), Intra- and Extra-Euro Area Import Demand for Manufactures, presented at the IV European Trade Study Group Annual Conference, Kiel, September 13-15.

Anderton R., di Mauro F., Moneta F. (2004), Understanding the Impact of the External Dimension of the Euro Area: Trade, Capital Flows and other International Macroeconomic Linkages, *ECB Occasional Paper* **12**, Frankfurt, European Central Bank.

Antonucci D., Girardi A. (2005), Currency Shocks and Dynamics of Trade Flows in the Euro Area, *European Review of Economics and Finance* **4** (3), 3-21.

Backus D. K., Kehoe P. J., Kydland F. E. (1994), Dynamics of the Trade Balance and the Terms of Trade: the J-Curve?, *American Economic Review* **84** (1), 84-103.

Bagnai A. (2004), Dynamic Paths of the European Economy: Simulations with an Aggregate Model of the EMU as a Part of the World Economy, in Deardorff A. (eds), *Past, Present, and Future of the European Union*, New York, Palgrave MacMillan.

Benkwitz A., Lütkepohl H., Neumann M. (2000), Problems Related to Confidence Intervals for Impulse Responses of Autoregressive Processes, *Econometric Reviews* **19**, 69-103.

Boyd D., Caporale G., Smith R. (2001), Real Exchange Rate Effects on the Balance of Trade: Cointegration and the Marshall-Lerner Condition, *International Journal of Finance and Economics* **6** (3), 187-200.

Brüggemann R., Lütkepohl H. (2001), Lag Selection in Subset VAR Models with an Application to a U.S. Monetary System, in Friedmann R., Knüppel L., Lütkepohl H. (eds), *Econometric Studies: A Festschrift in Honour of Joachim Frohn*, Münster, LIT Verlag.

Fagan G., Henry J., Mestre R. (2001), An Area-wide Model (AWM) for the Euro Area, *ECB Working Paper* **42**, Frankfurt, European Central Bank.

Goldstein M., Khan M. (1985), Income and Price Effects in Foreign Trade, in Jones R. Kenen P. (eds) *Handbook of International Economics*, Amsterdam, Elsevier.

Gupta-Kapoor A., Ramakrishnan U. (1999), Is There a J-Curve? A New Estimation for Japan, *International Economic Journal* **13** (4), 71-79.

Hall P. (1992), *The Bootstrap and Edgeworth Expansion*, New York, Springer Verlag.

Hamilton J. (2003), What is an Oil Shock?, *Journal of Econometrics* **113** (2), 363-398.

Houthakker H. S., Magee S. (1969), Income and Price Elasticities in World Trade, *Review of Economics and Statistics* **51** (2), 111-125.

Jiménez-Rodríguez R., Sánchez M. (2004), Oil Price Shocks and Real GDP Growth: Empirical Evidence for some OECD Countries, *ECB Working Paper* **362**, Frankfurt, European Central Bank.

Johansen S. (1992), Determination of the Cointegration Rank in the Presence of a Linear Trend, *Oxford Bulletin of Economics and Statistics* **54** (3), 383-397.

Johansen S. (1995), *Likelihood-Based Inference in Cointegrated Vector Autoregressive Models*, Oxford, Oxford University Press.

Kim I., Lougani P. (1992), The Role of Energy in Real Business Cycle Models, *Journal of Monetary Economics* **29** (2), 173-189.

King R. G., Plosser C. I., Stock J. H., Watson M. W. (1991), Stochastic Trends and Economic Fluctuations, *American Economic Review* **81** (4), 819-840.

Monti F. V. (2003), Implementing Optimal Control in Cointegrated I(1) Structural VAR Models, *ECB Working Paper* **288**, Frankfurt, European Central Bank.

Onafowora O. (2003), Exchange Rate and Trade Balance in East Asia: Is there a J-curve?, *Economics Bulletin* **5** (18), 1-13.

Pesaran H. M., Shin Y. (1998), Generalized Impulse Response Analysis in Linear Multivariate Models, *Economics Letters* **58** (1), 17-29.

Pesaran M. H., Shuermann T., Weiner, S. M. (2004), Modeling Regional Interdependencies Using a Global Error-Correcting Macroeconometric Model, *Journal of Business & Economic Statistics* **22** (2), 129-162.

Roberts M. A. (1995), The Second J-curve and Trade Account Dynamics, *Applied Economics Letters* **2** (2), 31-33.

Rotember J., Woodford M. (1996), Imperfect Competition and the Effects of Energy Price Increases, *Journal of Money, Credit, and Banking* **28** (4), 549-577.

Sims C. A. (1980), Macroeconomics and Reality, *Econometrica* **48** (1), 1-48.

Smets F., Wouters R. (2003), An Estimated Stochastic Dynamic General Equilibrium Model of the Euro Area, *Journal of the European Economic Association* **5** (1), 1123-1175.

In: New Developments in Macroeconomics Research
Editor: Lawrence Z. Pelzer, pp. 101-121
ISBN: 1-59454-663-0

Chapter 4

ORGANIC PAGE INFORMATION FOR INTERNATIONAL TRADE AND FINANCE

Olufemi A. Yesufu *

Department of Agricultural Economics,
Obafemi Awolowo University, Ile-Ife, Nigeria.

Thomas K. Yesufu **

Department of Electronic and Electrical Engineering,
Obafemi Awolowo University, Ile-Ife, Nigeria.

Abstract

Active involvement in international trade and finance is typical of sovereign entities with a track record of significant involvement in the large-scale production of a commodity that is widely consumed and appreciated across international boundaries. However, many economies do not have the tools that recognize budgetary provisions as the totality of policy instruments to address the current macroeconomic realities. This attracts a loss of information on the socio-economic reading of history on past and future interventions. It also results in dramatic changes in social policy, unfolding conflict and dwindling market economy, which threaten and weaken the society with dehumanization and poverty despite huge investments and the often use of irrecoverable resources. There is therefore a need to provide the necessary information to all stakeholders involved in development so as to avert the creation of failed states, unpredictable regimes and the attendant distortion of social and political structures meant for discharging intervention schemes. This chapter shows how the market paradigm can be used to obtain the poverty and gender equilibrium (PAGE) information with a view to achieving cooperation, creativity and synergy between stakeholders and intervention programs.

* E-mail address: olufemi_yesufu@hotmail.com, Phone: +2348053514471
** E-mail address: thomas_yesufu@yahoo.com, Phone: +2348034720266

Introduction

Trade between nations consists of the transfer of goods and services produced, the granting of capital loans, the payment of interest on loans and dividends on investment in foreign countries, and expenditures by tourists in foreign countries (Bishop and Tossaint, 1958). Accordingly, the continuation of a large volume of international trade cannot be maintained at a high level without outright grants of money or goods to foreign nations. Hence, a genuine integration of the global economy must take into account the fact that the world is economically and politically interdependent in terms of maintaining poverty and gender equilibrium respectively.

A balance must be struck between the drive for greater trade liberalization often entailing the dismantling of domestic regulation and the urgent need to counter accelerating environmental degradation, through regulatory and other measures meant to improve the quality of life. The effects of trade liberalization and/or policy on the environment must be carefully considered. The guiding principles of sustainable development tell us that core economic policies, including trade, finance and environmental objectives must be compatible by being World Trade Organization Principles' compliant, that is reciprocal, non-discriminatory and transparent.

A prescribed economic theory will go a long way, therefore, in making it possible to predict the consequences of actions yet to be taken and describe facts that are yet to be collected. Hence, economic theories are based upon the scientific method of theory formulation, collection of relevant data (observation), and testing of theories (modeling). In most cases, there is no true convergence between the results of this scientific method and the real system in focus due to the defective logic(s) employed (Fig. 1).

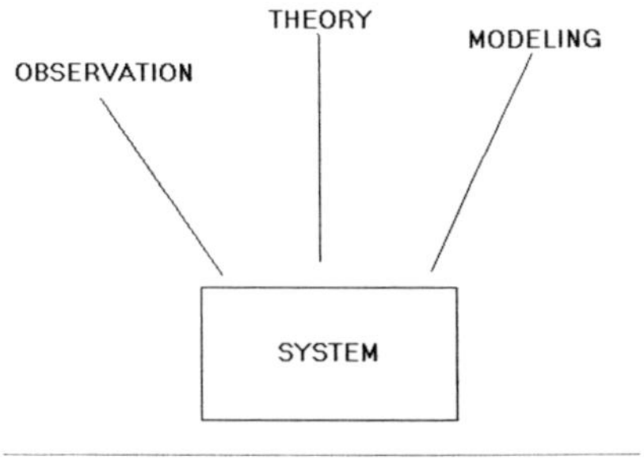

Fig. 1: Object of Economic Theory

Myth and Reality in Debt Management

The study of economics has nurtured the trend to own up to indigenous views at the expense of the development of the subject. This is not unconnected with the degree of randomness or uncertainty within it and the far-reaching implications of the results on socio-economic systems. Outright accusations, many of which are backed by evidences that seem not to be unfounded, and suspicion are common stock-in-trade as it is with the practice of a mysterious art that is looked upon to explain growth in all branches of the economy.

According to Ruffin and Gregory (1983), conflict in macroeconomic goals make a society to have trade-offs between inflation and unemployment, income distribution gap and living standards, and economic fluctuation and unemployment. These macroeconomic goals can be attained if the root of the conflict is known and measured. In this regard, the health of any sector of the economy is determined based on the relative conflict resolution status between it and the system of these goals.

It is true that in an economy where the prices of goods/services have increased may lead to a demand for an increase in wages. This demand may be a hoax if the goods/services in the nation are not locally produced and have prices that are fixed in the international market. Hence, adjusting internal wages because of this imported inflation, without tinkering with internal productivity, triggers the conflict envisaged to be associated with these macroeconomic goals. Furthermore, the gross national product (GNP) of an economy can rise when the quantity and/or price of goods/services produced increases.

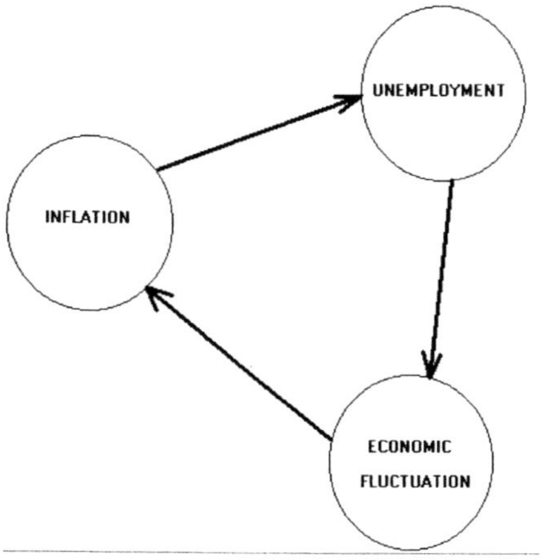

Fig. 2: Macroeconomic System of Relationships

A macroeconomic balance can be struck between the respective goals by determining the system of inter-relationships. In essence, high unemployment figures coupled with high living standards mean high productivity whilst a low inflation rate translates into an increase in productivity and a decrease in income distribution gap (or economic fluctuation) in an economy (Fig. 2). Hence, economies are in cycles like systems normally experience when they are celebrating a relationship. For instance, rapid population growth inhibits increases in per capita income; without substantial increases in per capita income it is difficult to bring about substantial reductions in birth rates. In addition, capital formation problems due to political uncertainties and the apparently poor development prospects of their countries make the wealthy and poor, whilst reaching to the realities of least developed country (LDC) life, invest their savings into non-productive areas (such as land, precious metals and foreign bank accounts) and save little or nothing. Consequently, the poor and affluent that live in LDCs do not save!

Economists first became interested in economic growth in the late 18th and early 19th centuries. Economies grow when the total amount of land, labor and capital input expands and/or available inputs are used more effectively. Balanced growth is a broad-based simultaneous advancement of all branches of the economy. Economic branches are interdependent and, therefore, other scenarios of growth leading to unbalanced growth of branches may subsist to achieve balanced growth in others. Balanced growth is yet to be experienced anywhere in the world as the poor (and the unemployed) have always been with us; they deserve a regular show of forgiveness. Moreover, balanced growth requires enormous resources that can only be sourced through a wise combination of export, import and support measures. In other words, a sustainable market is established when we have a production base, a preparedness to restructure it and a learning to impart on the larger society. Moreover, the fact that successes in a country cannot be attributed to the receiving or giving of foreign assistance alone, financial support must be backed by exports and imports in order to maintain a circular flow (Figs. 3a and 3b).

Pressure or stress on economic indicators relative to the basic cycle ultimately determines the nature of strain on the business cycle. Moreover, no two business cycles are identical making the nature of economic events to be random or unpredictable in spite of the knowledge of the indicators or universal differences. A business cycle may move from the state of indebtedness to buoyancy due to stress on the relevant economic indicators. Indebtedness is a major problem facing development in all spheres of economies. There is a need to give further insight into how debts have been managed, explain the role of financial assistance or support to economies and what to do in order to manage/avoid socio-economic conflicts directly or indirectly connected with a debt crisis of global dimension.

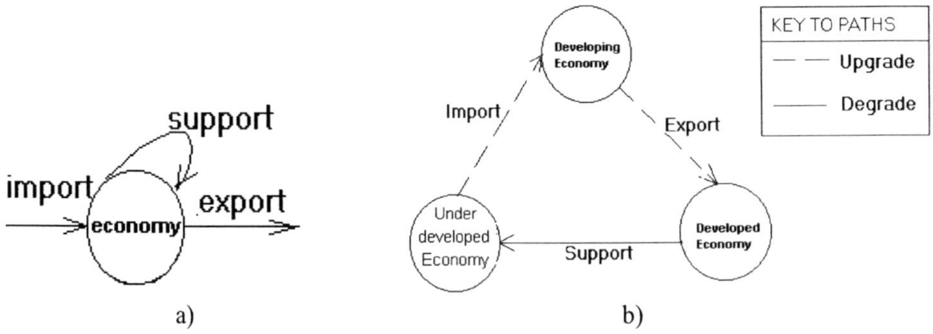

Fig. 3: Impact of Support, Export and Import on Economies

According to Fakiyesi (1991), debt management can take the following forms:

1. By stretching out the repayment of the debt while noting that most debts grow faster than a country's revenues and the need to take appropriate low credit ceilings to avoid default setting in. Furthermore, countries must not reduce their debt to export ratio or stretch out the service of her debt so as to keep the debt to resource ratio constant. It must be noted that debt to export (or resource) ratio has implication on the security or regenerative mode of an economy and hence inadequate to use as an index for debt management.
2. By monitoring the levels of exports and gross domestic product (GDP) through an appropriate measure of resources in such a way that it is invariant with the real exchange rate. It must be noted that GDP is too broad to be sensitive while

exports are too narrow as measures of resources and could respectively lead to over estimation and under estimation (all forms of spurious results).

3. By ignoring the creditor's capital loss in the form of discounted debts in the international financial markets. It is also worth noting that discounted debts are a loss to debtors if they are dependent on their creditor for the economy of goods and services.
4. By watching government deficit in the form of increase in surplus, domestic money creation and increase in government domestic debt. However, government surplus, domestic debt and domestic money creation does not necessarily mean a sufficient index for deficit.

It is very alarming to note that there is no sufficient index for carrying out debt management and/or the study of growth in an economy. Moreover, a successful debt management through economic decisions may result in growth, debt forgiveness and security or the eventual re-unification of an entity with life source(s) enthroned by a social justice system.

Scientific Method

According to Ruffin and Gregory (1983), three logical fallacies plague economic analysis: the false-cause or observational (output specification) fallacy (assuming that Event A has caused Event B because A is associated with B); the fallacy of composition (components/theory) or conceptualization (assuming that what is true for each part taken separately is true for the whole or, conversely, assuming that what is true for the whole is also true for each part); the *ceteris paribus* or modeling (input specification) fallacy (incorrectly attributing to one variable effects that are caused by another). The primary objective of finding the logic in a flow at maturity is the acquisition of the information for the universal differences (indicators) that give a description of the system. This is because a chaotic system can only be predictable if we always have the operating information for its universal differences or, according to Chua (1987), its initial conditions. A standard method of economic analysis needed to address these fallacies, therefore, requires obtaining the information for universal differences in the economy.

It is pertinent to note that indicators employed in any economic activity give a description of the disturbance due to phase changes (business cycles or oscillations) associated with the circular flow of goods and services. It is expected that the indicators connected as points in a basic cycle represent the circular flow of the economic activity. In other words, an economic activity is analogous to a flowing charge in a bid to adapting a perception with a goal.

The principle of circular flow for economic growth is derivable from the steps employed in Yesufu & Yesufu (1999) to explain a self-evident pattern recognition technique. These steps include the understanding that in a capacitive circuit (with just a resistor and a capacitor), the determination of its current (or flowing /falling charge), as in the International Centre for Theoretical Physics (1987), is not a local problem. This problem therefore requires an encompassing framework offered by Maxwell's equation for electromagnetism to understand the production of fields associated with this system as explosive, damped or perpetual oscillations. Hence, we can define the relationship between the cause and effect of the electromagnetic field generated by this system as

$$\nabla \times \vec{H} = jw\varepsilon\vec{E}\left(1 - j\sigma/_{w\varepsilon}\right) \tag{1}$$

Where ∇ and j are the del and complex operators respectively, w is the frequency of the number of cycles per second, H and E are the respective electric and magnetic field intensities, σ and ε are the respective conductivity and permittivity of the system, and the characteristic equation of the system is

$$1 - j\sigma/_{w\varepsilon} \tag{2}$$

and it is of the form

$$1 + BD \tag{3}$$

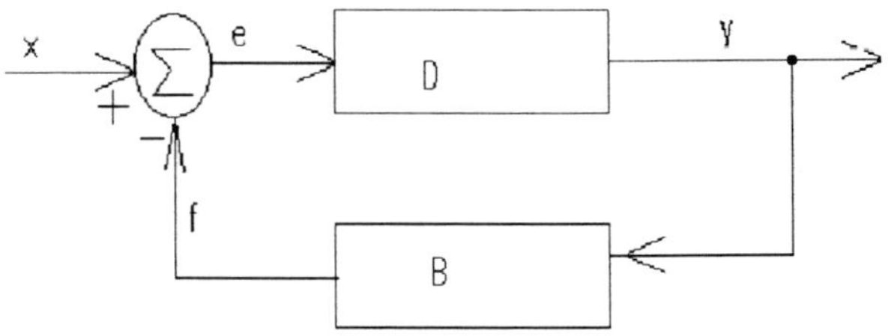

Fig. 4: A System

B and D are the accelerator's and the multiplier's characteristics of a typical system (in which there is an output (y) for a corresponding input (x), feedback (f) and error (e) as shown in Fig. 4) respectively and BD = $-j\sigma/_{w\varepsilon}$. Subsequently, the double transients associated with charge and current in an R-C circuit or system is based on charge reception and storage for the multiplier and accelerator arms (Fig. 5). The respective expressions defining the behavior of the multiplier (feed forward) arm as purely capacitive and the accelerator (feedback) arm as purely inductive (with inductance (L)) are as follows (in this case q = x and y = i):

$$\frac{dq}{dt} = i \tag{4}$$

$$v = -L\frac{di}{dt} \tag{5}$$

Or

$$q = -\frac{1}{w^2}\frac{di}{dt} \tag{6}$$

Where $w^2 = \frac{1}{\sqrt{LC}}$, the charge $q = Cv$ for a given current (i) and voltage (v) at any time (t).

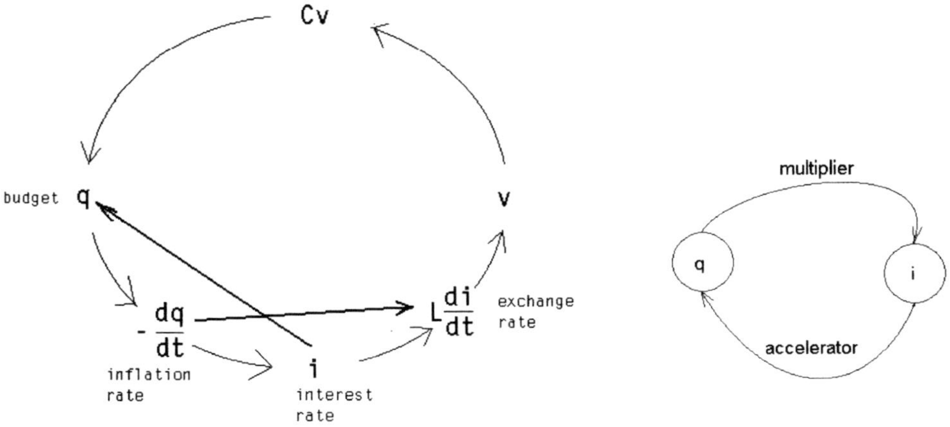

a) Circular Flow in Physical and Social Sciences b) Charge – Current Control

Fig. 5: Concept and Application of Circular flow

We can, therefore, derive the following based on the product (in the form of BD) of the transfer relationships of both arms compared to the value of BD for the system:

$$jw^2 \frac{\sigma}{w\varepsilon} = \frac{1}{qi}\frac{di}{dt}\frac{dq}{dt} \tag{7}$$

It is important to note that the annual budget figures eventually determine the returns for that year subject to a commensurate regime of inflation rate, interest rate and exchange rate; the inflation rate effectively reduces the policy charge in the budget, the interpretation of a reduction in the policy charge is reflected in the interest rate and the fluctuation in the interest rate naturally yields the controlling parameter (L) in the exchange rate.

Based on the hyperbolic connection between q and i in (7), we can obtain two separate expressions for their manifestations as follows:

$$\frac{1}{G_q}\frac{dq}{q} = \frac{dt}{T_q} \tag{8}$$

$$\frac{1}{G_i}\frac{di}{i} = \frac{dt}{T_i} \tag{9}$$

Where $G_q T_i = G_i T_q$, G and T are also separation constants in the resource (either q or i) and time domain respectively.

Hence,

$$dq = \frac{G_q}{T_q}(q\,dt) \tag{10}$$

or

$$di = \frac{G_i}{T_i}(i\,dt) \tag{11}$$

Hence, investment (q) accelerates the savings (i) and vice-versa.

The English Economist Sir Roy Harrod and Evsey Domar studied in the 1950s the relationship between a nation's rate of saving and economic growth. Their work is summarized in the Harrod-Domar growth model (Ruffin & Gregory, 1983). This model is based on two definitions and an identity:

Definitions

1. Investment (I) is the addition to the stock of capital or I = ΔK, where ΔK denotes the change in the stock of capital.
2. Marginal output to capital ratio (MOCR) is the change in output per unit change in capital.

Identity

This is based on the circular flow or the capture of a reciprocal attribute in a system meant to give the operational framework or information about the system.

If we know the system's devices and the circular flow associated with it then we can prescribe the operational facilities for the system. Hence, the identity of the Harrod-Domar model is the macroeconomic equality of investment (I) and saving (S).

But

$$\text{MOCR} = \left(\frac{\Delta K}{\Delta Q}\right) \tag{12}$$

Or

$$\frac{\Delta Q}{Q} = \text{MOCR}\left(\frac{\Delta K}{Q}\right) \tag{13}$$

Define $\frac{\Delta K}{Q}$ = saving rate = S and $\frac{\Delta Q}{Q}$ = growth rate of output

Hence, the growth rate of output equals the MOCR times the saving rate. Equations (10) and (11) are in the form of the Harrod-Domar model (where MOCR = $\frac{G_i}{T_i}$ and di = ΔQ and idt = ΔK) and the derivation shows the nature of MOCR in the growth model (note that the cyclic nature of the model is latent).

Three issues immediately emerge from this model:

1. The Harrod-Domar growth model implies that the LDCs could solve their problems by raising national saving rates. Usually, MOCR is frequently thought of as being dependent on the technological improvements and labor inputs. It is, therefore, required that the Harrod-Domar model be rigorously proved in order to substantiate this thought or any other one.
2. Sustainable growth is a desirable experience for all natural systems. It is, therefore, required that the universality and rationality of this identity be determined.
3. Using this growth equation, we also expect that the rate of economic growth is simply going to increase when foreign assistance (fa) is made available i.e.

$$\frac{\Delta Q}{Q} = \text{MOCR}\left(\frac{\Delta K}{Q} + \text{fa}\right) \tag{14}$$

However, most of fa has had a complex relationship with the actual value of S or $\frac{\Delta K}{Q}$ such that [S + fa] is mostly designed to be negative in developing countries since most of the support they attract from developed countries erodes any savings in the long run. It is, therefore, expected that obtaining a relationship between S and fa is necessary to stem the tide of confusion and conflict arising from what foreign assistance imply.

The equality of actual saving (S) and investment (I) is an important cornerstone of macroeconomics. Some mechanism is required to bring the two into equality in spite of the disparate wishes of savers and investors. This mechanism is based on the MOCR as Fig. 6 implies. As I increase, MOCR increases while S decreases sending counter signals to the original increase in I. This is followed by a decrease in MOCR and the circuital flow continues. However, output versus capital (debt or equity) is such that the MOCR is positive (Fig. 7). According to Carzo & Yanouzas (1967), rationality in decision-making is based on the ability to formulate alternatives and to make choices that optimize results.

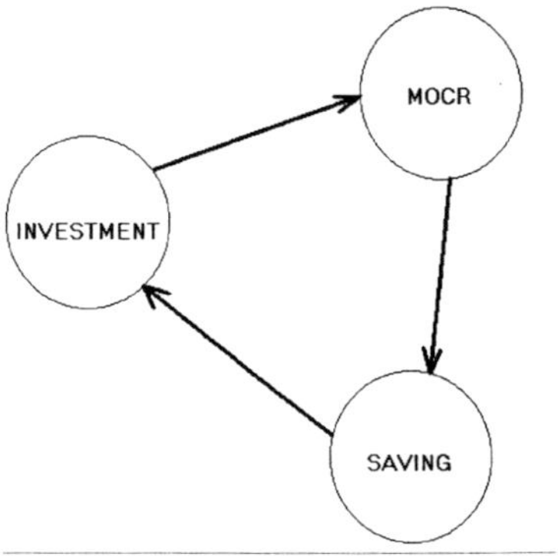

Fig. 6: Investment Dynamics

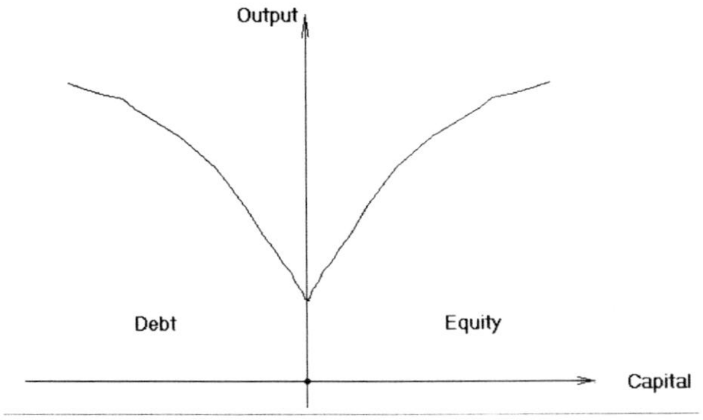

Fig. 7: Debt – Equity Transformation of Output

Sustainable or natural growth theory has connections with the Fibonacci sequences which is defined as

$$N_n = N_{n-1} + N_{n-2} \quad \text{where} \quad N_0 = N_1 = 1 \tag{15}$$

The relation gives a universal attribute (α) of this sequence for sustainable growth, called the divine ratio; it is expressed as

$$\frac{N_{n+1}}{N_n} = \alpha \quad \text{for large n} \quad \text{and} \quad \alpha = 1 + \frac{1}{\alpha} \tag{16}$$

α is a universal constant given by 0.6181……

Or

$$\alpha - \beta = \gamma + \frac{1}{\alpha} \tag{17}$$

where

$$\gamma + \beta = 1 \tag{18}$$

On rearranging, we have

$$\frac{\alpha}{\alpha\gamma + 1} = \frac{1}{\alpha - \beta} \tag{19}$$

Comparing (13) and (19) such that we have

MOCR = α, $\frac{1}{\alpha\gamma+1} = \frac{\Delta K}{Q}$ and $\frac{\Delta Q}{Q} = \frac{1}{\alpha - \beta}$

Hence, α or MOCR is a dynamic constant that is also connected with business information rate and the universal mechanism or universality that brings the rational response of the system to equity. MOCR shows that speed or number of rounds is required to ensure that an appropriate saving rate befits a growth rate assumed. According to Wik (1997), universality is based on the constraints offered by information and knowledge in decision-making.

Convergence

Definitions are based on coherent logic, which may be expressed in mathematical theories, empirical observations, periodontal models and systemic forms. A definition paradigm is therefore expected to reflect a marketing-mix of these expressions into homologous-based iconic motifs for describing the closure, predicting the limit and prescribing the unit of real systems. This typifies the convenience with which basic mathematical definitions appear in the open literature. For example, the differentiation of the financial price (P) as a function of the quantity demanded (Q) of a traded item, described as a form of price elasticity of demand, is given by

$$\frac{dP}{dQ} = {}_{Q \xrightarrow{\lim} 0} \frac{\Delta P}{\Delta Q} \tag{20}$$

In this situation:

- the limit of the definition paradigm depends on the analog or digital handle that hard computing requires of professionals amongst stakeholders in an activity.
- the unit in the flip-flop of the definition paradigm qualifies the soft computing integration of low and high level models or generalizations adapted by decision-makers.
- the micro and macro-applications or closure of the definition paradigm gives expressions to the scientific results in budgeting for reformation.

Generally, stakeholders may be market-defined as a family (in gender equilibrium) of professionals, scientists and decision-makers that are communicating with educators by either having a reactive (inorganic) or cooperative (organic) pursuit of information. The information in the language of stakeholders is, therefore, an economic resource that requires organization into an organic page for intensification available through the formulation of physical, computational and social media. Moreover, the position of a stakeholder is estimated based on the poverty (data-rich-information-poor [DRIP] or interference, hump-and-dump or preference, and Chameleon or indifference states) and gender equilibrium in finance and trade respectively. Stakeholders, at various levels of participation in trade and finance of switched economies, require operating information in order to be effectively networked through web pages of the international community. The summation of decisions on the web pages of switched economies is known as organic page information.

It is, therefore, a requirement for stakeholders to acquire the needed organic poverty and gender equilibrium (PAGE) information in order to participate meaningfully in all issues involving international trade and finance (Table 1). This information will allow stakeholders to attain synergy and be able to assess each other through the stages of motivation, cooperation and creativity following the respective interplay amongst budget (debt repayment mechanism on the road map from poverty to surplus), inflation rate, interest rate and exchange rate regimes. A successful budget is therefore expected to carry out the scientific transformation of a targeted microeconomic myth into the future realities of the macroeconomic environment.

The family unit or household is where poverty and gender equilibrium information are shaped by the reflexive signals it produces as the household agents interacts with social change. The basic socioeconomic reading of history often suggests that poverty is enthroned by pathological headship in any ramification of social significance. At various levels, the effect of social change is actually determined by the visionary use of policy instruments expressed in the respective budgets employed. In this case, policy instruments employed by a family of stakeholders have outcomes that literarily assume human faces that may be expressed along an organic poverty and gender equilibrium (PAGE) scale or information. This approach advances the customary way of expressing political, economic, social and psychological theory in words that is, policy – in the vernacular of the times - over the past centuries (Knight et al., 1971). With the development of mathematics, scholars had to use simulations or lower level generalizations in a bid to contend with the serial nature of verbal exposition as well as the intractability of many mathematical systems that involve nonlinear formulations. Simulations may serve in three ways as formats, which we may use to strengthen knowledge policy at the individual, sociological, cultural and environmental levels:

Table 1: Combining Myth, Science and Reality of Trade and Finance

1	**ACTIVITY**	Hard computing	Marketing	Soft computing	Servicing
2	**PARADIGM**	Limit	Definition	Unit	Closure
3	**APPLICATION**	Electronics	Page	Language	Economy
4	**SCIENCE**	Physical	Information	Computational	Social
5	**REALITY**	Analog/ Digital	Inorganic/ organic	Low/high level	Micro/macro
6	**COMPONENTS OF BEHAVIOR**	Power	Communication	Adaptation	Input/output
7	**STAKEHOLDER**	Professionals	Educators	Decision-Makers	Scientists
8	**MENTAL PROCESSING**	Motivation	Creativity	Cooperation	Synergy
9	**INSTRUMENTS**	Inflation rate	Exchange rate	Interest rate	Budget/Debt
10	**ANALYSIS**	Theoretical	Experimental	Modeling	Holistic

- Simulations may be used as techniques for increasing the coherence within and among models.

- Simulations may be used as construction in terms of which empirical research may be organized, so that the validity of our assertions may be appraised.
- Simulations may be used by members of the decision-making community in the development of policy, both as devices for making systematic critiques, through "box-scoring" its failures and successes, and as formats for the exploration of alternative plans for action.

This, therefore, presents a high level generalization of the convergence in modes of information production with the effectiveness of policy instruments in the transformation of poverty and gender equilibrium witnessed by the family (of stakeholders).

Social change is a multi-dimensional concept existing in a dialectical partnership with many international and inter-temporal contexts. Subsequently, the adequacy and relevance of existing theories of social change to the development of a social policy research methodology are problems (Afonja & Pearce, 1986). Previous theories link up systematically with their contexts from either an exemplary window or an analytic shadow. Moreover, it is very instructive to use this exemplary window and analytic shadow to proceed from the particular to the general, to understand the dynamics of each society before attempting to formulate a macro-level theory.

The belief that economic factors determine structural change leading to a superficial definition of the concept of economic surplus is central to the theory and to the errors in the explanation of the determinants of social change. A major criticism from Taylor in Afonja & Pearce (1986) is that the definition of Economic surplus, simply in terms of the difference between what a society produces and the costs of producing it, does not adequately explain how surplus is generated within different modes of production. Taylor argued that the specific combination of production and productive forces, which determine the amount of surplus produced, differs from one mode of production to another. In addition, Taylor noted that this restriction does not allow in depth analysis of the structures, reproduction and development of different modes of production.

Taylor went beyond studying social change merely in terms of analyzing society and the processes which ensure its maintenance but applied the concept of social formation to link historical changes in the dominant practice (social formation) to the dominant practice in other social formations. Each social formation contains different practices – economic, political, ideological and theoretical. But one of these is usually the dominant practice that determines the inter relation of all of them at a particular point of time. The nature of the determinant instance is determined by the degree of correspondence between the ownership of the means of production and the relations of extraction of labor surplus. There is therefore reason to consider the analytic shadow in the modes of production along with the exemplary window of social change in a three-generation family open to these contexts.

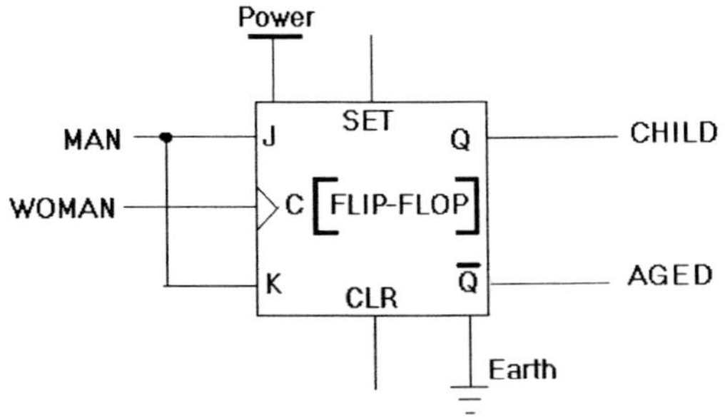

Fig. 8: The Social Unit Versus Signals in an Electronic Flip-Flop

According to Afonja & Pearce (1986) open systems paradigms are those whose analytic component, that is its basic unit of analysis, is open to the basic unit of analysis of other paradigms. An open system paradigm is characterized by the formulation of the inter relationships among the components of social order in such a way that each element, though relatively autonomous, also constitutes a basic referent of the other components. Open systems paradigms give up the idea of a fixed relationship between sub-components and are directed towards the analysis of the internal system dynamics, interconnections and continuous feedback processes among the components of social order. According to Haken (2002), open systems are pattern recognition and decision making systems that are composed of many individual parts that produce spatio-temporal or functional structures via self organization. Self - organization means that the resulting structures or functions are not imposed on the system from the outside but are developed by the system in response to rather unspecific control parameters. These open system paradigms have nonlinear dynamics, which are changing former paradigms by showing that many phenomena observed in nature and society are neither completely deterministic nor completely random. While looking random or chaotic, they are governed by strict deterministic laws hence may easily be controlled and changed in a desirable direction.

A suitable lower level generalization can, therefore, be conceptualized from Fig. 8, which shows the exemplary window of social change as a unit interacts, reproduces and keeps track of the past under a favorable balance in the available power. This situation is similar to the behavior of a fundamental logic circuit called the J-K Flip-Flop (FF). The J-K FF is basically used as a memory element in a computer environment. It has the J and K inputs linked together, the Q and inverted Q ($\overline{Q}$) output and the clock, C. Subsequently, J and K are taken to represent steady gender activity in a man while C represents the cyclic gender activity in a woman; the man and woman are of the present generation. Furthermore, the outputs (Q and $\overline{Q}$) are regarded as taken out of one another such that Q represents the child (new generation) and $\overline{Q}$ represents the aged (the old generation). Also, the FF is powered (with reference to the Earth) and the outputs may be untimely set (SET) that is, Q = 1 or cleared (CLR) that is, Q = 0 by environmental conditions dictated by policy instruments. The subsequent development of this unit is reflexively driven by the social environment, which is adjusted by the policy instruments stimulating their interactions. The larger fabric of society is, therefore, seen to come from this lower level generalization as the children develop into either a man or woman and the aged refrains from going on to produce another child as a man or woman.

The frequency in the production of gametes in this normal family, resulting in either dehumanization or gender balance, is in the following increasing order: balanced, man, woman, child, aged and dead or dehumanized. The man, woman, child and the aged can be seen as heterogeneous interacting agents and, hence, the key determinants of the social change observed. This scenario affords us the ability to have the historical and materialistic perspectives of development in a specified mode of production. It also accounts for change as a function of one continuous historical process in which the most dominant factors in one period are specified and are at the same time linked with those of the following periods. Moreover, this scenario is able to cope with internal contradictions, conflicts, exploitative relations and revolutions. This makes it to be like the much to be desired open systems paradigms right from the onset.

Method of Analysis

Random Walk Model will be used to determine the random interaction effect of the total budget on physical inflation rate, facilitating interest rate and exchange rate functions, which are organically related and involved in steering trade and finance in an economic system. This is because the concept of household key determinant of production/security suggests that the components employed in its implementation are prepared for any social change and hence must follow the "random walk" pattern. The one – way random effect model for this situation is given by (Hays & Winkler, 1971):

$$Y_{ij} = u + a_{ij} + e_{ij} \qquad (21)$$

Where; u = Grand Mean of all the J different population

$i = 1, \ldots, n_j$
n_j = sample size in the jth group
$j = 1, \ldots, J$
J = J different samples or groups
e_{ij} = Random Error
a_{ij} = Random Effect Variable
Y_{ij} = Observable measurement

An effect is a reflection of a difference among population means on the condition that the random error cancels out in the long – run, that is, having long standing relationship.

The assumptions made about a_{ij} are:

i) The possible values a_{ij} represent a random variable having a distribution with a mean of zero and a variance of σ_A^2.
ii) The (i) values of the random variable a_{ij} occurring in the experiment are completely independent of each other.
iii) Each pair of random variables a_{ij} and e_{ij} is completely independent.

This represents the variance of the treatment effects. The hypothesis of no treatment effects is true when, and only when, the value of σ_A^2 is zero or $a_{ij} = 1$.

Hence a_{ij} can be obtained using the Random Walk Model given as (Hallam et al., 1992):

$$Y_{ij} = a_{ij} Y_{i\,j-1} + e_{ij} \tag{22}$$

Subsequently, a_{ij} in the long run is given by (Yesufu & Yesufu (2002))

$$a_{ij} = 2(Y_{ij} - Y_{i\,j-1})Y_{ij}^{-1} Y_{i\,j-1}^{-2} \tag{23}$$

When

$a_{ij} = 1$, it means no effect
$a_{ij} < 1$, it means reduction of effect
$a_{ij} > 1$, it means increase of effect

These give six (6) outcomes for the production system corresponding to the determinant of social change being expressed by one of these: no stimulation of the system, productive stimulation of the system, either one of the two exchange functions, the physical function or the facilitating function). The variable / observable with the highest aggregate effect (e.g. we assume this to be the a_{i1} series of Y_1) is used as a point of reference to ensure consistency/correspondence in comparative analysis of effects among the observable as:

$$nY_1 = Y_2\sum_{i=1}^{n-1}(a_{i1} - a_{i2} - 1) + Y_3\sum_{i=1}^{n-1}(a_{i1} - a_{i3} - 1) + Y_4\sum_{i=1}^{n-1}(a_{i1} - a_{i4} - 1) \tag{24}$$

Where n = number of respondents

Y_1 = exchange function (input)
Y_2 = exchange function (output)
Y_3 = facilitating function
Y_4 = physical function

Alternatively, the history of the motivation (a_{ij}) of a policy instrument can indicate to us the key determinant by computing appreciation of social change (A) and the inertia (I) as follows (for $j > 0$):

$$A_j = a_{ij} - a_{ij-1} \tag{25}$$

And

$$I_j = A_j + A_{j-1} \tag{26}$$

Family reaction, therefore, belongs to a set of normative patterns or decisions based on their stimulation and information through the gratification, application and purification of distresses and intentions in policy instruments. Each decision takes into account all available information that bears on the decision, both information concerning the state of the world and information concerning the consequences of the potential decisions. The associated normative marketing scenarios of the consequences of the decisions vis-à-vis the state of the world are as follows (Yesufu & Yesufu, 2003):

When $A = 0$, this implies that price (supply) will maintain a perpetual oscillation resulting in specialization or extinction given a respective positive or negative climate of incentives. Specialization involves the clear demarcation of the market area into commodity zones, functions, etc. Specialization is the universal characteristics of markets, primitive or advanced. There can be functional, product or institutional specialization. Specialization increases the interdependency of the producers/farmers, marketing firms and consumers, increase the volume of exchange and thereby the importance of marketing activity and tend to lead to larger firms. It corresponds to $A = 0, I > 0$. Extinction ($A = 0, I < 0$) is the stage in which marketers embark on a withdrawal from the market having resorted to all means of attracting customers and failed.

When $A > 0$, the marketing system will exhibit explosive oscillation as price (supply) increase and become infinite as t increases without limit resulting in diversification or mutation given a respective positive or negative climate of incentives. Each new value of price and quantity is farther from equilibrium than the preceding. Diversification involves the use of assigned market areas without any specific categorization. Marketers freely engage in selling what they choose to sell at their assigned location. This is due to the onset of bifurcation ($A > 0, I > 0$) in market growth and location factors. This contributes to the flexibility in market decisions and reduces market risks. It protects from risks of price changes and market losses for a single product. Diversification can be functional, product or institutional. Households carry out an insurance of their own by diversifying their production. It is the production and sale of several products at the same time or the production and sale of the same product at different times during the year. Mutation ($A > 0, I < 0$) is the state whereby marketers convert the market area to some other ventures not originally intended.

When $A < 0$, the system will exhibit damped oscillation resulting in hawking or touting given a respective positive or negative climate of incentives and thus, the value for the equilibrium price is approached as j approaches infinity. Hawking ($A < 0, I > 0$) is associated with marketers at the mid-stream of bifurcation due to growth and location factors. In this case, they freely resort to employing more hands involved in hawking at any location in and around the vicinity of the market. They provide extra positive incentives to consumers at no extra cost to them. Touting ($A < 0, I < 0$) is a scenario whereby the marketers through various means of attracting them physically harass customers. Here, very aggressive hands are employed in a bid to attract elusive customers. The incentives employed are usually at the expense of the consumer unlike in hawking.

The gender scales in these scenarios are respectively balanced, man, woman, child, aged and poverty (dehumanized) for specialization, diversification, hawking, touting, extinction and mutation. Comparative analysis with these normative typologies is, therefore, required in order to understand the reactions expressed with a view to making possible improvements by detecting statistical relevance of the data through an unbiased or neutral analysis. In addition, all the agents involved in the family are undergoing revolutions that must be handled simultaneously in order to obtain the actual preferences, interferences and indifferences expressed. Moreover, it is possible to reveal the consequences of power fluctuations and/or interruptions as the revolutions, if not significantly different in impact, ultimately synchronize with an inertia that sustains the socioeconomic realities of the times under investigation.

Nigeria's Budget (1977 – 1996)

The total Nigerian budget (recurrent and capital estimates) for the period 1977 to 1996 was obtained from the report/publication of the Central Bank of Nigeria. These data were analyzed using the budget for 1977 (₦15328.9 million) as the starting year and tabulated in Table 2. The PAGE information as shown in Table 2 exhibited the child, man and woman scenarios, which are the distributional consequences of the pathological scenarios in Nigeria and a fall-out from the inability to achieve a productive economy; they all reflect a scenario of missed opportunities for development as also in Arinze (1991). The pathological scenarios also show the dominant group in the drive towards development and, subsequently, those suffering significant deprivations due to their pathological headship in the years concerned. The search for a productive base in Nigeria is seen in the man scenario where resources are characteristically spread too thin to generate significant social change.

Table 2: Organic PAGE Information in the Nigerian Budget 1977 –1996

YEAR (j)	TOTAL BUDGET (₦million)	a_{ij}	A_j	I_j	PAGE
1978	12452.4	-1.966162E-9	6.909277E-9	6.909277E-9	MAN
1979	20190.2	4.943115E-9	-6.4545E-9	4.547771E-10	WOMAN
1980	15435.3	-1.511385E-9	-1.449224E-9	-9.944469E-10	CHILD
1981	11410.9	-2.960609E-9	4.688761E-9	3.694314E-9	MAN
1982	12857.5	1.728152E-9	-2.500318E-9	1.193996E-9	WOMAN
1983	12086.1	-7.721659E-10	4.099585E-9	5.293581E-9	MAN
1984	15966.3	3.327419E-9	-2.537353E-9	2.756228E-9	WOMAN
1985	17754.2	7.900661E-10	-4.610385E-9	-1.854157E-9	CHILD
1986	11081.8	-3.820318E-9	8.468967E-9	6.61481E-9	MAN
1987	15508.6	4.648649E-9	-1.640853E-9	4.973957E-9	WOMAN
1988	24297.2	3.007795E-9	-2.354037E-9	2.61992E-9	WOMAN
1989	30107.1	6.537585E-10	-1.179127E-10	2.502007E-9	WOMAN
1990	39764.0	5.358458E-10	-5.717681E-10	1.930239E-9	WOMAN
1991	38665.9	-3.592231E-11	3.796402E-10	2.30988E-9	MAN
1992	52035.9	3.437179E-10	5.204484E-11	2.361924E-9	MAN
1993	112100.5	3.957628E-10	-3.985075E-10	1.963417E-9	WOMAN
1994	110200.0	-2.74474E-12	4.919783E-11	2.012615E-9	MAN
1995	153495.6	4.645309E-11	-3.050684E-11	1.982108E-9	WOMAN
1996	189000.0	1.594625E-11	1.100473E-11	1.993113E-9	MAN

- Yearly Total Budget were compiled from the Statistical Bulletin of the Central Bank of Nigeria, 1998
- a_{ij} MOTIVATION
- A_j APPRECIATION
- I_j INERTIA

This search is occasionally and fixedly (1987 –1990) abandoned for the regular base of subsistence exhibited in the woman scenario, which attracts both legal and illegal international finance and trade in many dimensions. The child scenario is a case needing a recovery from over exploitation or deep erosion below the base for subsistence (1980 and 1985). It is usually characterized by large administrative overhead and/poor returns from the base for subsistence. On two occasions, the woman-child-man transitions were observed to have come from the onset of new regimes presumably seeking to settle public concerns about presumed past difficulties. These results show that despite all the policy instruments announced and summed up in the budget of Nigeria to attaining development, the wheel of the developmental process did not find its theme from 1977 to 1996. It is also worth noting that the woman has had far more significant stress from the policy instruments in Nigeria having worn the crown of a pathological headship (also interestingly refused in many individualistic, sociologic, national, cultural, financial and environmental contexts) for a longer time than the man and child beneficiaries of public policies. The balanced, aged and dehumanized scenarios did not manifest in all the years investigated.

The method of analysis, called the market or definition paradigm, can be used for analyzing complex systems like policies, societies and governments, by helping to reveal the dominance (signatures) of the different physiological and pathological states therein. Following this, the link between gender and poverty, as epitomized by the prevalence of pathological headship in the Nigerian society, is established in this work based on a generalization that encompasses an analytic or logic shadow of reasoning and a real operating system based on the market (definition) paradigm, a new open paradigm in social policy research. The distributional consequence of a pathological leadership or policy is in the degree of poverty indicated by the market paradigm in terms of the organic page information. Furthermore, the rigorous question asked by Soyinka (1982), on what should be our contribution to society whilst awaiting the revolution, is seen to be very pertinent to our attitude to social policy in view of the potentially disruptive tendencies of policy instruments and all types of headship in community level participation. Accordingly, this approach reduces the power of sycophancy and clothes leadership with the advisory responsibility of self-criticism as a strategy for contributing to society. Moreover, Soyinka (1982) opined that we cannot rest upon any categories of ideas in which any observable patterns, within societies which have produced those ideas, have not been taken into full dialectical partnership – this would be to perpetuate the habit of excision which obscured the socioeconomic reading of history in its time, enthroning the dictatorship of the mutant or the pathological in the realm of human ideas. This framework is therefore suitable for planning a route map out of poverty and, also, help in fostering researches in social policy amongst researchers, agencies and other organizations.

Conclusion

This chapter has shown how the market (definition) paradigm can be used to obtain the poverty and gender equilibrium (PAGE) information with a view to enhancing cooperation, creativity and synergy between stakeholders and intervention programs. The method employed involved the use of a representative theory, observation, model and system of macroeconomic indicators to obtain the limit, unit and closure of development scenarios in a market economy. Further more, a low-level generalization was developed on how conflict history tracks social changes and converges with policy and marketing. Following this, the market paradigm was used to obtain the homologous PAGE information of observed budgetary contributions from a mixed grill of interventions in governance. The results obtained showed that budgetary interventions have usual organic interpretations in development, including the entry, tenure and exit of unpredictable regimes.

This chapter, therefore, concludes that the market paradigm is not too slogan in the plaudit definition of the nature of open systems employed in intervention programs and brings organic realities into the realm of social policy, conflict history and market economy analysis. It also emphasizes the various roles of stakeholders in fashioning a gender sensitive road map out of poverty through a concerted recovery from debt burden, avoidance of cosmetic intervention programs and the repair of ailing structures for a regime of favorable international trade and finance.

References

Afonja, S. & Pearce, T.O. (Eds.) (1983): *Social Change in Nigeria*, London: Longman.

Arinze, A.I. (1991): Human Development Report 1990 by United Nations Development Programme (UNDP) New York, Oxford University Press, 1990. In: *Central Bank of Nigeria Economic and Financial Review, Vol. 29,* (No. 2), pp. 208 – 212.

Bishop, C.C. & Toussaint, W.D. (1958): *Introduction to Agricultural Economic Analysis*, New York, USA: John Wiley & Sons Inc.

Carzo, R. Jr. & Yanouzas, J.N. (1967): *Formal Organizations: A Systems Approach*, Richard D. Irwin Inc. and The Dorsey Press, Homewood, Illinois, USA.

Chua, L.O. (ed.)(1987): Special Issue on Chaotic Systems, *Proceedings of the IEEE*, Vol. 75, (No. 8), pp. 979 – 1133.

Fakiyesi, O.M. (1991): Cohen, Daniel: The Management of the developing Countries' Debt: Guidelines and Application to Brazil, *The World Bank Economic Review,* Vol. 2, No. 1, January 1988, *Central Bank of Nigeria, Economic and Financial Review,* Vol. 29, (No. 4), pp. 314 – 315.

Hallam, D., Machado, F. & Rapsomanikis, G. (1992): Co-integration Analysis and the Determinants of Land Prices, *Journal of Agricultural Economics*, Vol. 41, (No. 3), pp. 28–37.

Haken, H. (2002): Synergetics: The Past, Present and Future. In: W. Klonowski (Ed.): Attractors, Signals and Synergetics, *Proceedings of the 1st European Interdisciplinary School on Nonlinear Dynamics for System and Signal Analysis EUROATTRACTOR 2000,* (pp. 18 – 19). Warsaw: Pabst Science Publishers.

Hays, W.L. & Winkler, R.L. (1971): *Statistics: Probability, Inference and Decision*, New York, USA: Holt, Rinehart and Winston Inc.

International Centre for Theoretical Physics (1988): *The Dirac Medals of the ICTP 1987*, p.13 – 27: Miramare-Trieste, IT

Knight, D.E., Curtis, H.W. & Fogel, L.J. (1971)(Eds): Cybernetics, Simulation and Conflict Resolution, *Third Annual Symposium of the American Society for Cybernetics*, New York, USA: Spartan Macmillan Co. Ltd.

Ruffin, R.J. & Gregory, P.R. (1983): *Principles of Macroeconomics*, Illinois, USA: Scott, Foresman and Co.

Soyinka, W. (1982): The Critic and Society: Barthes, Leftocracy and Other Mythologies, *Inaugural Lecture Series* **49**, Ile-Ife, NG: University of Ife Press.

Wik, M.W. (1997): Global Information Infrastructure: Threats, In R. Struzak (Ed.), *Global Communications Interactive '97* (p.280–287) London, UK Hanson Cooke Publishers Ltd.

Yesufu, T.K. & Yesufu, O.A. (1999): Pattern Recognition in Time Series Data, *Proceedings of the International Symposium on Nonlinear Theory and Applications*, Hawaii (USA), Nov. 28 – Dec. 2, pp. 543 – 544.

Yesufu, T.K. and O.A. Yesufu (2002): Development of a Methodology for Studying Nonlinear Dynamics. In: W. Klonoski (ed.): *Attractors, Signals and Synergetics, Proceedings of the 1st European Interdisciplinary School on Nonlinear Dynamics for System and Signal Analysis EUROATTRACTOR 2000* (pp. 231 – 239). Lengerich, DE: Pabst Science Publishers.

Yesufu, O.A. & Yesufu, T.K. (2003): Development of the Market Paradigm for Analyzing Systems, Available Online: http://www.ssrn.com/abstract=437181.

In: New Developments in Macroeconomics Research
Editor: Lawrence Z. Pelzer, pp. 123-139
ISBN: 1-59454-663-0

Chapter 5

Mathematical Model of Stock Market Fluctuations in the Absence of Economic Growth

Alexei Krouglov[*]
796 Caboto Trail, Markham, Ontario L3R 4X1,
Canada

Abstract

Here presented is a mathematical model inferring the stock market fluctuations from the business fluctuations. There are shown the ordinary differential equations describing the fluctuations of equities, derivatives, and second derivatives on the stock market.

Journal of Economic Literature Classification Numbers: E 32, G 12
Keywords: business fluctuations, stock market fluctuations

1 Introduction

Earlier author described the dynamics of business fluctuations both on the market of goods and services, and on the money market based on ordinary differential equations related such categories as supply, demand, and price in his previous articles [1, 2, 3, 4, 5]. In the latest work [5] author described two distinct markets: market of goods and services and money market, and investigated how these markets interrelate with each other.

In the current paper author projects both business fluctuations on the market of goods and services, and business fluctuations on the monetary market on the fluctuations experiencing by the underlying stock.

At first author examines the equities' fluctuations. Then he shows how fluctuations on the equities market induce the fluctuations on the market of derivatives.

[*] E-mail address: alexkrouglov@hotmail.com

All results are based on the mathematical models expressing equilibrium forces acting on markets through the ordinary differential equations of the second order, and solutions of some these equations are presented and examined.

The problems associated with economic growth are left behind of this article. Author is planning to examine them in his future work.

2 Primary Market: Goods and Services

Here we describe the closed 'imaginary' market with one only product. At the beginning we assume that market is in equilibrium position, there is no economic growth, and market has product's supply and demand, which both are developing with a constant rate and the product's price is fixed.

When the balance between the product's supply and demand is broken the product's market is experienced the economic forces, which act to bring the market to a new equilibrium position.

These market forces are described by the following ordinary differential equations regarding to the product's supply $V_S(t)$, demand $V_D(t)$, and price $P_C(t)$.

$$\frac{d^2 V_S(t)}{dt^2} = \lambda_1 \cdot \frac{dP_C(t)}{dt} \tag{1}$$

$$\frac{dP_C(t)}{dt} = \lambda_2 \cdot (V_D(t) - V_S(t)) \tag{2}$$

$$\frac{d^2 V_D(t)}{dt^2} = -\lambda_3 \cdot \frac{d^2 P_C(t)}{dt^2} \tag{3}$$

In the equations above the values $\lambda_1, \lambda_2, \lambda_3 \geq 0$ are constants.

The meaning of equations (1) – (3) was described in [5] as follows.

Let us define the product's deficit at each point in time as the positive difference between the product's demand and the one's supply. Similarly the product's surplus at the same time stands for the negative difference between the product's demand and supply. In situation when the product's demand and supply are equal, the market for product is at the equilibrium position.

When the product's demand and supply are not equal, the price of product changes. If the product's demand exceeds the one's supply, the price goes up, and it goes down in another circumstances. The rate of the changes in the product's price at each point in time is developing with the speed linearly proportional to the product's deficit (or surplus) at the same time.

When the product's price changes, the product's supply undergoes changes as well. When the price increases, the product's supply goes up, and it goes down in another circumstances. The acceleration (or deceleration) of changes in the product's supply at each point in time is linearly proportional to the rate of the changes in the product's price at the same time.

Also when the product's price changes, the product's demand experiences the oppressive effect. When the price increases, the product's demand goes down, and it goes up in another circumstances. The acceleration (or deceleration) of changes in the product's demand at each point in time is inversely-linearly proportional to the acceleration (or deceleration) of changes in the product's price at the same time.

3 Primary Market: Money

Similarly here we describe the closed market with only one peculiar product – money. At the beginning we assume that monetary market is in equilibrium position, there is no growth, and monetary market has the money's supply and demand, which both are developing with a constant rate and the money's price is fixed. The price of money is universally represented by an interest rate.

When such balance between the money's supply and demand is broken, the money's market is experienced the economic forces, which act to bring the market to a new equilibrium position.

These market forces are described by the following ordinary differential equations regarding to the money's supply $M_S(t)$, demand $M_D(t)$, and price $P_M(t)$.

$$\frac{d^2 M_S(t)}{dt^2} = \mu_1 \cdot \frac{dP_M(t)}{dt} \tag{4}$$

$$\frac{dP_M(t)}{dt} = \mu_2 \cdot (M_D(t) - M_S(t)) \tag{5}$$

$$\frac{d^2 M_D(t)}{dt^2} = -\mu_3 \cdot \frac{d^2 P_M(t)}{dt^2} \tag{6}$$

In the equations (4) – (6) above the values $\mu_1, \mu_2, \mu_3 \geq 0$ are constants.

The meaning of equations (4) – (6) was described in [5] as follows.

Let me define the positive difference between the money's demand and the one's supply at each point in time as the money's deficit. Likewise the money's surplus at the same time denotes the negative difference between the money's demand and supply. As earlier when money's demand and supply are equal, the money's market lies at the equilibrium position.

In situation when money's demand and supply are not equal, the price of money experiences changes. As it was said previously the price of money is expressed through the interest rate. If the money's demand exceeds the one's supply on the market, the price of money goes up, and it goes down in another circumstances. The rate of changes in the money's price at each point in time is developing with the speed linearly proportional to the money's deficit (or surplus) at the same time.

When the money's price changes, the money's supply undergoes changes. Correspondingly when the money's price increases, the money's supply goes up, and it goes down in another circumstances. The acceleration (or deceleration) of the changes in the money's supply at each point in time is linearly proportional to the rate of changes in the money's price at the same time.

Also when the money's price changes, the money's demand experiences the oppressive effect. When the money's price increases, the money's demand goes down, and it goes up in another circumstances. The acceleration (or deceleration) of changes in the money's demand at each point in time is inversely-linearly proportional to the acceleration (or deceleration) of the changes in the money's price at the same time.

4 Primary Market: Monetary Economy

Here we describe the closed 'imaginary' market with two commodities – the first one is real product and the second one is money.

At the beginning we assume that market is in equilibrium position. Again there is no economic growth. The money's supply and demand on the market are both developing with a constant rate and the money's price is fixed. The product's supply and demand on the market are both developing with a constant rate and the product's price is fixed. The above-mentioned rate, which regards to real product, equals to the similar rate, which regards to money.

When either the balance between the product's supply and demand or the balance between the money's supply and demand is broken the market is experienced the economic forces, which act to bring the market to a new equilibrium position.

These market forces are described by the following ordinary differential equations regarding to the product's supply $V_S(t)$, demand $V_D(t)$, and price $P_C(t)$ and the money's supply $M_S(t)$, demand $M_D(t)$, and price $P_M(t)$.

$$\frac{d^2V_S(t)}{dt^2} = \lambda_1 \cdot \frac{dP_C(t)}{dt} \tag{7}$$

$$\frac{dP_C(t)}{dt} = \lambda_2 \cdot (M_S(t) - V_S(t)) \tag{8}$$

$$\frac{d^2M_S(t)}{dt^2} = \mu_1 \cdot \frac{dP_M(t)}{dt} - \lambda_3 \cdot \frac{d^2P_C(t)}{dt^2} \tag{9}$$

$$\frac{dP_M(t)}{dt} = \mu_2 \cdot (M_D(t) - M_S(t)) \tag{10}$$

$$\frac{d^2 M_D(t)}{dt^2} = -\mu_3 \cdot \frac{d^2 P_M(t)}{dt^2} \tag{11}$$

$$V_D(t) = M_S(t) \tag{12}$$

Meaning of equations (7) – (12) was described in [5] as follows.

As formerly the product's deficit at each point in time is the positive difference between the product's demand and the one's supply. Similarly the product's surplus at the same time stands for the negative difference between the product's demand and supply. Likewise the positive difference between the money's demand and the one's supply at each point in time is the money's deficit. Equally the money's surplus at the same time denotes the negative difference between the money's demand and supply.

Here we are identifying the money's supply with the product's demand. Really it follows from the fact that we are actually interested in the solvent demand for a product.

In situation when the product's demand and supply are equal, the market for product is at the equilibrium position. As well when the money's demand and supply are equal, the money's market lies at the equilibrium position.

When the product's demand (i.e. money's supply) and the product's supply are not equal, the price of product changes. If the product's demand exceeds the one's supply, the price goes up, and it goes down in another circumstances. The rate of the changes in the product's price at each point in time is developing with the speed linearly proportional to the product's deficit (or surplus) at the same time.

When the product's price changes, the product's supply undergoes changes as well. When the price increases, the product's supply goes up, and it goes down in another circumstances. The acceleration (or deceleration) of changes in the product's supply at each point in time is linearly proportional to the rate of changes in the product's price at the same time.

Also when the product's price changes, the product's demand (i.e. money's supply) experiences the oppressive effect. When the price increases, the product's demand goes down, and it goes up in another circumstances. The acceleration (or deceleration) of changes in the product's demand at each point in time is inversely-linearly proportional to the acceleration (or deceleration) of changes in the product's price at the same time.

But distinct from the product's supply the product's demand (i.e. money's supply) experiences the impact from the money's market.

In situation when the money's demand and the money's supply (i.e. product's demand) are not equal, the price of money experiences changes. As it was said at an earlier time the price of money is expressed through the interest rate. If the money's demand exceeds the one's supply (i.e. product's demand) on the market, the price of money goes up, and it goes down in another circumstances. The rate of changes in the money's price at each point in time is developing with the speed linearly proportional to the money's deficit (or surplus) at the same time.

When the money's price changes, the money's supply (i.e. product's demand) undergoes changes. Correspondingly when the money's price increases, the money's supply (i.e. product's demand) goes up, and it goes down in another circumstances. The acceleration (or deceleration) of changes in the money's supply (i.e. product's demand) at each point in time is linearly proportional to the rate of changes in the money's price at the same time.

Also when the money's price changes, the money's demand experiences the oppressive effect. When the money's price increases, the money's demand goes down, and it goes up in another circumstances. The acceleration (or deceleration) of changes in the money's demand at each point in time is inversely-linearly proportional to the acceleration (or deceleration) of the changes in the money's price at the same time.

Here I give an illustrative example showing activities of the equilibrium forces.

Let me assume in this example for simplicity that $\lambda_3 = 0$ and $\mu_3 = 0$.

I assume that at time $t = t_0$ we have the following conditions on the market – with regard to money $\frac{dM_S(t_0)}{dt} = \frac{dM_D(t_0)}{dt} = 0$, $M_D(t_0) = \Delta$, $M_S(t_0) = 0$, $P_M(t_0) = I_0$, and $\Delta \neq 0$, and with regard to real product $\frac{dV_S(t_0)}{dt} = \frac{dV_D(t_0)}{dt} = 0$, $V_S(t_0) = V_D(t_0) = 0$, $P_C(t_0) = P_0$.

It was shown in [5] based on [7, 8] that aforesaid change in the money demand $M_D(t_0) = \Delta$ creates the following fluctuations in the product's supply $V_S(t)$,

$$V_S(t - t_0) = \Delta \cdot \left[\frac{\mu_1 \cdot \mu_2}{\lambda_1 \cdot \lambda_2 - \mu_1 \cdot \mu_2} \cdot \cos\left(\sqrt{\lambda_1 \cdot \lambda_2}(t - t_0)\right) - \frac{\lambda_1 \cdot \lambda_2}{\lambda_1 \cdot \lambda_2 - \mu_1 \cdot \mu_2} \cdot \cos\left(\sqrt{\mu_1 \cdot \mu_2}(t - t_0)\right) + 1 \right] \quad (13)$$

The solution (13) of this illustrative example represents the sum of two sinusoids.

5 Secondary Market: Equities in Monetary Economy

The markets forces performing the valuation of equities in the monetary economy relate the demand, supply, and price of equities to the demand, supply, and price of underlying products where we are expressing these forces through the following ordinary differential equations.

At first we define (in the limits of this theoretical model) the equities in regard to one of two commodities, which we are using in the model – real product and money, as an ownership rights to the part of an entity producing the commodity in question and as consequence an ownership right to corresponding part of the commodity in question as well.

Let us denote $V_S^{II}(t)$ – be supply of equities in regard to the product, $V_D^{II}(t)$ – be demand for equities in regard to the product, and $P_C^{II}(t)$ – be price of equities in regard to the product. Similarly we denote $M_S^{II}(t)$ – be supply of equities in regard to the money, $M_D^{II}(t)$ – be demand for equities in regard to the money, and $P_M^{II}(t)$ – be price of equities in regard to the money.

Then we have the following expressions in regard to the equities of entity supplying the money,

$$\frac{dP_M(t)}{dt} = \mu_2 \cdot (M_D(t) - M_S(t)) \tag{14}$$

$$\frac{d^2 M_S^{II}(t)}{dt^2} = \mu_1^{II} \cdot \frac{dP_M^{II}(t)}{dt} \tag{15}$$

$$\frac{dP_M^{II}(t)}{dt} = \mu_2^{II} \cdot (M_D^{II}(t) - M_S^{II}(t)) \tag{16}$$

$$\frac{d^2 M_D^{II}(t)}{dt^2} = \mu_4 \cdot \frac{dP_M(t)}{dt} - \mu_3^{II} \cdot \frac{d^2 P_M^{II}(t)}{dt^2} \tag{17}$$

In the equations (15) – (17) above the values μ_4, μ_1^{II}, μ_2^{II}, $\mu_3^{II} \geq 0$ are constants.

The meaning of equations (14) – (17) is following.

As we said ahead when the money's demand and supply are not equal, the price of money experiences changes. If the money's demand exceeds the one's supply on the market, the price of money goes up, and it goes down in another circumstances. The rate of changes in the money's price at each point in time is developing with the speed linearly proportional to the money's deficit (or surplus) at the same time.

When the money's price changes, the demand for underlying equities undergoes changes. Correspondingly when the money's price increases, the demand for underlying equities goes up, and it goes down in another circumstances. The acceleration (or deceleration) of changes in the underlying equities' demand at each point in time is linearly proportional to the rate of changes in the money's price at the same time.

Let us define the positive difference between the equities' demand and the ones' supply at each point in time as the equities' deficit. Likewise the equities' surplus at the same time denotes the negative difference between the equities' demand and supply. As before when the equities' demand and supply are equal, the equities' market lies at the equilibrium position.

In situation when the equities' demand and supply are not equal, the price of equities experiences changes. If the equities' demand exceeds the ones' supply on the market, the price of equities goes up, and it goes down in another circumstances. The rate of changes in the equities' price at each point in time is developing with the speed linearly proportional to the equities' deficit (or surplus) at the same time.

When the equities' price changes, the equities' supply undergoes changes. Correspondingly when the equities' price increases, the equities' supply goes up, and it goes down in another circumstances. The acceleration (or deceleration) of changes in the equities' supply at each point in time is linearly proportional to the rate of changes in the equities' price at the same time.

Also when the equities' price changes, the equities' demand experiences the oppressive effect. When the equities' price increases, the equities' demand goes down, and it goes up in another circumstances. The acceleration (or deceleration) of changes in the equities' demand at each point in time is inversely-linearly proportional to the acceleration (or deceleration) of changes in the equities' price at the same time.

Analogously we have the following expressions in regard to the equities of entity making the real product,

$$\frac{dP_C(t)}{dt} = \lambda_2 \cdot (V_D(t) - V_S(t)) \tag{18}$$

$$\frac{d^2 V_S^{II}(t)}{dt^2} = \lambda_1^{II} \cdot \frac{dP_C^{II}(t)}{dt} \tag{19}$$

$$\frac{dP_C^{II}(t)}{dt} = \lambda_2^{II} \cdot \left(V_D^{II}(t) - V_S^{II}(t)\right) \tag{20}$$

$$\frac{d^2 V_D^{II}(t)}{dt^2} = \lambda_4 \cdot \frac{dP_C(t)}{dt} - \lambda_3^{II} \cdot \frac{d^2 P_C^{II}(t)}{dt^2} \tag{21}$$

In the equations (19) – (21) above the values $\lambda_4, \lambda_1^{II}, \lambda_2^{II}, \lambda_3^{II} \geq 0$ are constants.

The meaning of equations (18) – (21) is following.

When the product's demand and supply are not equal, the price of product experiences changes. If the product's demand exceeds the one's supply on the market, the price of product goes up, and it goes down in another circumstances. The rate of changes in the product's price at each point in time is developing with the speed linearly proportional to the product's deficit (or surplus) at the same time.

When the product's price changes, the demand for underlying equities undergoes changes. Correspondingly when the product's price increases, the demand for underlying equities goes up, and it goes down in another circumstances. The acceleration (or deceleration) of changes in the underlying equities' demand at each point in time is linearly proportional to the rate of changes in the product's price at the same time.

As previously when the equities' demand and supply are equal, the equities' market lies at the equilibrium position.

In situation when the equities' demand and supply are not equal, the price of equities experiences changes. If the equities' demand exceeds the ones' supply on the market, the price of equities goes up, and it goes down in another circumstances. The rate of changes in the equities' price at each point in time is developing with the speed linearly proportional to the equities' deficit (or surplus) at the same time.

When the equities' price changes, the equities' supply undergoes changes. Correspondingly when the equities' price increases, the equities' supply goes up, and it goes down in another circumstances. The acceleration (or deceleration) of changes in the equities' supply at each point in time is linearly proportional to the rate of changes in the equities' price at the same time.

Also when the equities' price changes, the equities' demand experiences the oppressive effect. When the equities' price increases, the equities' demand goes down, and it goes up in another circumstances. The acceleration (or deceleration) of changes in the equities' demand at each point in time is inversely-linearly proportional to the acceleration (or deceleration) of changes in the equities' price at the same time.

Here we give an illustrative example showing activities of the equilibrium forces.

Let us assume in this example for simplicity that $\lambda_3 = 0$, $\mu_3 = 0$, and $\mu_3^{II} = 0$.

We assume that at time $t = t_0$ we have the following conditions on the primary and secondary markets – with regard to money $\frac{dM_S(t_0)}{dt} = \frac{dM_D(t_0)}{dt} = 0$, $M_D(t_0) = \Delta$, $M_S(t_0) = 0$, $P_M(t_0) = I_0$, and $\Delta \neq 0$, and with regard to equities of the entity supplying the money $\frac{dM_S^{II}(t_0)}{dt} = \frac{dM_D^{II}(t_0)}{dt} = 0$, $M_S^{II}(t_0) = M_D^{II}(t_0) = 0$, $P_M^{II}(t_0) = I_0^{II}$.

Based on [7, 8] the aforesaid change in the money demand $M_D(t_0) = \Delta$ creates the fluctuating disbalance in the difference between the money's supply and demand,

$$M_S(t - t_0) - M_D(t - t_0) = -\Delta \cdot \cos\left(\sqrt{\mu_1 \cdot \mu_2}\,(t - t_0)\right) \tag{22}$$

that produces the fluctuating disbalance in the difference between the underlying equities' supply and balance,

$$\begin{aligned} &M_S^{II}(t-t_0) - M_D^{II}(t-t_0) = \\ &= \frac{\Delta \cdot \mu_2 \cdot \mu_4}{\mu_1 \cdot \mu_2 - \mu_1^{II} \cdot \mu_2^{II}} \cdot \cos\left(\sqrt{\mu_1 \cdot \mu_2}\,(t-t_0)\right) - \frac{\Delta \cdot \mu_2 \cdot \mu_4}{\mu_1 \cdot \mu_2 - \mu_1^{II} \cdot \mu_2^{II}} \cdot \cos\left(\sqrt{\mu_1^{II} \cdot \mu_2^{II}}\,(t-t_0)\right) \end{aligned} \tag{23}$$

Therefore the price of equities supplying the money will also fluctuate as follows,

$$\begin{aligned} P_M^{II}(t - t_0) = I_0^{II} &- \frac{\Delta \cdot \mu_2^{II}}{\sqrt{\mu_1 \cdot \mu_2}} \cdot \frac{\mu_2 \cdot \mu_4}{\mu_1 \cdot \mu_2 - \mu_1^{II} \cdot \mu_2^{II}} \cdot \sin\left(\sqrt{\mu_1 \cdot \mu_2}\,(t - t_0)\right) \\ &+ \frac{\Delta \cdot \mu_2^{II}}{\sqrt{\mu_1^{II} \cdot \mu_2^{II}}} \cdot \frac{\mu_2 \cdot \mu_4}{\mu_1 \cdot \mu_2 - \mu_1^{II} \cdot \mu_2^{II}} \cdot \sin\left(\sqrt{\mu_1^{II} \cdot \mu_2^{II}}\,(t - t_0)\right) \end{aligned} \tag{24}$$

The solution (24) of this illustrative example represents the sum of two sinusoids.

6 Tertiary Market: Derivatives in Monetary Economy

The markets forces performing the valuation of derivatives in the monetary economy relate the demand, supply, and price of derivatives to the demand, supply, and price of both underlying equities and corresponding products where we are expressing these forces through the following ordinary differential equations.

At first we define (in the limits of this theoretical model) the derivatives of equities in regard to one of two commodities, which we are using in the model – real product and money, as an ownership rights to the part of equities for an entity producing the commodity in question, and as consequence an ownership right to corresponding part of the entity itself, and as consequence an ownership rights to the matching part of the commodity in question as well.

Let us denote $V_S^{III}(t)$ – be supply of derivatives in regard to the product, $V_D^{III}(t)$ – be demand for derivatives in regard to the product, and $P_C^{III}(t)$ – be price of derivatives in regard to the product. Similarly we denote $M_S^{III}(t)$ – be supply of derivatives in regard to the money, $M_D^{III}(t)$ – be demand for derivatives in regard to the money, and $P_M^{III}(t)$ – be price of derivatives in regard to the money.

Then we have the following expressions in regard to the derivatives for equities of an entity supplying the money,

$$\frac{dP_M(t)}{dt} = \mu_2 \cdot \left(M_D(t) - M_S(t)\right) \tag{25}$$

$$\frac{dP_M^{II}(t)}{dt} = \mu_2^{II} \cdot \left(M_D^{II}(t) - M_S^{II}(t)\right) \tag{26}$$

$$\frac{d^2 M_S^{III}(t)}{dt^2} = \mu_1^{III} \cdot \frac{dP_M^{III}(t)}{dt} \tag{27}$$

$$\frac{dP_M^{III}(t)}{dt} = \mu_2^{III} \cdot \left(M_D^{III}(t) - M_S^{III}(t)\right) \tag{28}$$

$$\frac{d^2 M_D^{III}(t)}{dt^2} = \mu_5 \cdot \frac{dP_M(t)}{dt} + \mu_4^{II} \cdot \frac{dP_M^{II}(t)}{dt} - \mu_3^{III} \cdot \frac{d^2 P_M^{III}(t)}{dt^2} \tag{29}$$

In the equations (27) – (29) above the values $\mu_5, \mu_4^{II}, \mu_1^{III}, \mu_2^{III}, \mu_3^{III} \geq 0$ are constants.

The meaning of equations (25) – (29) is following.

When the money's demand and supply are not equal, the price of money experiences changes. If the money's demand exceeds the one's supply on the market, the price of money goes up, and it goes down in another circumstances. The rate of changes in the money's price at each point in time is developing with the speed linearly proportional to the money's deficit (or surplus) at the same time.

Similarly when the equities' demand and supply are not equal, the price of equities experiences changes. If the equities' demand exceeds the ones' supply on the market, the price of equities goes up, and it goes down in another circumstances. The rate of changes in the equities' price at each point in time is developing with the speed linearly proportional to the equities' deficit (or surplus) at the same time.

When the price of money or the price of equities changes, the demand for underlying derivatives undergoes changes. Correspondingly when the price of money or the price of equities increases, the demand for underlying derivatives goes up, and it goes down in another circumstances. The acceleration (or deceleration) of the changes in the underlying derivatives' demand at each point in time is linearly proportional to the rate of changes in the price of money or the price of equities at the same time.

Let us define the positive difference between the derivatives' demand and the ones' supply at each point in time as the derivatives' deficit. Likewise the derivatives' surplus at the same time denotes the negative difference between the derivatives' demand and supply. As earlier when the derivatives' demand and supply are equal, the derivatives' market lies at the equilibrium position.

In situation when the derivatives' demand and supply are not equal, the price of derivatives experiences changes. If the derivatives' demand exceeds the ones' supply on the market, the price of derivatives goes up, and it goes down in another circumstances. The rate of changes in the derivatives' price at each point in time is developing with the speed linearly proportional to the derivatives' deficit (or surplus) at the same time.

When the derivatives' price changes, the derivatives' supply undergoes changes. Correspondingly when the derivatives' price increases, the derivatives' supply goes up, and it goes down in another circumstances. The acceleration (or deceleration) of changes in the derivatives' supply at each point in time is linearly proportional to the rate of changes in the derivatives' price at the same time.

Also when the derivatives' price changes, the derivatives' demand experiences the oppressive effect. When the derivatives' price increases, the derivatives' demand goes down, and it goes up in another circumstances. The acceleration (or deceleration) of changes in the derivatives' demand at each point in time is inversely-linearly proportional to the acceleration (or deceleration) of changes in the derivatives' price at the same time.

Analogously we have the following expressions in regard to the derivatives for equities of an entity making the real product,

$$\frac{dP_C(t)}{dt} = \lambda_2 \cdot (V_D(t) - V_S(t)) \tag{30}$$

$$\frac{dP_C^{II}(t)}{dt} = \lambda_2^{II} \cdot \left(V_D^{II}(t) - V_S^{II}(t)\right) \tag{31}$$

$$\frac{d^2 V_S^{III}(t)}{dt^2} = \lambda_1^{III} \cdot \frac{dP_C^{III}(t)}{dt} \tag{32}$$

$$\frac{dP_C^{III}(t)}{dt} = \lambda_2^{III} \cdot \left(V_D^{III}(t) - V_S^{III}(t)\right) \tag{33}$$

$$\frac{d^2V_D^{III}(t)}{dt^2} = \lambda_5 \cdot \frac{dP_C(t)}{dt} + \lambda_4^{II} \cdot \frac{dP_C^{II}(t)}{dt} - \lambda_3^{III} \cdot \frac{d^2P_C^{III}(t)}{dt^2} \tag{34}$$

In the equations (32) – (34) above the values $\lambda_5, \lambda_4^{II}, \lambda_1^{III}, \lambda_2^{III}, \lambda_3^{III} \geq 0$ are constants.

The meaning of equations (30) – (34) is following.

When the product's demand and supply are not equal, the price of product experiences changes. If the product's demand exceeds the one's supply on the market, the price of product goes up, and it goes down in another circumstances. The rate of changes in the product's price at each point in time is developing with the speed linearly proportional to the product's deficit (or surplus) at the same time.

Similarly when the equities' demand and supply are not equal, the price of equities experiences changes. If the equities' demand exceeds the ones' supply on the market, the price of equities goes up, and it goes down in another circumstances. The rate of changes in the equities' price at each point in time is developing with the speed linearly proportional to the equities' deficit (or surplus) at the same time.

When the price of product or the price of equities changes, the demand for underlying derivatives undergoes changes. Correspondingly when the price of product or the price of equities increases, the demand for underlying derivatives goes up, and it goes down in another circumstances. The acceleration (or deceleration) of changes in the underlying derivatives' demand at each point in time is linearly proportional to the rate of changes in the price of product or the price of equities at the same time.

As formerly when the derivatives' demand and supply are not equal, the price of derivatives experiences changes. If the derivatives' demand exceeds the ones' supply on the market, the price of derivatives goes up, and it goes down in another circumstances. The rate of changes in the derivatives' price at each point in time is developing with the speed linearly proportional to the derivatives' deficit (or surplus) at the same time.

When the derivatives' price changes, the derivatives' supply undergoes changes. Correspondingly when the derivatives' price increases, the derivatives' supply goes up, and it goes down in another circumstances. The acceleration (or deceleration) of changes in the derivatives' supply at each point in time is linearly proportional to the rate of the changes in the derivatives' price at the same time.

Also when the derivatives' price changes, the derivatives' demand experiences the oppressive effect. When the derivatives' price increases, the derivatives' demand goes down, and it goes up in another circumstances. The acceleration (or deceleration) of the changes in the derivatives' demand at each point in time is inversely-linearly proportional to the acceleration (or deceleration) of changes in the derivatives' price at the same time.

Here it is also possible to give an illustrative example showing activities of the equilibrium forces in regard to the derivatives.

7 Quaternary Market: Second Derivatives

The markets forces performing the valuation of second derivatives in the monetary economy relate the demand, supply, and price of derivatives to the demand, supply, and price of all underlying derivatives, equities and corresponding products where we are expressing these forces through the following ordinary differential equations.

At first we define (in the limits of this theoretical model) the second derivatives of equities in regard to one of two commodities, which we are using in the model – real product and money, as an ownership rights to the part of derivatives for equities of an entity producing the commodity in question, and as consequence an ownership right to corresponding part of the equities itself, and as consequence an ownership right to matching part of the entity itself, and as consequence an ownership rights to the equivalent part of the commodity in question as well.

Let us denote $V_S^{IV}(t)$ – be supply of second derivatives in regard to the product, $V_D^{IV}(t)$ – be demand for second derivatives in regard to the product, and $P_C^{IV}(t)$ – be price of second derivatives in regard to the product. Similarly I denote $M_S^{IV}(t)$ – be supply of second derivatives in regard to the money, $M_D^{IV}(t)$ – be demand for second derivatives in regard to the money, and $P_M^{IV}(t)$ – be price of second derivatives in regard to the money.

Then we have the following expressions in regard to the second derivatives for derivatives for equities of an entity supplying the money,

$$\frac{dP_M(t)}{dt} = \mu_2 \cdot (M_D(t) - M_S(t)) \tag{35}$$

$$\frac{dP_M^{II}(t)}{dt} = \mu_2^{II} \cdot (M_D^{II}(t) - M_S^{II}(t)) \tag{36}$$

$$\frac{dP_M^{III}(t)}{dt} = \mu_2^{III} \cdot (M_D^{III}(t) - M_S^{III}(t)) \tag{37}$$

$$\frac{d^2 M_S^{IV}(t)}{dt^2} = \mu_1^{IV} \cdot \frac{dP_M^{IV}(t)}{dt} \tag{38}$$

$$\frac{dP_M^{IV}(t)}{dt} = \mu_2^{IV} \cdot (M_D^{IV}(t) - M_S^{IV}(t)) \tag{39}$$

$$\frac{d^2 M_D^{IV}(t)}{dt^2} = \mu_6 \cdot \frac{dP_M(t)}{dt} + \mu_5^{II} \cdot \frac{dP_M^{II}(t)}{dt} + \mu_4^{III} \cdot \frac{dP_M^{III}(t)}{dt} - \mu_3^{IV} \cdot \frac{d^2 P_M^{IV}(t)}{dt^2} \tag{40}$$

In the equations (38) – (40) above the values $\mu_6, \mu_5^{II}, \mu_4^{III}, \mu_1^{IV}, \mu_2^{IV}, \mu_3^{IV} \geq 0$ are constants.

The meaning of equations (35) – (40) is following.

When the money's demand and supply are not equal, the price of money experiences changes. If the money's demand exceeds the one's supply on the market, the price of money goes up, and it goes down in another circumstances. The rate of changes in the money's price at each point in time is developing with the speed linearly proportional to the money's deficit (or surplus) at the same time.

Similarly when the equities' demand and supply are not equal, the price of equities experiences changes. If the equities' demand exceeds the ones' supply on the market, the price of equities goes up, and it goes down in another circumstances. The rate of changes in the equities' price at each point in time is developing with the speed linearly proportional to the equities' deficit (or surplus) at the same time.

Likewise when the derivatives' demand and supply are not equal, the price of derivatives experiences changes. If the derivatives' demand exceeds the ones' supply on the market, the price of derivatives goes up, and it goes down in another circumstances. The rate of changes in the derivatives' price at each point in time is developing with the speed linearly proportional to the derivatives' deficit (or surplus) at the same time.

When the price of money, the price of equities or the price of derivatives changes, the demand for underlying second derivatives undergoes changes. Correspondingly when the price of money, the price of equities or the price of derivatives increases, the demand for underlying second derivatives goes up, and it goes down in another circumstances. The acceleration (or deceleration) of changes in the underlying second derivatives' demand at each point in time is linearly proportional to the rate of changes in the price of money, the price of equities or the price of derivatives at the same time.

Let us define the positive difference between the second derivatives' demand and the ones' supply at each point in time as the second derivatives' deficit. Likewise the second derivatives' surplus at the same time denotes the negative difference between the second derivatives' demand and supply. As beforehand when the second derivatives' demand and supply are equal, the second derivatives' market lies at the equilibrium position.

In situation when the second derivatives' demand and supply are not equal, the price of second derivatives experiences changes. If the second derivatives' demand exceeds the ones' supply on the market, the price of second derivatives goes up, and it goes down in another circumstances. The rate of changes in the second derivatives' price at each point in time is developing with the speed linearly proportional to the second derivatives' deficit (or surplus) at the same time.

When the second derivatives' price changes, the second derivatives' supply undergoes changes. Correspondingly when the second derivatives' price increases, the second derivatives' supply goes up, and it goes down in another circumstances. The acceleration (or deceleration) of changes in the second derivatives' supply at each point in time is linearly proportional to the rate of changes in the second derivatives' price at the same time.

Also when the second derivatives' price changes, the second derivatives' demand experiences the oppressive effect. When the second derivatives' price increases, the second derivatives' demand goes down, and it goes up in another circumstances. The acceleration (or deceleration) of changes in the second derivatives' demand at each point in time is inversely-linearly proportional to the acceleration (or deceleration) of changes in the second derivatives' price at the same time.

Analogously we have the following expressions in regard to the second derivatives for derivatives for equities of an entity making the product,

$$\frac{dP_C(t)}{dt} = \lambda_2 \cdot \left(V_D(t) - V_S(t)\right) \tag{41}$$

$$\frac{dP_C^{II}(t)}{dt} = \lambda_2^{II} \cdot \left(V_D^{II}(t) - V_S^{II}(t)\right) \tag{42}$$

$$\frac{dP_C^{III}(t)}{dt} = \lambda_2^{III} \cdot \left(V_D^{III}(t) - V_S^{III}(t)\right) \tag{43}$$

$$\frac{d^2 V_S^{IV}(t)}{dt^2} = \lambda_1^{IV} \cdot \frac{dP_C^{IV}(t)}{dt} \tag{44}$$

$$\frac{dP_C^{IV}(t)}{dt} = \lambda_2^{IV} \cdot \left(V_D^{IV}(t) - V_S^{IV}(t)\right) \tag{45}$$

$$\frac{d^2 V_D^{IV}(t)}{dt^2} = \lambda_6 \cdot \frac{dP_C(t)}{dt} + \lambda_5^{II} \cdot \frac{dP_C^{II}(t)}{dt} + \lambda_4^{III} \cdot \frac{dP_C^{III}(t)}{dt} - \lambda_3^{IV} \cdot \frac{d^2 P_C^{IV}(t)}{dt^2} \tag{46}$$

In the equations (44) – (46) above the values $\lambda_6, \lambda_5^{II}, \lambda_4^{III}, \lambda_1^{IV}, \lambda_2^{IV}, \lambda_3^{IV} \geq 0$ are constants.

The meaning of equations (41) – (46) is following.

When the product's demand and supply are not equal, the price of product experiences changes. If the product's demand exceeds the one's supply on the market, the price of product goes up, and it goes down in another circumstances. The rate of changes in the product's price at each point in time is developing with the speed linearly proportional to the product's deficit (or surplus) at the same time.

Similarly when the equities' demand and supply are not equal, the price of equities experiences changes. If the equities' demand exceeds the ones' supply on the market, the price of equities goes up, and it goes down in another circumstances. The rate of changes in the equities' price at each point in time is developing with the speed linearly proportional to the equities' deficit (or surplus) at the same time.

Likewise when the derivatives' demand and supply are not equal, the price of derivatives experiences changes. If the derivatives' demand exceeds the ones' supply on the market, the price of derivatives goes up, and it goes down in another circumstances. The rate of changes in the derivatives' price at each point in time is developing with the speed linearly proportional to the derivatives' deficit (or surplus) at the same time.

When the price of product, the price of equities or the price of derivatives changes, the demand for underlying second derivatives undergoes changes. Correspondingly when the price of product, the price of equities or the price of derivatives increases, the demand for underlying second derivatives goes up, and it goes down in another circumstances. The acceleration (or deceleration) of changes in the underlying second derivatives' demand at each point in time is linearly proportional to the rate of changes in the price of product, the price of equities or the price of derivatives at the same time.

As earlier when the second derivatives' demand and supply are not equal, the price of second derivatives experiences changes. If the second derivatives' demand exceeds the ones' supply on the market, the price of second derivatives goes up, and it goes down in another circumstances. The rate of changes in the second derivatives' price at each point in time is developing with the speed linearly proportional to the second derivatives' deficit (or surplus) at the same time.

When the second derivatives' price changes, the second derivatives' supply undergoes changes. Correspondingly when the second derivatives' price increases, the second derivatives' supply goes up, and it goes down in another circumstances. The acceleration (or deceleration) of changes in the second derivatives' supply at each point in time is linearly proportional to the rate of changes in the second derivatives' price at the same time.

Also when the second derivatives' price changes, the second derivatives' demand experiences the oppressive effect. When the second derivatives' price increases, the second derivatives' demand goes down, and it goes up in another circumstances. The acceleration (or deceleration) of changes in the second derivatives' demand at each point in time is inversely-linearly proportional to the acceleration (or deceleration) of changes in the second derivatives' price at the same time.

8 Conclusion

In the current paper I inferred the fluctuations observed on the stock market from the business fluctuations observed on the markets of products and monetary market. Based on this approach I expressed the economic forces driving the stock market fluctuations through ordinary differential equations of the second order connecting the supply, demand, and prices of underlying products.

This model can be used as theoretical explanation of a financial mechanism responsible for price formation on the stock markets.

I am planning to continue my efforts devoted to stock market problems. Here I introduced the mathematical model with two interrelated products, the real product and money, in situation when underlying entities don't experience growth and stock market products used in the model are rather theoretical ones than the ones commercially available on the market. It looks like the inclusion into the current stock market model the possibilities for multiple products can be straightforwardly done by following the approach outlined in [5, 6] but accommodation into the stock market model concept of economic growth represent quite significant theoretical challenge requiring modeling and description at first of the market forces providing an economic growth itself.

References

[1] A. Krouglov, "Mathematical Model of Simple Business Fluctuations," *ewp-mac/9706009*, available at http://econwpa.wustl.edu.

[2] A. Krouglov, "Mathematical Description of Business Fluctuations," *ewp-mac/9710002*, available at http://econwpa.wustl.edu.

[3] A. Krouglov, "Mathematical Model of the Inflationary Process," *ewp-mac/9804001*, available at http://econwpa.wustl.edu.

[4] A. Krouglov, "Mathematical Model of the Inflationary Process (Part II)," *ewp-mac/0301010*, available at http://econwpa.wustl.edu.

[5] A. Krouglov, "Dynamical Elements of the Monetary Theory," *ewp-mac/0306013*, available at http://econwpa.wustl.edu.

[6] A. Krouglov, "Dynamics of Business Fluctuations in the Leontief-type Economy," *ewp-mac/9807007*, available at http://econwpa.wustl.edu.

[7] N. S. Piskunov, *Differential and Integral Calculus*, Groningen P. Noordhoff, 1965.

[8] I. G. Petrovski, *Ordinary Differential Equations*, Prentice Hall, Englewoods Cliffs, N.J., 1966.

In: New Developments in Macroeconomics Research
Editor: Lawrence Z. Pelzer, pp. 141-175
ISBN 1-59454-663-0

Chapter 6

THE STATISTICAL APPROACH TO THE AGGREGATION PROBLEM

Isabelle Maret*
B.E.T.A., Theme, UMR 7522 du CNRS, Université Louis Pasteur, 61, avenue de la Forêt Noire, 67085 STRASBOURG CEDEX, France

Abstract

These last two decades many authors have pointed out that the way to develop appropriate microfoundations for macroeconomics is not to be found from the study of individuals in isolation but rests in an essential way on studying the aggregate activity resulting from the interaction between different individuals. An alternative approach to the neoclassical paradigm based on individual rationality has been developed. The fundamentals of the models remain individual behaviors described by individual characteristics. However, the assumptions formalized at the individual level are very weak so that individual rationality might even be redundant. The major assumptions rely on the whole population and, more precisely, on the distribution of agents' characteristics. The purpose of this paper is to give an overview of this approach that we call the "statistical approach" [1]and to present it in an unified framework with the hope that its assumptions will be more systematically used in macroeconomic models.

Keywords: Distribution of agents' characteristics; Heterogeneous Individual Characteristics; Behavioral heterogeneity; Aggregation; Market Demand; Aggregate Properties.
JEL Classification Numbers: D00; D11; D12; D30, D41, D50, E10.

---

*E-mail address: maret@cournot.u-strasbg.fr; The author would like to thank Pierre Dehez, Gaël Giraud, Jean-Michel Grandmont, Werner Hildenbrand, and Alois Kneip for some discussions on the topic of this paper.

1 Introduction

These last two decades many authors have pointed out that the way to develop appropriate microfoundations for macroeconomics is not to be found from the study of individuals in isolation but rests in an essential way on studying the aggregate activity resulting from the interaction between different individuals. Therefore, an alternative approach to the neoclassical paradigm based on individual rationality has been developed. The fundamentals of the models remain individual behaviors described by individual characteristics. However, the assumptions formalized at the individual level are very weak so that individual rationality might even be redundant. The major assumptions rely on the whole population and, more precisely, on the distribution of agents' characteristics. The purpose of this paper is to give an overview of this approach that we call the "statistical approach"[2] and to present it in an unified framework with the hope that it will be more systematically used in macroeconomic models. The framework could be applied to formalize the aggregate behavior of any population of competitive agents most of the illustrations are taken from demand theory.

Consider a market consisting of agents with different behaviors. The typical question in aggregation theory is to look for the conditions which guarantee that the macroeconomic model that describes the behavior of this population takes on a particular property. There are two mutually non-exclusive approaches to problems of this sort. The more obvious way is simply to ask for the conditions on individual behavior which guarantee that the aggregate property holds. This pure microeconomic approach is most useful when the property required can be straightforwardly aggregated and exact aggregation holds. So one way of ensuring that aggregate demand is a continuous function of price is to assume that individual demand is a continuous function of price, which in turn follows from preferences which are continuous and strictly convex. Sometimes the solution is less straightforward. For example, it is well known that aggregate demand need not satisfy the strong or weak axioms, even when the agents who make up that market satisfy those properties. In these instances, stronger properties have to be imposed at the individual level to obtain the desired aggregate properties. For example, the strong axiom (essentially the existence of a representative consumer) is guaranteed if all agents have preferences representable by the Gorman polar form; the weak axiom in the aggregate holds provided agents individually obey the Law of Demand.

As pointed out by Giraud and Quah (2004), the pure microeconomic approach to aggregation problems is distinguished by three features: First, the property required at the individual level is at least as strong as the aggregate property required. Second, once it is satisfied and therefore the support of the distribution is restricted, the precise shape of the distribution of individual characteristics on this support does not matter. However, the aggregate property is sensitive to perturbations of this support. This motivates the statistical approach where these features are reversed. In this alternative approach, the assumptions made at the individual level are weaker than, or at least different from the aggregate property required. The aggregate property arises because of the distributional assumptions imposed

[2]This terminology was introduced by Malinvaud (1993).

and it is, in addition, robust to small perturbations of the distribution.

In section 2, we introduce the general framework. We point out that economic models need to formalize simultaneously the individual behavior and the aggregate behavior, since the two might significantly diverge.

Section 3 and section 4 present the limits of the pure microeconomic approach that have motivated the statistical approach. In section 3, we recall that for the microeconomic structure to be transposed to the macroeconomic model, one often needs to restrict drastically the set of feasible individual characteristics. In section 4, we point out that when the set of individual characteristics is enlarged to include any standard rational behavior, the properties that emerge in the aggregate are often very weak, as underlined by the theory of disaggregation.

In section 5, we point out that the statistical approach allows a formal justification to structured macroeconomic models left unexplained by individual rationality. In contrast to the theory of exact aggregation, restrictions are no longer introduced on the support of the distribution of individual characteristics, but rather on the shape of this distribution. Furthermore, the results are robust to small perturbations of the distribution.

In section 6, we underline how the diversity of individual characteristics is crucial in this approach where both the assumption of a high number of agents and the fact that their characteristics are distinct play a role. If, in addition, the distribution of agents' characteristics is restricted to have a specific shape, additional properties might be introduced in the macroeconomic model as exemplified by Houthakker (1955). The main interest of this approach is to orientate the theory towards assumptions that can be tested empirically. However, it is important to note that as long as there exists a relationship between the distribution of observable characteristics and the distribution of non-observable characteristics these assumptions cannot be directly tested. This is enlightened in section 7, where the theoretical conditions that allow to build falsifiable assumptions are specified.

An alternative solution offered by the statistical approach is to define, following Grandmont (1992), a specific type of behavioral heterogeneity and study the aggregate properties that emerge for a sufficient degree of behavioral heterogeneity. Grandmont considers a population consisting of agents with the same income and different demand functions generated by a given demand function through a specific class of transformations such that an agent and its transformed react differently to price changes. Assuming that there are l commodities in the economy, demand functions can then be parametrized by elements in $\mathbb{R}^l$. When the density function on the parameter is sufficiently flat in some precise sense, market budget share of each commodity becomes increasingly insensitive to changes in prices. Kneip (1999) extended this formalism to a non parametric set-up.

An issue which has attracted some debate recently in demand theory is the precise nature of behavioral heterogeneity at work in this family of models. First, the approximate insensitivity of the market budget shares might follow from an almost insensitivity at the individual level. A second possible view, where the statistical approach is more fully used, is that the insensitivity property in the aggregate is induced by a "balancing effect" (The term is borrowed from Maret (2003)). In other words, the mean budget share for each commodity is approximately constant because, while some agents may increase their budget share as prices and/or income change, this is balanced by other agent who choose to reduce their budget share. We shall present intuitively, in section 7, the mathematical conditions and their economic interpretations that allow to formalize these two types of behavioral heterogeneity.

For a soundly argued criticism of the representative agent hypothesis that has motivated the statistical approach the reader is referred to Kirman (1991). In this paper, we shall focus on the statistical approach presented with the economist point of view. For a very detailed study of the econometric methods that allow to take into account assumptions on the distribution of agents' characteristics one should refer to the very complete survey by Stoker (1993), where one can find, in particular, a detailed presentation of the hypotheses required to ensure that the aggregate behavior is similar to the individual behavior. Note that we shall not be concerned with the aggregation process within the decision problem of one agent, such as the aggregation of commodities or the aggregation of a two-stage decision problem. Nor shall we be concerned in demand theory by the aggregation of the decision problem within the household. This issue has been widely studied by the rich literature of the collective models initiated by Pollak (1985) and Chiappori (1988).

2 The Macroeconomic Model and the Distribution of Agents' Characteristics

In this section, we introduce the general framework to study the aggregate activity resulting from the interaction between different individuals. We point out that economic models need to formalize simultaneously the individual behavior and the aggregate behavior, since the two might significantly diverge. The main reason for this divergence is that aggregate properties are not only explained by properties at the individual level but they also fundamentally depend on the aggregation process itself. Hence, some properties will disappear in the aggregation process while others will emerge.

We assume that the notion of individual agent is sufficiently unambiguous to be formalized by a microeconomic model.

$$\mathbf{y}^i = f^i\left(\mathbf{p}, \mathbf{R}^i\right) \tag{1}$$

where $\mathbf{y}^i$ is the endogenous element (it could be a variable or a vector of variables) of agent i at a given date that depends on exogenous variables where some are specific to agent i, $\mathbf{R}^i$, others are not, $\mathbf{p}$.

As an illustration, the behavior of one household at a given date can be formalized by its demand function. More precisely, in this case the microeconomic model is the following. The household i spends her income $\mathbf{R}^i \geq 0$ at the consumption of L commodities which prices are $p_1 > 0, ..., p_L > 0$. She chooses a consumption bundle, $\mathbf{y}^i$, that belongs to her budget set $B\left(\mathbf{p}, \mathbf{R}^i\right) = \left\{y \in \mathbb{R}_+^L \mid \mathbf{p} \cdot y \leq \mathbf{R}^i\right\}$. This choice for each price-income pair, $\left(\mathbf{p}, \mathbf{R}^i\right)$, defines a demand function from $\mathbb{R}_{++}^L \times \mathbb{R}_+$ into $\mathbb{R}_+^L$. In the traditional microeconomic approach, the choice $f^i\left(\mathbf{p}, \mathbf{R}^i\right)$ is defined, in addition, as the solution of a maximization problem under constraint: Let $\succsim^i$ be the household preference relation over $\mathbb{R}^L_+$, then $f^i\left(\mathbf{p},\mathbf{R}^i\right)$ satisfies $p\cdot f^i\left(\mathbf{p},\mathbf{R}^i\right)\leq x$ and $f^i\left(\mathbf{p},\mathbf{R}^i\right)\succsim y$ for all $y\in B\left(\mathbf{p},\mathbf{R}^i\right)$. If the preference relation is continuous, strictly convex and monotone, then the assumption of preference maximization induces a continuous demand function $f^i\left(\mathbf{p},\mathbf{R}^i\right)$ over $\mathbb{R}^L_{++}\times\mathbb{R}_+$ which satisfies the budget constraint $\mathbf{p}\cdot f^i\left(\mathbf{p},\mathbf{R}^i\right)=\mathbf{R}^i$, is homogenous of degree zero with respect to $\left(\mathbf{p},\mathbf{R}^i\right)$ and satisfies the weak axiom. We shall see later on that for many results of the statistical approach in demand theory this individual rationality is not required.

To assume that the economy can be described by the behavior of one agent would be equivalent to assume that the aggregate behavior can be described by a macroeconomic model of the following type

$$\bar{y}=\bar{f}\left(\mathbf{p},\bar{\mathbf{R}}\right) \tag{2}$$

where $\bar{\mathbf{y}}$ is an aggregate of the individual variables y^i and $\bar{\mathbf{R}}$ is an aggregate of the individual variables $\mathbf{R}^i$ and $\bar{f}$ possesses the same properties as the individual functions f^i.

Let us prove with a very simple example that this representative agent hypothesis is very restrictive. Assume that we are concerned with the demand behavior of a population including $\#I$ households of two types, $\#I_0$ households of type 0 and $\#I_1$ households of type 1, which are described respectively by the two following microeconomic models

$$\begin{aligned}\mathbf{y}^i &= b_0\left(\mathbf{p}\right)\cdot\mathbf{R}^i\\ \text{and }\mathbf{y}^i &= b_1\left(\mathbf{p}\right)\cdot\mathbf{R}^i\end{aligned}$$

Hence, mean demand behaves according to the following macroeconomic model

$$\bar{y}=b_0\left(p\right)\Pi_0\bar{R}_0+b_1\left(p\right)\left(1-\Pi_0\right)\bar{R}_1$$

where $\Pi_0=\frac{\#I_0}{\#I}$, $\bar{R}_0$ is the mean income of type-0 households and $\bar{R}_1$ is the mean income of type-1 households. Note that the representative agent model would be written here

$$\bar{y}=\bar{b}\left(p\right)\bar{R},$$

where $\bar{b}\left(p\right)=b_0\left(p\right)\Pi_0+b_1\left(p\right)\left(1-\Pi_0\right)$. The latter is a good approximation of the macroeconomic model if and only if $\bar{R}_0=\bar{R}_1$. This condition should be preserved after any perturbation to ensure that representative agent model allows to make good predictions. As an illustration, assume that mean income increases by one unit where δ is allocated to households of type 0 and $(1-\delta)$ is allocated to households of type 1. The study of individual behaviors teaches us that mean demand will increase by $\triangle\bar{y}=\delta b_0\left(p\right)+\left(1-\delta\right)b_1\left(p\right)$. However, the representative agent model predicts that it increases by $\triangle\bar{y}=\bar{b}\left(p\right)$. Hence, the prediction is correct if and only if $\delta=\Pi_0$.

To conclude by restricting the analysis to the aggregate variables ($\bar{y}$ and $\bar{R}$) the representative agent model loses important information on the behavior of heterogenous agents. To take these heterogenous behaviors into account economic models should integrate not only the aggregate variables but also the distribution of the exogenous variables specific to individuals, such as $\left(\Pi_0, \bar{R}_0, \bar{R}_1\right)$, and more generally the distribution of individual characteristics.

Note that this implies, in particular, that the agents lose their identity. More precisely, a given agent is perfectly described by her economic characteristics : Two agents with identical characteristics behaves identically. This means that the joint distribution of individual characteristics does not only include the exogenous variables specific to the individual, but also the variables that describes implicitly her function $f^i(\cdot)$. To be more explicit, assume that

$$\mathbf{y}^i = f\left(\mathbf{p}, \mathbf{R}^i, a^i\right) \tag{3}$$

where the function f is identical for all individuals. Two distinct individual behaviors are formalized by two distinct vectors $a^i = \left(a_1^i, a_2^i, \ldots\right) \in A$. The vector a^i might include observable variables, α^i, as well as non observable variables $\beta^i \in \mathcal{A}$, we denote by $r^i = \left(R^i, \alpha^i\right) \in \mathbb{R}^k$ the vector of observable individual characteristics.

Note that this model could be static as well as dynamic. As an illustration, the microeconomic model could formalize intertemporal consumption. In this case, y^i is the household current consumption, R^i is the flow of future incomes, $\mathbf{p}$ is the interest rate and the information set, β^i, the household intertemporal preferences and α^i the stock of financial assets at the beginning of the period or demographic variables such as the age of the household head, the household size, and so on. The microeconomic model could formalize other competitive behaviors such as individual price expectations (see Calvet et al. (1998)). We shall keep the notation introduced in demand theory, however, the reader should keep in mind that $\mathbf{p}$ denotes more generally the vector of exogenous variables that affect all individual behaviors and (R^i, a^i) the vector of exogenous variables specific to individual i.

The mean behavior of a finite population of agents I defined by $\left\{r^i, \beta^i\right\}_{i \in I}$ is described by

$$\bar{y} = \frac{1}{\# I} \sum_i f\left(p, r^i, \beta^i\right) \tag{4}$$

More generally, mean behavior of a large population is defined by

$$\bar{y} = E(y) = \int_{\mathbb{R}^k \times \mathcal{A}} f(p, r, \beta)\, d\mu \equiv F(p, \mu) \tag{5}$$

where μ denotes a joint probability distribution of individual characteristics, thus μ is a distribution of (r, β) on $\mathbb{R}^k \times \mathcal{A}$. In demand theory, when a describes A, f describes $\mathcal{F}$, the set of household demand functions[3]. In this case, μ denotes the joint distribution of incomes and demand functions (R, f) on $\mathbb{R}_+ \times \mathcal{F}$ and $F(p, \mu)$ denotes the mean demand of this population of households with exogenous incomes. In a pure exchange economy, the household income is endogenous and defined as the nominal value of the household initial endowments, e, i.e. $R = p \cdot e$. In this pure exchange economy we shall also be interested by the behavior of the mean excess demand $Z(p, \nu) \equiv \int_{\mathbb{R}^L \times \mathcal{F}} \left(f(p, p \cdot e) - e\right) d\nu$, where ν denotes the joint distribution of initial endowments and demand functions on $\mathbb{R}^L \times \mathcal{F}$.

[3]The set $\mathcal{F}$ is endowed with a topology, for example, the topology of uniform convergence on compact sets.

In the sequel, it will be interesting to distinguish $\mathcal{F}_{\succsim}$ the subset of $\mathcal{F}$ which includes demand functions induced by preferences maximization under budget constraint, where the preference relation satisfies all standard assumptions (completeness, transitivity, continuity, monotonicity and convexity).

The typical question in aggregation theory is to ask for the conditions which will guarantee that the macroeconomic model that describes the behavior of this population takes on a particular property.

3 The Theory of Exact Aggregation : Severe Restrictions on Individual Behaviors

The more obvious way to solve this aggregation problem is to ask for conditions on individual characteristics which will guarantee that the aggregate property holds. This pure microeconomic approach is most useful when the property required can be straightforwardly aggregated and exact aggregation holds. As an illustration, one way of ensuring that aggregate demand is a continuous function of price is to assume that individual demand is a continuous function of price, which in turn follows from preferences which are continuous and strictly convex. The last section gave us the intuition that sometimes the solution is less straightforward. We recall in this section results of the theory of exact aggregation that confirm this intuition. We underline that for the microeconomic structure to be rightly transposed to the macroeconomic model, one often needs to restrict drastically the set of feasible individual characteristics. In addition, we point out that the microeconomic structure when transposed to the macroeconomic model often lacks of economic meaning.

The main issue of the theory of exact aggregation is how to define the set of individual characteristics $\mathbb{R}^k \times \mathcal{A}$ and how to aggregate the individual variables $\left(y^i, R^i, a^i\right)_i$ over this set – in other words how to define the aggregate variables $\bar{y}$ and $\bar{R}$ and the aggregate function $\bar{f}$ – to ensure that the representative agent model is valid. In other words, what are the conditions that guarantee that the representative agent model (2) is generated by the exact aggregation of the microeconomic model (3).

The consistency of this macroeconomic model requires that this exact aggregation result is valid whatever the exogenous individual characteristics and whatever the individual functions f^i, in other words whatever the distribution of the individual characteristics μ over $\mathbb{R}^k \times \mathcal{A}$. However, allowing for any distribution of individual characteristics cannot yield to the well structured macroeconomic model (2) without restricting significantly the set of feasible individual behaviors.

As an illustration, in demand theory when $\bar{R}$ denotes mean income, mean demand, $\bar{y}$, is described by (2) if and only if it does not vary with the distribution of household characteristics that preserves mean income. One can prove that this result is obtained if and only if individual demands are linear in income and the marginal propensity to consume is identical from one household to the other, i.e. $y^i = b(p)\, x^i$ for all i. When individual demand is explained by preferences maximization under budget constraint such a specific household behavior requires that all households possess identical homothetic preferences or preferences quasilinear with respect to the same commodity (see Eisenberg (1961)). These restrictions are far beyond the standard assumptions formalized on individual preferences [4]. They require a very specific type of household preferences (referred in the literature as the Gorman polar form). In general, aggregate demand need not satisfy the strong axiom, even when the agents who make up that market satisfy those properties. Nevertheless, the strong axiom (essentially the existence of a representative consumer) is guaranteed if all agents have preferences representable by the Gorman polar form. In addition, one can prove that the weak axiom in the aggregate holds provided agents individually obey the Law of Demand. To conclude, the theory of exact aggregation has proved in demand theory that stronger properties have often to be imposed at the individual level to obtain the desired aggregate properties.

More generally, the theory of exact aggregation focus on the macroeconomic model (5) and requires that this model depends on a bounded number of statistics of the distribution μ. Jorgensen et al. (1982), Lau (1982) and Lewbel (1989) show that this requires that the microeconomic models are strongly linear and the aggregate variables $\bar{y}$ and $\bar{R}$ are defined as arithmetical means. In this theory, one studies how the endogenous aggregate variable react to changes in the distribution μ. However, the difficulty is that μ is of infinite dimension. Hence, the purpose of the theory of exact aggregation is to reduce the complexity of this variable. This is done by restricting the domain, $\mathcal{D}$, of the distribution.

Hence, the purpose of the theory of exact aggregation can be expressed in the following way : To identify a domain $\mathcal{D}$ sufficiently large with the property that there exists a mapping $\gamma : \mathcal{D} \to \mathbb{R}^n$ and a function G such that the identity $F(p,\mu) = G(p,\gamma(\mu)) \in \mathbb{R}_+^L$ holds for all p and all $\mu \in \mathcal{D}$. The vector $\gamma(\mu)$ of dimension n can be interpreted as the vector of relevant statistics of the distribution μ. For this aggregation problem to be meaningful the domain $\mathcal{D}$ has to be sufficiently large and the integer n sufficiently small so that the mapping γ is not injective. Otherwise, the dimension of the explicative variable would not have been reduced. However, for the results mentioned previously this is not the case. In particular, the exact aggregation result in demand theory is obtained for $n = 1$, $\gamma(\mu) = \bar{x}$ and $\mathcal{D}$ defined by the domain of the probability distributions over $\mathbb{R} \times \{b(p)\}$, where $b(p)$ described the individual demand function $f(p, x^i) = b(p)\, x^i$ possessed by all households. In this example, the vector of relevant statistics is restricted to the mean income. This drastic reduction is allowed by a severe reduction of the support of the distribution of individual characteristics, which is of dimension one, since households are only allowed to diverge in terms of their income. For a very good survey on this issue, the reader should refer to Stoker (1993).

In addition to the restrictive conditions on individual behavior required for its validity, the theory of exact aggregation might lead to a macroeconomic model without economic meaning. As an illustration, let us assume that market demand follows from the exact aggregation of individual demands, where individual demand is explained by the maximization of preferences. The preferences of the representative household that give an account of aggregate demand do not correspond to social preferences. Effectively, Jerison (1984) gives

[4]Note that the latter include, in particular, the convexity requirement that is already rather controversial.

the example of a population where the representative agent prefers the alternative b to the alternative a while any agent in the population prefers a to b. Therefore, the preferences of this representative agent do not have any economic meaning. In particular, they cannot be used for positive purposes such as the evaluation of the social benefit of public policies.

4 The Theory of Disaggregation : The Neoclassical Paradigm Has Reached a Deadlock

In this section, the set of individual characteristics is enlarged to include any standard rational behavior. In this case, the theory of disaggregation proves that the properties that emerge in the aggregate are often very weak. We give three illustrations of this difficulty that lead us to conclude with Kirman (1991) that the extensive use in the macroeconomic models of the representative agent hypothesis is not only due to the desire to explain the aggregate behavior by individual behaviors but rather by the fact that individual rationality cannot explain structured macroeconomic models.

The first illustration can be given in the context of the general equilibrium model of a pure exchange economy, where individual rationality does not ensure uniqueness and stability of the competitive equilibrium. This result relies on the theory of disaggregation initiated by Sonnenschein (1972) (for a review of this literature see Shafer and Sonnenschein, 1982). An important result of this theory is the well known Debreu-Mantel-Sonnenschein theorem established independently by Sonnenschein (1972,1974), Debreu (1974) and Mantel (1974) which states the following.

Theorem 1 *Given any continuous function g from $\mathbb{R}^L_{++}$ into $\mathbb{R}^L$ homogenous of degree zero that satisfies Walras' Law, i.e. $p \cdot g(p) = 0$ for all $p \in \mathbb{R}^L_{++}$, then for every compact subset K of $\mathbb{R}^L_{++}$ there exists a probability distribution ν (which support is of finite cardinality L) on $\mathbb{R}^L_{++} \times \mathcal{F}_{\succsim}$ such that*

$$g(p) = Z(p, \nu)$$

for all $p \in K$.

Note that the support of the distribution ν is such that at the individual level the strongest assumptions commonly accepted in demand theory are required, namely that individual demand is explained by preference maximization where the preference relation satisfies all standard assumptions. Nevertheless, the only properties of mean excess demand ensured by this individual rationality are continuity, Walras' Law and homogeneity of degree zero. These properties are sufficient to guarantee existence of the competitive equilibrium but not its uniqueness and stability.

The conclusion of the theorem might even be strengthened by introducing additive restrictions on the support of the distribution ν. Effectively, for a differentiable function g, Mantel (1976) proves that when the set of individual preferences is restricted to homothetic preferences no additional property of mean excess demand is obtained.

Note that if the mean demand behavior was explained by a representative agent, mean excess demand would satisfy the weak axiom and this property would ensure uniqueness of equilibrium and its stability with respect to the walrasian tâtonnement. However, this result is not only unjustified within the neoclassical paradigm based on individual rationality but it is also not robust. Effectively, Kirman and Koch (1986) prove that for any function g that satisfies the three previous properties there always exists a finite population of rational agents with identical preferences but distinct incomes (defined by the nominal values of initial endowments colinear from one agent to the other) such that the mean excess demand is precisely the function g. In other words, while one gets arbitrarily close to an economy where all agents are identical no additional property of mean demand is generated. This is a stronger version of Debreu-Sonnenschein-Mantel theorem where the domain of the distribution ν is now restricted to $E(\bar{e}) \times \{f\}$, where given $\bar{e} \in \mathbb{R}^L_{++}$ one has $E(\bar{e}) = \{e \in \mathbb{R}^L_{++} \mid e = c\bar{e} \text{ with } c \in \mathbb{R}\}$ and $f \in \mathcal{F}_{\succsim}$.

The Debreu-Sonnenschein-Mantel theorem has, in addition, been extended to excess demand functions in economies with incomplete markets (Bottazzi and Hens (1996), Chiappori et Ekeland (1999b), Momi (2001)). This market structure typically emerge when several periods and uncertainty are introduced in the model.

A result similar to the Debreu-Sonnenschein-Mantel theorem can also be established for demand functions (rather than excess demand functions). This second result is nevertheless weaker and more difficult to prove. The difficulty lies in the fact that the set of feasible demand functions is smaller than the set of individual excess demands since demand functions have to be positive (see Shafer en Sonnenschein (1982), Chiappori (1999b)). Chiappori et Ekeland (1999a) recently proved that any analytic mapping in $\mathbb{R}^L$ satisfying Walras Law can be locally decomposed at the sum of L individual, utility-maximizing demand functions. This result can again be extended to exchange economies with incomplete markets (see Bottazzi et al. (1998) and Momi (2001)).

To conclude the theory of disaggregation underlines that one should abandon restrictions on the support of the distribution of household characteristics to explain properties of the mean functions $F(\cdot, \mu)$ and $Z(\cdot, v)$ since these assumptions are not only arbitrary but also the results they generate are not robust as exemplified by Kirman and Koch (1986).

A second compelling argument to give up this kind of assumptions is that the existence itself of the optimum of a rational agent is not guaranteed within this approach. Effectively, Roberts and Sonnenschein (1977) pointed out within a model of imperfect competition that the profit function of a firm for given prices of its competitors need not be quasi-concave. They show that this can happen even if quite severe restrictions are imposed on the set of feasible individual preferences. The reason is, of course, that restrictions imposed on individual behavior alone have hardly any consequence at all on the aggregate level if the distribution of households' characteristics can be arbitrary, as demonstrated by the Debreu-Sonnenschein-Mantel theorem.

In addition, even when the existence of the best response of each firm with respect to its competitors' strategies is ensured, the pure strategy Nash equilibrium might fail to exist. This is the case, in particular, for price competition under product differentiation.

The nature of the existence problem is seen clearly if one tries to base a proof of existence on a standard fixed-point argument. It is straightforward to build models where each firm's best response to other firms' prices is bounded and has standard continuity properties. Specifically, the best response correspondence is typically upper hemi-continuous, suggesting that Kakutani's theorem should be used to demonstrate existence. However, the fixed point argument requires that the best-response correspondence be convex valued. This condition may fail in the context of imperfect competition. Without any restriction on market demand, it may be that two extreme strategies, either charging a high price to select group of customers (for whom the product is well positioned) or charging a low price to a mass market, both dominate the strategy of setting an intermediate price. In response to this existence problem, several authors have explored special conditions under which a pure strategy price equilibrium exists (Economides (1989), Gabszewicz and Thisse (1979), Hauser (1988), Hauser and Wernerfelt (1988), Lane (1980) and Shaked and Sutton(1982)). In these models, demand functions are concave in own price (or log-price) so that there is a unique best-response, and a fixed point argument applies to prove existence. This approach requires strong arbitrary restrictions on individual behavior (in other words on the support of the distribution individual characteristics). More precisely, the concavity of market demand is obtained for specific utility functions, for populations where all households possess the same income or the same preferences. Hence, the existence result is again very sensitive to small perturbations of the support of the distribution of individual characteristics.

A third illustration of our aggregation problem can be given in social choice theory, where the modelling of group decision making also reaches a deadlock, brought to light by Arrow's impossibility theorem. For ordinal preferences, there does not exist any aggregation procedure of individual preferences that yields to social preferences fulfilling a consistent axiomatic. Assume, for example, that the aggregation rule of individual preferences for choices in pairwise comparisons is the majority rule. One can prove that, for any distribution of individual preferences, the majority rule induces social preferences that are not transitive. This is the well known Condorcet's paradox. Again, the only solution offered within the neoclassical paradigm based on individual rationality is to introduce arbitrary restrictions on the support of the distribution of individual characteristics (by requiring, for example, that all agents are identical) yielding to non robust results, as exemplified by Kirman and Koch (1986).

However, the difficulty common to these three illustrations of our aggregation problem, is that the aggregate property is required to hold whatever the distribution of individual characteristics, once the support of this distribution has been arbitrarily fixed. Intuitively, if the construction in Debreu (1974) is feasible this is because, for a predefined set of feasible individual behaviors, any type of behavior is allowed to emerge in the population with any frequency. This too large degree of freedom implies that no interesting property is obtained in the aggregate. Similarly, this is only because the aggregation rule is required to be valid whatever the distribution of individual preferences that this construction is doomed to failure.

5 The Statistical Approach : A Robust Answer

To justify a macroeconomic model for whatever the distribution of individual characteristics μ is more than required. When one is concerned with aggregate phenomena exogenous variables are not relevant individually but in terms of their distribution. In addition, some patterns are observed empirically in the distribution of individual characteristics. As an illustration, a population of households with identical characteristics except for income can often be represented by an income distribution with a lognormal density function (see Hildenbrand (1983)). Therefore, it is more useful when modeling aggregate variables to introduce restrictions on the shape of the distribution of individual characteristics rather than on the support of this distribution. These assumptions might be tested empirically or justified by heterogeneity requirements. Hence, we shall enlarge the pure microeconomic approach to allow for such restrictions and adopt a "statistical approach".

In the statistical approach, the issue is no longer the validity of the macroeconomic model described by (5) that is assumed, but rather, for a given distribution of individual characteristics, what are the properties of this macroeconomic relationship. The main contribution of this approach is to give an account of properties of the macroeconomic model that are not shared by the microeconomic model. Hence the issue is no longer : What are the properties preserved by the aggregation process ? but : What are the properties that emerge with aggregation ?

Note that, in this approach, the distribution of individual characteristics μ is now an exogenous data. Hence, the differences between individuals are exogenous. In addition, the knowledge of the distribution of individual characteristics is sufficient to determine the endogenous aggregate variables. Hence, the knowledge of the aggregate exogenous variable becomes redundant.

Let us now underline that the statistical approach can give an answer to the three aggregation problems left unanswered by the pure microeconomic approach.

This approach has essentially been developed in demand theory to offer an answer to the questions raised by the Debreu-Sonnenschein-Mantel theorem. The first step was to allow for a very large support of the distribution of consumers' characteristics and to show that this heterogeneity introduces on its own properties of market demand. An application of Lyapunov's theorem guarantees that when the measure space of agents is atomless, the aggregate demand correspondence is convex valued, even when each agent may not have a convex valued demand correspondence (see Hildenbrand (1974)). Beyond this, there is a substantial literature on when a market will have a continuous and smooth demand function, even when non-convexities are present at the individual level (see, for example, Dierker et al. (1980a, 1980b)).

The second step was to restrict the shape of the distribution of consumers' characteristics. This decisive step has been taken by Hildenbrand (1983) who gives a first answer to the Debreu-Sonnenschein-Mantel theorem. It says that a market in which all agents have the same demand function f which obeys the weak axiom will satisfy a stronger property – the Law of Demand – provided the conditional income distribution μ/f has a downward sloping density function. More precisely, this assumption on the income distribution ensures that individual income effects induced by a price change are more frequently positive than negative in the subpopulation so that the aggregate income effect is positive. Since the aggregate substitution effect is negative by assumption (thanks to the weak axiom), the Law of demand follows for the subpopulation from the Slutsky decomposition The crucial point is that individual demand functions are not assumed to be monotone, the monotonicity of $F(\cdot, \mu/f)$ emerges from the aggregation process itself. The additivity of the monotonicity of $F(\cdot, \mu/f)$ over subpopulations with distinct demand functions ensures that $F(\cdot, \mu)$ is also monotone. To the extend that the share of mean income allocated to each household is independent of prices (this holds when initial endowments are collinear), this result when applied to a pure exchange economy ensures the weak axiom in the aggregate and uniqueness and stability (under Walrasian tâtonnement) follow. In this case, the assumption of the decreasing density concerns the conditional distribution of the share of mean income. Despite the assumption required on the income distribution is not very realistic, this result is crucial for economic theory. It demonstrates unambiguously the structural contribution in macroeconomic modelling of assumptions on the distribution of individual characteristics. This decisive result has been followed by a rich literature on which we shall come back in section 7.

In particular, the model introduced by Grandmont (1992) and its successors illustrates how the statistical approach allows to enlarge significantly the support of the distribution of households' characteristics ; that is to weaken drastically the assumptions at the individual level. More precisely, it is proved that when households are heterogenous in terms of their reaction to changes in prices and/or income and that the distribution of the population tend to be "uniform" (each type of behavior emerge with approximately the same probability) over the set of budget share functions, aggregate market budget shares become independent of prices and/or income. This has strong consequences for the prevalence, in the aggregate, of the weak axiom of revealed preference, of gross substitutability, and on uniqueness and stability of the Walrasian exchange equilibrium. The advantage of this second answer to the Debreu-Sonnenschein-Mantel theorem is that no additional assumption on the support of the marginal distribution of initial endowments is required; to be more specific, initial endowments do not need any longer to be collinear. Above all, the crucial result is that the strong aggregate structure is obtained for very weak assumptions on individual behavior, Kneip (1999)'s development of Grandmont's model only require the individual budget shares to be bounded. In other words, in these models, individual rationality becomes redundant: The household demand function is not necessarily the outcome of a utility maximization program under budget constraint.

A direct consequence of this second answer to the Debreu-Sonnenschein-Mantel theorem is that the statistical approach can also be applied to the aggregation problem in the theory of imperfect competition, and in particular, to study imperfect competition on the market of an homogenous product. Grandmont (1993) applies his assumption on the distribution of individual demand parameters (introduced in Grandmont, 1992) to a market for a single commodity and proves that for a sufficiently "uniform" distribution of households' parameters, aggregate demand is not only downward sloping but it has also an elasticity close to -1. In the context of a partial equilibrium in which firms compete in quantities this generates concave revenue functions and therefore existence and uniqueness of a Cournot oligopoly equilibrium.

The statistical approach also helps to study price competition among differentiated products. Caplin and Nalebuff (1991b), followed by Dierker (1991), Dierker and Podczeck (1992), use this technique to demonstrate the existence of a pure-strategy price equilibrium for any number of firms producing any set of products. In addition, they provide conditions for uniqueness. These models allow for a larger support of the distribution of individual preferences than in the related literature, in particular, the traditional one-dimensional framework is expanded to allow for multi-dimensional product differentiation. This is allowed by restricting the distribution preferences across society : Preferences are parametrized and the distribution of the parameter vector is described by a density function that satisfies a weak-form of concavity. This assumption generates concave market demand functions in own price (or log-price) so that for each firm there is a unique best-response at any price vector, and a fixed point argument applies to prove existence of the pure Nash equilibrium.

Our third aggregation problem can also be solved with this approach. More precisely, one can identify a class of distributions of individual preferences such that their aggregation is feasible.

Note that a solution to the aggregation of individual preferences can first be obtained by restricting mainly the support of the distribution of individual characteristics rather than the shape of this distribution. In this sense this first solution is closely related to the microeconomic approach. Assume that the choice set is one-dimensional (this is the case, for example, when agents of one country have to choose their president) and agents' utility is unimodal in this dimension. Individuals can then be identified by their most preferred alternative. The median agent's optimum secures a majority over all alternatives (see Black (1948)). Under the additional assumption that at the individual level no two distinct alternatives are indifferent and that there is an odd number of agents (in other words the population is described by a uniform distribution over a finite set with odd cardinality), pairwise majority voting generates a well defined social relation (complete and transitive), see Mas-Colell et al. (1995, p.803). Note that this result crucially depends on the number of agents in the economy, when this number is even the result is no longer valid. Hence, this result is not robust to a small perturbation of the support of the distribution of individual characteristics. More generally, the property that the social preference relation is not acyclic, which is ensured for the pairwise majority by the existence of a 50%-majority winner, is very sensitive to small perturbations of the support of individual characteristics. We recall that a δ-majority winner is a proposal preferred by more than a fraction $(1 - \delta)$ of the population to any other alternative in pairwise comparison. Condorcet's paradox demonstrates the possibility that there may be no 50%-majority winner. In fact, the works of Kramer (1973), Plott (1967) and Rubinstein (1979) show that this possibility is almost a certainty: The set of societies for which there exists a 50%-majority winner is of measure zero.

Hence, the shortcomings of this first solution and its extensions to a multidimensional framework (offered by Davis et al. (1967), Grandmont (1978), Plott (1967) and Tullock (1967)) to the aggregation of individual preferences is that assumptions restrict arbitrarily the individual behavior. In addition, the generated result is not robust.

Nevertheless, if one considers a distinct aggregation rule that requires more than the majority one can build a social ordering, which is acyclic, with weaker assumptions on the distribution of individual characteristics. These assumptions allow for a larger support of the distribution but restrict the shape of the distribution. In addition, the result is robust to small perturbations of the distribution. Effectively, Caplin and Nalebuff (1988) extend the support of the distribution of individual preferences to the set of euclidean preferences (Individual ranks their propositions according to their Euclidean distance from a most preferred point). They prove that if the density function of individuals' most preferred points is concave then there exists an unbeatable proposal according to 64%-majority rule and no electoral cycles are possible. In addition, this result remain valid for density functions close to concave functions. The requirement of a concave (or close to concave) density can even be relaxed to allow for all log-concave densities, see Caplin and Nalebuff (1991a). These authors provide a general bound of the minimum majority rule needed to support the mean voter's most preferred outcome. The bound depends on a concavity index for the distribution of preferences and on the dimensionality of the choice space.

It is important to point out that the solution offered by the statistical approach to these three aggregation problems is robust in the sense that it is not sensitive to small perturbations of the distribution of individual characteristics. For the two first illustrations, it is also robust in the sense that the aggregate property (the monotonicity of aggregate demand) is additive over subpopulations, adding two macroeconomic models fulfilling the aggregate property, one gets a macroeconomic model with the same property.

Note that the representative agent model can be justified following this approach for a very specific class of distributions of individual characteristics, namely for any atomic distribution where the support of the distribution is restricted to one single element of the set of individual characteristics, or at least to a very small subset of the set of feasible characteristics where the theory of exact aggregation holds. However, the motivation of this approach is precisely to avoid such arbitrary assumptions. In the literature of the statistical approach, one important feature of the models is to include any individual behavior considered as feasible by the microeconomic theory. More precisely, the restrictions introduced on the distribution of individual characteristics should be such that any open subset of the set defined by the microeconomic theory has a strictly positive measure (see Giraud and Maret (2002))[5]. In other words, assumptions will allow for the largest support of the distribution

[5]Note however that for technical reasons, minimum assumptions have to be introduced on the set individual characteristics to ensure the existence of a probability distribution over this set. Effectively, it might be the case that the set of individual characteristics has not the required structure so that the restriction to a metric space introduced previously yields to focus on a subset of the feasible set defined by the microeconomic theory. For example, in demand theory when the microeconomic behavior is explained by the maximisation of (strictly convex) preferences under budget constraint, the individual demand function is differentiable, homogenous of degree zero and satisfies the budget identity and the weak axiom. However, the set of these individual functions

of individual characteristics and the restrictions will essentially concern the shape of this distribution.

To conclude the main contribution of the statistical approach is to show that it is not only wrong to follow the theory of exact aggregation and transpose the microeconomic structure to the macroeconomic model but it might also be very misleading. The arguments are twofold. First, the pure microeconomic approach has severe limits : The properties at the microeconomic level are not necessarily preserved by aggregation, and standard individual rationality yields to weak properties in the aggregate. Second, some properties might emerge with the aggregation process in such a way that the requirement of individual rationality might become redundant. The statistical approach has given many illustrations of this phenomenon. The most significative result was obtained by Kneip (1999).

6 The Large Support of the Distribution of Individual Characteristics

The introduction of a large support of the distribution of individual characteristics (without any assumption on the shape of this distribution) allows on its own to introduce structure in the macroeconomic model. This structure depends both on the presence of a large number of agents and on their diversity.

Let us initially look at the structural impact of a large number of agents.

To this end we begin with an observation to the effect that the pertinence of a theory might depend on the existence of a continuum of agents (even identical). The concept of perfect competition, for example, gets all its legitimacy in such a framework. Effectively, the assumption that agents are "price takers", in other words that no agent has a negotiation power and is able to influence the price determination, presumes a large number of agents. This idea that the weight of each agent in the economy is negligible while the economy has a strictly positive weight lies at the heart of measure theory and is formalized by a non atomic probability measure on $\mathbb{R}^k \times \mathcal{A}$. This analytical framework has been introduced by Aumann (1964) but the use of a continuum of (identical) agents is already present in Allen and Bowley (1935); see also Shapley (1953) for an application to game theory. For a detailed study of the applications of measure theory to economics the reader is referred to Kirman (1982).

The existence of a continuum of identical agents also introduces new properties of the macroeconomic model so that these properties have no longer to be required on the microeconomic model.

Consider, for example, that the microeconomic model describes the demand of one household induced by the maximization of non-convex preferences. For the pair (p, R) that corresponds to the budget line on figure 1, the household a is indifferent between the two consumptions bundles A and B, i.e. $f(p, R, a) = \{A, B\}$. As long as the economy contains a finite number of agents with these identical preferences the graph of mean demand

is not a metric space.

remains non-convex (For (p, R) mean demand is represented by a finite number of points on the segment $[A, B]$). However, when the number of households with these preferences become infinite the graph of mean demand is convexified. Effectively, for the price-income pair (p, R) the mean demand graph is the segment $[A, B]$. The mean demand vector evolves on $[A, B]$ from A to B with the percentage of households choosing B rather than A.

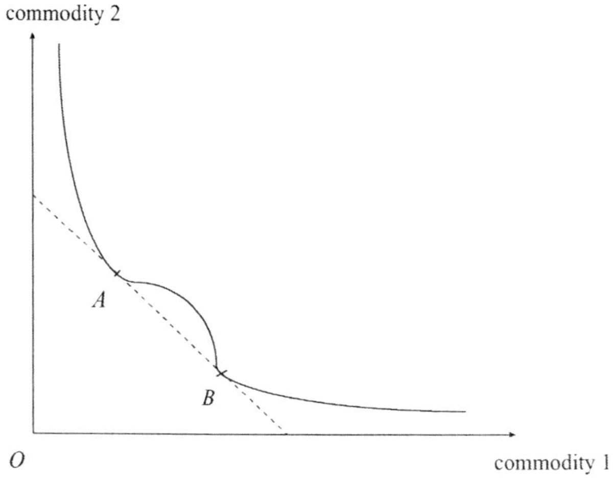

Figure 1: [6]

Let us now recall that the convexity of the graph of mean demand is a crucial assumption to prove existence of the competitive equilibrium in a pure exchange economy. This property of the macroeconomic model is traditionally obtained in a finite economy by requiring convex individual preferences, i.e. the convexity of the individual demand graph. The introduction of an infinite number of households allow to relax this assumption and to prove the existence of the competitive equilibrium with weaker assumptions on the microeconomic model (see Aumann (1966) and Hildenbrand (1970)).

If, in addition to the large number of agents, one requires now that these agents possess distinct characteristics, additional structure can be introduced in the macroeconomic model.

First, the diversity of individual characteristics might give more realism to some economic concepts. A constant criticism addressed to economics is its use of abstract tools to formalize agents' behavior. The assessment of the assumptions that formalize individual rationality are left to the economist's discretion, but more often they do not correspond to any economic reality and cannot be tested empirically. Consider, for example, the demand function that describes the consumption choices of a household i at a given period as a function of prices and income. The theory of general equilibrium assumes that transactions only take place at equilibrium values, an equilibrium being a state where agents' choices are compatible. Hence, outside the equilibrium values (p^*, R^{i*}), the household demand function does not describe any effective economic activity. However, the criticism collapses when there is a sufficiently large number of distinct agents such that for any price system

$p \neq p^*$ there exists a household j such that

$$f\left(p^*, R^{j*}, a^j\right) = f\left(p, R^{i*}, a^i\right) \tag{6}$$

Thus, the hypothetical demand of household i at the price system $p \neq p^*$ matches household j's demand that is effective at the equilibrium price system p^*. This demand can, therefore, be observed.

A second structural effect of the diversity of individual characteristics is to introduce additional properties of the macroeconomic model.

As an illustration, the introduction of such assumptions in demand theory does not only generate the convexity of the graph of mean demand but it does also ensure that mean demand can be formalized by a function and not a correspondence. Assume that individual demand $f(p, R, a)$ is induced by the maximization of preferences. If these preferences, described by the parameter vector a, are non strictly convex, for a given price vector, p, the consumption bundle chosen by the household is not necessarily unique. However, if there exists a large number of distinct households such that the weight of households indifferent between more than one consumption bundle at the price vector p is negligible, uniqueness might be obtained "on average". Formally, mean demand is unique if the probability measure of the characteristics (R, a) yielding a multiple demand is equal to zero. In other words the support of the distribution μ over $\mathbb{R}^k \times \mathcal{A}$ has to be sufficiently large to ensure that the measure of the "undesirable" characteristics (R, a) is equal to zero.

Using the same line of argument, Sondermann (1975, 1976, 1980), Araujo and Mas-Colell (1978) prove that mean demand of a population with a large number of households that possess sufficiently distinct preferences is almost everywhere continuous. Dierker et al. (1980a) prove a similar result for a population of households that also possess distinct incomes. These results require a slightly specific structure of the set of preference relations that has been extended by Hildenbrand (1980) and Trockel (1983). The differentiability of mean demand can also be deduced from this type of arguments. Trockel (1984) and Dierker et al. (1980b, 1984) add to the previous models the assumption that the distribution of individual characteristics is continuous and get a mean demand that is not only continuous but also differentiable. Intuitively, the continuity assumption forbids the arbitrary exclusion of any individual behavior ; any non empty open subset of the set of individual characteristics has a strictly positive measure. It is important to note that this assumption concerns more the support of the distribution of individual characteristics rather than the shape of this distribution. It requires that the support of the distribution is as large as feasible, formally that it is dense within the set of feasible individual characteristics.

To conclude the requirement that agents are numerous and sufficiently distinct is fully formalized by a large set of individual characteristics $\mathbb{R}^k \times \mathcal{A}$ and the assumption that the distribution μ of agents over this set is non atomic and continuous. Such a distribution of individual characteristics can be considered as a good approximation of a competitive world where numerous and heterogenous agents interact.

7 Assumptions on the Shape of the Distribution of Individual Characteristics

As underlined by Malinvaud (1991) the introduction of assumptions on the shape of the distribution of individual characteristics leads the economist to build more specific but also more useful macro-economic models. This is exemplified by the initiatic model of Houthakker (1955) where a strong property of a macroeconomic model emerges from an assumption on the distribution of individual characteristics. The author shows that the short-run aggregate production function has a very specific shape (of the Cobb-Douglas type) when the distribution of the fixed coefficient of the firms' (Leontieff) technologies is Pareto. The main difficulty is to avoid to substitute arbitrary assumptions on the shape of the distribution of individual characteristics to the strong assumptions on individual behavior of the pure microeconomic approach. Hence, the crucial issue is what kind of assumptions the economist can reasonably introduce on μ. as pointed out, in particular, by Hildenbrand (1994).

7.1 To What Extend can we Observe the Distribution of Individual Characteristics ?

The main motivation of the statistical approach is to introduce assumptions that can be (to some extend) tested empirically rather than assumptions on abstract notions such as the utility function that are left to the theorist's own appraisal. Hence, the first methodology developed by the statistical approach has focused on assumptions that constraint the distribution of observable characteristics. Nevertheless, the vector of theoretical characteristics (R, a) include both observable variables (R, α) and non observable variables β. Hence, assumptions on the distribution of (R, α) cannot be directly tested empirically as long as there exists a dependence between the latter and the distribution of β. More generally, to build an empirical test of assumptions on the conditional distributions $\mu_{(R,\alpha)/\beta}$ one has to define a theoretical link between these distributions and observable distributions. What is at stake within this methodology is to formulate assumptions such that this theoretical link is in accordance with our economic intuition.

To make this point clearer, we begin with assumptions on the conditional distributions of the exogenous variable R, $\mu_{R/a}$, since the parameter vector a describing individual behavior includes unobservable variables. This type of assumptions was initially introduced by Hildenbrand (1983). He derived the monotonicity of aggregate demand by restricting the distribution of individual income. Let us give the intuition of the structural impact of this type of assumption. Consider a group of individuals who differ in their income but all of whom have the same consumption behavior described by a common demand function $f(p, R, a)$ (or equivalently by the demand parameters a), which is assumed to satisfy the weak axiom of revealed preference. Formally, the distribution of households' characteristics μ is decomposed into $\mu_{x/a}$ over $\mathbb{R}_+$, the distributions of income conditional to the demand parameters a, and μ_a over A, the marginal distribution of a. Hildenbrand (1983) focuses on a subpopulation described by a given a and shows that if the distribution $\mu_{R/a}$ is given by a decreasing density then the mean demand of this subpopulation $F\left(\cdot, \mu_{R/a}, a\right)$ is monotone.

If no additional assumption is made on the form of the common demand, then the income effect of a price change might be positive for some individuals (i.e., for some values of income) while for the others it will be negative. However, and this is the crucial point, the average income effect is always negative if, for example, the income of the households is distributed uniformly over the interval $[0, 1]$.

In fact, the income effect corresponding to a price change of commodity h of an individual with expenditure R is given by

$$-f_h(p, R, a) \cdot \frac{\partial}{\partial R} f_h(p, R, a).$$

Hence the average income effect of the subpopulation described by a is given by

$$\begin{aligned} -\int_0^1 f_h(p, R, a) \cdot \frac{\partial}{\partial R} f_h(p, R, a)\, dR &= -\frac{1}{2} \int_0^1 \frac{\partial}{\partial R} \left[f_h^2(p, R, a)\right] dR \\ &= -\frac{1}{2} f_h^2(p, 1, a) \leq 0. \end{aligned}$$

Since the substitution effect for every individual is negative, we obtain from Slutsky's equation

$$\frac{\partial}{\partial p_h} f_h(p, R, a) < -f_h(p, R, a) \cdot \frac{\partial}{\partial R} f_h(p, R, a).$$

Hence

$$\frac{\partial}{\partial p_h} F_h\left(p, \mu_{R/a}, a\right) = \int_0^1 \frac{\partial}{\partial p_h} f_h(p, R, a)\, dR < 0.$$

Consequently, the partial mean demand curve for every commodity is strictly decreasing.

This result can easily be extended ; the assumptions can be weakened to allow for any $\mu_{R/a}$ given by a decreasing density on $\mathbb{R}_+$ and the conclusion can be strengthened to obtain the strict monotonicity of $F\left(\cdot, \mu_{R/a}, a\right)$.

It is important to make two observations about the nature of the macroeconomic property that emerge from assumptions on the shape of the conditional distributions of the exogenous variable R.

Firstly, the property deals with the dependence of the mean function $F\left(\cdot, \mu_{R/a}, a\right)$ with respect to the conditional distribution of this variable $\mu_{R/a}$, any general property that restrict the dependence of $F\left(p, \mu_{R/a}, a\right)$ with respect to the exogenous variable p require assumptions on individual behavior. In the above example, the assumption on the conditional distributions of income only restricts the average income effect of a price change. One can draw a general conclusion about the global effect on demand of a price change to the extend that the average substitution effect is negative. This additional property is explained by standard individual rationality.

Secondly, the induced macroeconomic property is not directly valid for the whole population but only for subgroups. Nevertheless, to the extend that the property is additive, it is preserved when aggregating over subgroups along μ_a. Here, the monotonicity is effectively an additive property, hence market demand $F(\cdot, \mu)$ is also monotone.

It is now crucial to understand to what extend the above assumption on $\mu_{R/a}$ can be tested empirically. Clearly, it cannot be directly tested since the characteristics a are not all observable. To build an empirical test of this hypothesis one should be able to establish a link between $\mu_{R/a}$ and an observable distribution. This is obtained, for example, if for a given vector α of the observable elements of a, the income distribution is independent of the distribution of β, the vector of unobservable elements of a. In this case the density of $\mu_{R/a}$ is non increasing if and only if the density of $\mu_{R/\alpha}$ is non increasing. To the extend that the vector of variables α includes any observable variable that is known to affect demand behavior independently of prices and income (such as the age of the household head, the occupation of the household head, the household size, and so on ...), the independence of the two previous distributions can be considered as a plausible approximation. In the sense that the unobservable distribution $\mu_{R/a}$ describes a subgroup of households with an identical consumption behavior while the observable distribution $\mu_{R/\alpha}$ includes households with fairly similar consumption behaviors. Hence, the two distributions should have similar shapes.

We turn to the empirical validation of our assumption. Firstly, we should note that the existence of a density of $\mu_{R/\alpha}$ strictly speaking implies that we consider a group with a continuum of individuals. As underlined in section 6, this continuum is generally introduced in the models of the statistical approach. Consequently the empirical distribution of any finite group of individuals can never fulfills exactly the requirements of the statistical approach. Since it is known that the mean function $F(\cdot, \mu)$ depends continuously on the distribution μ (with respect to weak convergence) the relevant question is whether the empirical distribution of a large but finite population belongs to a neighborhood of a distribution with the required shape. If this were the case, for the previous issue, then the actual mean demand function would not necessarily be monotone but would belong to a neighborhood of a monotone function F. To conclude the continuity of the distribution might be considered in certain situations as an acceptable approximation.[7] However, the assumption of a decreasing density of $\mu_{R/\alpha}$ is of a different nature.

Empirical studies do not validate the latter assumption and the distributions $\mu_{R/\alpha}$ generally appear to be closer to lognormal distributions. By limiting consideration to assumptions on the conditional distributions of income, the analysis cannot give an account of the Law of Demand. To provide an explanation of the Law of Demand, Chiappori (1985), Grodal and Hildenbrand (1992), Marhuenda (1995) and Quah (2000) show that one has to add to the realistic assumption of lognormal conditional distributions of income, assumptions that restrict a priori the aggregate substitution effect beyond the negative semi-definiteness obtained under standard individual rationality. As to this result in demand theory, in gen-

[7] In addition, recent developments of the statistical approach have obtained the required property of the mean function $F(\cdot, \mu)$ for finite group of individuals. Their discussion is postponed until the next section.

eral the statistical approach needs to formalize assumptions on the non observable marginal distribution of individual behaviors μ_a.

We shall focus now on assumptions on the conditional distributions of individual behaviors $\mu_{a/R}$. Two methodologies have been followed in the literature to deduce properties of the macroeconomic model, which is described by (5), from assumptions on $\mu_{a/R}$. The first methodology is the one followed in this section where the purpose is to establish a link between the theoretical distribution and an observable distribution. A discussion of the second methodology is postponed to the next section.

Let us give an illustration of these alternative assumptions when F denotes market demand and $\mu_{a/R}$ the distribution of households' consumptions behaviors a conditional on the income level R. Hildenbrand (1994) applies our first methodology to deduce the Law of Demand at the macroeconomic level from the theoretical assumption that in a given subgroup of households described by the income R ($R-$households), the dispersion of demand vectors is assumed to increase (in a specific way) with an hypothetical increase Δ of income. The Law of Demand is again derived from the Slutsky decomposition under the additional assumption that the average substitution effect is negative since the increasing dispersion only restricts the average income effect. Hildenbrand's assumption is a direct extension of the increasing dispersion of household Engel curves (as income goes up) introduced by Jerison (1982, 1984, 1992) used to explain the weak axiom of revealed preference in the aggregate. For a discussion of this result and its application to a pure exchange economy the reader is referred to Hildenbrand (1995).

The increasing dispersion cannot be directly tested empirically since what R-households would demand if they could spend $R+\Delta$ cannot be observed. However, an empirical test can be built if one believes that for the hypothetical price-income pair $(p, R+\Delta)$ the distribution of the demand vectors of households with the effective income R, $\mu^{(p,R)}/\,(R+\Delta)$, is sufficiently close to the distribution of the demand vectors of households with the effective income $R+\Delta$, $\mu^{(p,R+\Delta)}/\,(R+\Delta)$. More precisely, Hildenbrand (1994) requires that the observable covariance of the distribution $\mu^{(p,R+\Delta)}/\,(R+\Delta)$ is a good approximation of the unobservable covariance of $\mu^{(p,R)}/\,(R+\Delta)$. Under this hypothesis of metonymy, the increasing dispersion is well supported empirically (see Haerdle et al.(1991), Hildenbrand and Kneip (1993) and Hildenbrand (1989, 1994)).

Jerison (1999) introduces a similar assumption in a general equilibrium model. More precisely, he requires an "increasing dispersion of excess demands"[8] that constraint the joint distribution ν of individual demand functions and initial endowments. This hypothesis ensures that the mean consumer excess demand $Z(\cdot,\nu)$ satisfies the weak axiom and therefore the competitive equilibrium of a production economy with constant returns to scale is unique. Again, to the extend that one believes in a second metonymy hypothesis introduced by Marhuenda (1995), this assumption is falsifiable using cross-section data on

[8]This is an extension of Freixas and Mas-Colell (1987), in the sense that one substitutes to severe restrictions on the support of the distribution ν an assumption on the shape of this distribution. Effectively, Freixas and Mas-Colell consider a group of households with similar consumption behaviors described by an identical Engel curve and collinear endowments. These authors deduce the weak axiom in the aggregate from a priori assumptions on the shape of the common Engel curve.

consumer expenditures and endowments.

To recapitulate one can substitute arbitrary assumption at the individual level by falsifiable assumptions on the distribution of individual characteristics and give an account of properties dealing with the dependence of the mean function $F\left(\cdot, \mu_{R/a}, a\right)$ with respect to the conditional distribution of the exogenous variable R. This is done to the extend that either the observable variables α are sufficiently significant to describe the individual behavior for a fixed level of the exogenous variable R, either one believes in metonymy hypotheses.

7.2 Assumptions of Behavioral Heterogeneity

As underlined in section 3, for many theoretical purposes it is of great interest to obtain general conclusions about the dependence of the mean function $F(\cdot, \mu)$ with respect the exogenous variables p non specific to agents. To this end, one can again substitute to a priori assumptions on the individual behavior assumptions on the conditional distributions of individual behaviors $\mu_{a/R}$ over $\mathcal{A}$. However, since the exogenous variables p are not specific to agents it is difficult to build falsifiable assumptions on these distributions that lead to relevant properties of the macroeconomic model. Hence, a second methodology of the statistical approach focuses on assumptions that can be interpreted in terms of behavioral heterogeneity. The results established within this methodology state that for a sufficiently high degree of behavioral heterogeneity mean function satisfies a given property.

This methodology was developed around the concept of the equivalence class of households used in applied demand analysis (see Prais and Houthakker, 1955, Barten, 1964, Jorgenson and Slesnik, 1987) and introduced in general equilibrium theory by Mas-Colell and Neuefind (1977) and Dierker et al. (1984). The idea is to generate the set of feasible individual behaviors (described by $\mathcal{F}$ or equivalently by $\mathcal{A}$) through transformations of a given individual behavior (described by an initial individual function $\bar{f}$). This subgroup of individuals is called the equivalence class of $\bar{f}$. The population might include an infinite number of equivalence classes. However, the macroeconomic property is required for any equivalence and is preserved for the entire population by additivity. It is obtained for distributions $\mu_{f/R}$ over $\mathcal{F}$ sufficiently close to "uniform" distributions.

From now on, we shall be interested by the behavior of market budget shares. For any demand function f, the budget share spent by the household for the commodity l is

$$s_l(p, R) = \frac{p_l f_l(p, R)}{R}.$$

We shall focus on conditional distributions $\mu_{s/R}$ of individual budget share functions rather than individual demand functions. To define uniform distributions $\mu_{s/R}$ one has to introduce a distance on the probability space of individual budget share functions $\left(S, \mu_{s/R}\right)$ and a class $\mathcal{T}$ of distance preserving transformations over this space. By construction

$$S = \{s : s = T(\bar{s}), T \in \mathcal{T}\},$$

where $\bar{s}$ is a given budget share function generating the subgroup of households. A uniform distribution over S is an invariant probability measure with respect to any transformation $T \in \mathcal{T}$, since the latter distribution gives to any two subsets of equal size, $A \subset S$ and $T(A) \subset S$, the same weight. Such a uniform distribution defines in this set-up the perfectly heterogeneous population. The specific type of behavioral heterogeneity that emerges depends on the class of transformations at hand and on the distance introduced on the probability space $\left(S, \mu_{s/R}\right)$. Note that any assumption required on $\bar{s}$ defined in this model the restrictions introduced on individual behavior.[9] The crucial issue is what kind of behavioral heterogeneity is it legitimate to introduce?

Initially the literature has focused on behavioral heterogeneity of individuals that might be rational. Therefore, the class of transformations was restricted to the class of affine transformations that is well known to preserve individual rationality. This is the case of the initiatic model of Grandmont (1992), where each subgroup of households is generated through affine transformations of the price system of an initial budget share function $\bar{s}(p, R)$. The demand behavior parametrized by $a \in \mathbb{R}^L$ is written

$$s(p, R, a) = \bar{s}(e^a \otimes p, R).$$

Hence, any two distinct households a and a' react heterogeneously to a change in the price system. Despite the model allows for standard individual rationality, the assumptions required at the individual level are limited to the continuity of the demand function, the absence of money illusion and the budget identity.

In this set-up, a very strong property is obtained in the aggregate when the density function of the parameter distribution is sufficiently flat in some precise sense: Market budget share of each commodity becomes increasingly insensitive to changes in prices, in other words market demand behaves almost like a Cobb-Douglas demand function.

It is important to mention two extensions of this result. Firstly, Quah (1997) extends Grandmont's formalism to allow for the possibility of atoms. This gives more realism to the result that remains true for finite populations. Secondly, Kneip (1999) extends Grandmont's formalism to a non parametric set-up. The novelty is twofold. First, the result does no longer rely on a specific parametrization of consumption behaviors. Second, it is pointed out that the formalism can be used to define a behavioral heterogeneity of households in terms of their reaction to income changes rather than to price changes (when the affine transformations apply to income rather than to prices). In the latter case, the property that emerge in the aggregate is the insensitivity of mean budget shares to changes in income. Hence, the average income effect of a price change is negative. Put differently the increasing dispersion introduced by Hildenbrand (1994) can be interpreted as a sufficient heterogeneity of households' budget share functions in terms of their reaction to changes in income. Note that this type of behavioral heterogeneity was also implicit in Grandmont (1992). Effectively, under the absence of money illusion required at the individual level, affine transformations applied to the income of the initial budget share function are equiv-

[9]To the extend that these properties of $\bar{s}$ are preserved by any transformation $T \in \mathcal{T}$.

alent to specific affine transformations applied to the price vector (where $a_l = a$ for any $l = 1, \ldots, L$).

An issue which has attracted some debate, initiated by B. de Villemeur (1998, 1999) and Hildenbrand (1998), is the precise nature of behavioral heterogeneity at work in this family of models. To grasp the problem that emerges, consider the following parametric model of consumption used by Quah (1997). The space of households' budget share functions is parametrized by a real number $a \in \mathbb{R}$. More precisely, the behavior of household a is described by $s(p, R, a) = \bar{s}(p, e^{-\alpha}R)$. In this set-up the behavioral heterogeneity (of households' budget share functions in terms of their reaction to a change in income) is said to increase as the probability distribution converge to the "uniform" distribution over $\mathbb{R}$. Nevertheless, such a probability distribution does not exist. In addition the limit measure gives all the weight to two limit behaviors $\{+\infty\}$ and $\{-\infty\}$, while any subset of the group of households that is described by a compact interval has measure zero. Due to this concentration phenomenon, two opposite types of behavioral heterogeneity can give an account of the insensitivity property in the aggregate. The behavioral heterogeneity at work crucially depends on what are the limit behaviors of the generating budget share function.

The first explanation relies on the assumption, commonly done in demand theory, that the generator $\bar{s}$ is almost insensitive to changes in income outside a compact interval $[c, C]$. Note that this property holds, in particular, for the class of CES budget share functions. Indeed, it holds for any function $\bar{s}$ with the property that $\lim_{R\to 0} \bar{s}(p, R)$ and $\lim_{R\to +\infty} \bar{s}(p, R)$ exist for any $p \in \mathbb{R}^L_+$. Consequently, by construction $s(p, \cdot, a)$ is almost insensitive to changes in income outside the compact interval $[e^{-\alpha}c, e^{-\alpha}C]$. Hence, distinct agents are sensitive to income changes on distinct intervals. In addition, as the probability distribution of the parameters a becomes more flat, at any price-income vector, the weight of the population sensitive to changes in income tends towards zero. This implies that at each price-income level almost all households are insensitive to changes in income. This type of behavioral heterogeneity has been formalized for a finite population by Hildenbrand and Kneip (1999b). These authors show that Grandmont's model, with some additional assumptions [10], can effectively be understood as an example of such a behavioral heterogeneity where the insensitivity in the aggregate emerges because at each price-income vector almost all households are insensitive to price changes.

This is a legitimate view of the type of behavioral heterogeneity that might induces the insensitivity property in the aggregate, but it is not the only possible view. A second possible view, where the statistical approach is fully used, is that the insensitivity property in the aggregate is induced by a "balancing effect" (The term is borrowed from Maret (2003)). In other words, the mean budget share for each commodity is approximately constant because, while some agents may increase their budget share as prices and/or income change, this is balanced by other agent who choose to reduce their budget share. Note that a very similar

[10] The crucial assumption in Hildenbrand and Kneip's (1999) interpretation of Grandmont's result is that the budget share function generating the affine class has, in certain sense, finitely many turning points (Assumption 3 in their paper). Note that this assumption is fulfilled when the generator is insensitive to price changes outside a compact subset of the price space.

type of behavioral heterogeneity was already introduced by Hicks (1953)(p.64) to give an account of the Law of Demand. Hicks underlines that the property emerges in the aggregate for the excess demand function if income effects cancel out when aggregating over buyers and sellers.

This second type of behavioral heterogeneity is at the heart of the statistical approach, and it is therefore of great interest to make precise the conditions for its emergence. Giraud and Maret (2001, 2002, 2005) build a general analytical framework that formalizes this type of behavioral heterogeneity. We shall present now intuitively their conclusions.

The first important conclusion is that if one focuses on the behavioral heterogeneity of possibly rational households a necessary condition for the balancing effect to emerge is that the budget share function of each household behaves erratically on the price-income boundary. (The budget share of each commodity has no limit when the price of some commodity or income converges towards zero or infinity.) This is a direct consequence of the previous discussion and the fact that any affine transformation preserves individual rationality.

However, this condition is not sufficient. As underlined previously, the difficulty is that for the limit measure (defining the perfectly heterogeneous population) any non empty (compact) subset of individual behaviors has a measure equal to zero. In other words, for the perfectly heterogenous population the set of feasible individual behaviors becomes drastically smaller. A sufficient condition to avoid this difficulty, which gives an economic meaning to the uniform distribution $\mu_{\bar{s}/R}$, is to assume that the set of individual behaviors S is compact. For the previous illustration, this requires that S is described by a compact interval of the real line. This seems an priori reasonable assumption : if one wants to allow for a large set of feasible individual behaviors it is still reasonable to assume that this set is bounded. Many economic models with a continuum of agents make this assumption. However, in our example, this require that the behavior of any budget share function when income varies over the real line is perfectly described by its behavior when income varies over a compact subset of the real line. This is obtained, for example, if one adds at the individual level the following periodicity requirement : There exists γ such that

$$\bar{s}\left(p, e^{n\gamma}R\right) = \bar{s}\left(p, R\right)$$

The function represented on figure 2 fulfills this assumption. Note that if one can find rational households that maximize a utility function under budget constraint fulfilling this requirement, the latter is clearly not a necessary condition for individual rationality. One easily checks that this property induces the previously mentioned erratic behavior.

To recapitulate, if one focuses on the behavioral heterogeneity of possibly rational households a sufficient condition for the balancing effect to emerge is that the budget share function of each household fulfills a periodicity requirement. Note that this requirement is stronger than standard individual rationality. Effectively, many budget share functions induced by utility maximization, such as CES budget share functions, do not fulfill this periodicity requirement.

However, one might also be interested in the macroeconomic behavior of a population

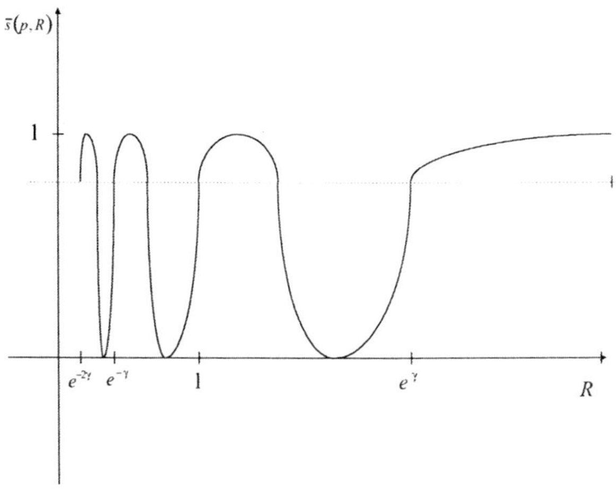

Figure 2:

of non rational agents. The main argument is that, in Grandmont (1992) and its successors, the macroeconomic property is obtained without the standard rationality assumption that each household solves a utility maximization program under budget constraint. Therefore, individual rationality might become redundant.

Consider first the case where household behavior is entirely arbitrary except for the budget identity. The insensitivity property is induced in the aggregate by the balancing effect for the example of a population of households given by Becker (1962) and rigorously formalized by John (2001). The idea is that the distribution of individual behaviors $\mu_{/R}$ is such that at each price-income pair (p, R) it induces a uniform distribution of individual budget share vectors over the set $\left\{s \in \mathbb{R}_+^L : \sum_{l=1}^L s_l = 1\right\}$. Hence the mean budget share function is the Cobb-Douglas function $S_l(p, R) = \frac{1}{L}\frac{R}{p_l}$ for any $l = 1, \ldots, L$.

Nevertheless, this solution cannot be applied if household behaviors are not arbitrary. This second case needs to be considered, since the collective approach (see for example Chiappori, 1988, 1992) has pointed out that if the WARP is not well supported empirically at the household level (when the household includes more than one member), other properties of the budget share function will hold. This legitimizes to consider a compact set of budget share functions that do not satisfy the WARP but are not arbitrary in contrast to Becker (1962). Given any such compact set, Giraud and Maret (2001, 2002, 2005) build a general analytical framework where the insensitivity property of the mean budget share function is explained by the "balancing effect". They give the example of a population obtained by applying to the generating function a new class of transformations defined through rotations of the price-income vector (rather than the class of affine transformations). With this new type of heterogeneous reactions to changes in prices and/or income they prove that the balancing effect is generated with an individual rationality essentially restricted to the absence of money illusion.[11] In addition, the heterogeneity of the individual budget share functions is now explicitly formalized in contrast to Becker (1962).

Another contribution of Giraud and Maret (2001, 2002, 2005) is to prove the exact insensitivity result for the limit probability distribution. This gives coherence to the theory when the degree of behavioral heterogeneity is pushed up to the limit.[12] Furthermore, an approximate Cobb-Douglas behavior is still obtained for a probability distribution sufficiently close to the limit. This approximate result is quite realistic in the sense that it is established for a finite population of households.

8 Extensions to an Intertemporal Framework

In the literature the statistical approach was essentially applied to demand theory in a static framework. Nevertheless, the structural impact of assumptions on the distribution of individual characteristics carries through a dynamic set-up. As an illustration, the behavioral heterogeneity of Grandmont and its successors is adapted by Maret (1998) to an intertemporal framework in the overlapping generations model of a pure exchange economy. Approximate bounds for the derivative of market demand that depend upon specific measure of the degree of behavioral heterogeneity of households' budget share functions in terms of their reaction changes in the expected real interest rate are provided. To the extend that price expectations are observed, the assumption of behavioral heterogeneity can be tested empirically since the expected real interest rate is specific to individuals. To this end one has to introduce a metonymy assumption and use cross-section data of consumption expenditures partitioned with respect to price expectations. The aggregate property has strong consequences for the prevalence in the aggregate of gross substitutability between current and future consumption while this property does not hold at the household level. Note that this property solves the indeterminacy of the dynamics of a sequence of temporary competitive equilibria with perfect foresight by forbidding the emergence of endogenous cycles. Following this approach, Hildenbrand and Kneip (1999a) introduce assumptions of structural invariance over time of the distribution of individual characteristics to give an account of properties of the mean consumption expenditure of a large and heterogeneous population of households. It is shown that the change in the aggregate consumption expenditure ratio can be decomposed into an effect of changing income dispersion, an effect of income growth, an effect of price-inflation and an effect of changing the distribution of individual behaviors.

[11] A first step in this direction was made by Maret (2003). The author introduces a new class of distance preserving transformations that ensures that the concentration phenomenon cannot emerge in subpopulations of households. However, since any subpopulation might have a measure zero, this result does not prevent the concentration phenomenon over the whole space S.

[12] The exact insensitivity has been obtained under weaker assumptions by Giraud and Quah (2004) when the class of affine transformations is used to formalize behavioral heterogenity. In particular, these authors do not introduce any periodicity requirement at the household level. The counterbalancing effect is that in their framework nothing ensure that the aggregate insensitivity is not induced by an insensitivity at the household level.

The next step would be to apply the statistical approach to study the properties of another aggregate function. It seems more reasonable to focus on demand theory since the statistical approach approximates the population by a continuum of agents which are therefore implicitly assumed to be perfectly competitive. In a dynamic model of demand one could introduce heterogeneous price expectations. If the requirement of perfect foresight is perfectly legitimate in a repetitive environment, in particular at a stationary state or along any periodic orbit, it is more severe outside such trajectories. Price expectations could be formalized as functions of current and past prices. Since these exogenous variables that affect price expectations are not specific to individuals it is difficult to build falsifiable assumptions on the distribution of the price expectations functions. One should therefore exploit behavioral heterogeneity of individual functions to give an account of properties of the aggregate price expectation function, when the set of feasible individual expectation functions remains as wide as possible. Depending on these structural properties, some properties of the market demand function could then be established as well as some relationship between stability with learning and stability of the perfect foresight dynamics. First attempts in this direction have been made by Maret (1995a, 1995b) and more recently by Calvet et al. (1998). In Maret (1995a) the monotonicity of market demand is deduced from distributional requirements of household demand functions combined with distributional requirements of household price expectation rules. In Maret (1995b) a specific heterogeneity of the price expectation functions between households is shown to reverse the stability property of the unique monetary stationary state. A deeper examination of these issues would be useful.

References

[Allen, R.G.D. and Bowley, A.L.] (1935), "Family expenditure: A study of its variation", Staples Press, Lond on.

[Araujo, A. and Mas-Colell, A.] (1978), "Notes on the Smoothing of Aggregate Demand", *Journal of Mathematical Economics* **5**, 113-127.

[Aumann R.J.] (1964), 'Markets with a continuum of traders', *Econometrica* **32**, 39-50.

[Aumann R.J.] (1966), 'Existence of competitive equilibria in markets with a continuum of traders', *Econometrica* **34**, 1-17.

[Barten, A.P.] , 'Family Composition, Prices and Expenditure Patterns, in Econometric Analysis for National Economic Planning : 16th Symposium of the Colston Society', P. Hart, G. Mills and J.K. Whitaker (eds), Butterworth, London, 1964.

[Becker, G.S.] (1962), "Irrational Behavior and Economic Theory", *Journal of Political Economy* **70**, 1-13.

[Black, D.] (1948), "On the Rationale Group Decision-Making", *Journal of Political Economy* **56**, 23-34.

[Billette de Villemeur, E.] (1998), "Heterogeneity and Stability : Variations on Scarf's Processes", Florence: European University Institute, Working Paper ECO No. 98/38.

[Billette de Villemeur, E.] (1999), "Aggregation of Demand and Distribution of Characteristics: a Difficulty in Modelling Behavioural Heterogeneity", Université de Cergy-Pontoise: Document de travail 99/38.

[Bottazi, J.-M., Hens T.] : On the Excess Demand Functions with Incomplete Markets. Journal of Economic Theory **68** (1), 149-163 (1996).

[Bottazi, J.-M., Löffler, A., Hens T.] : Market Demand in the CAPM, *Journal of Economic Theory* **79**, 192-206 (1998).

[Calvet L., Grandmont, J.-M., Lemaire, I.] : Heterogeneous Probabilities in Complete Asset Markets. Université Catholique de Louvain-la-Neuve : CORE, DP 9819 (1998).

[Caplin A. and B. Nalebuff] (1988), "On 64%-Majority Rule", *Econometrica* **56,** 25-59.

[Caplin A. and B. Nalebuff] (1991a), "Aggregation and Social Choice : A Mean Voter Theorem", *Econometrica* **59**, 1-23.

[Caplin A. and B. Nalebuff] (1991b), 'Aggregation and the Imperfect Competition: on the Existence of Equilibrium', *Econometrica* **59**, 25-59.

[Chiappori P.A.] (1985), 'Distribution of income and the "Law of Demand"', *Econometrica*, **53**, No. 1, 109-127.

[Chiappori P.A.] (1988), 'Rational household labor supply', *Econometrica* **56,** 63-89.

[Chiappori P. A. and I. Ekeland] (1999a), 'Aggregation and Market Demand : an Exterior Differential Calculus Viewpoint', *Econometrica* **67**, 1435-1457.

[Chiappori P. A. and I. Ekeland] (1999b), 'Disaggregation of excess demand functions in incomplete markets', *Journal of Mathematical Economics* **31**, 111-129.

[Davis, O., Degroot, M., and Hinich, M.] (1967), "Social Preference Orderings and Majority Rule", *Econometrica* **40**, 147-157.

[Debreu, G.] (1974), "Excess Demand Functions", *Journal of Mathematical Econonomics* **1**, 15-21.

[Dierker E., H.Dierker and W.Trockel] (1980a), 'Continuous Mean Demand Functions Derived from non Convex Preferences', *Journal of Mathematical Economics* **7**, 27-33.

[Dierker E., H.Dierker and W.Trockel] (1980b), 'Smoothing Demand by Aggregation with Respect to Wealth', *Journal of Mathematical Economics* **7**, 227-247.

[Dierker E., H. Dierker and W. Trockel] (1984), 'Price Dispersed Preferences and C^1 Mean Demand', *Journal of Mathematical Economics* **13**, 11-42.

[Dierker. E] (1991), 'Competition for Costumers', in Equilibrium Theory and Application, W.A. Barnett, B. Cornet, C. D'Aspremont, J. Gabszewicz and A. Mas-Colell (eds), Cambridge: Cambridge University Press.

[Dierker E. and K. Podczeck] (1992), 'The Distribution of Consumers' Tastes and the Quasiconcavity of the Profit Function', University of Vienna.

[Economides, N.S.] (1989), "Symmetric Equilibrium Existence and Optimality in a Differentiated Product Market", *Journal of Economic Theory* **47**, 178-194.

[Eisenberg E.] (1961), 'Aggregation of Utility Functions', *Management Science* **7,** 337-350.

[Gabszewicz, J.J. and Thisse, J.-F.] (1979), "Price Competition, Quality, and Income Disparities", *Journal of Economic Theory* **20**, 340-359.

[Giraud, G. and Maret, I.] (2001), "Behavioral Heterogeneity in Large Economies", BETA, Université Louis Pasteur, *Working Paper* n.2001-08.

[Giraud, G. and Maret, I.] (2002), "Modelling Behavioral Heterogeneity", BETA, Université Louis Pasteur, *Working Paper* n.2002-22.

[Giraud, G. and Maret, I.] (2005), "The Exact Insensitivity of Market Budget Shares and the 'Balancing Effect'", BETA, Université Louis Pasteur, *Working Paper* n.2005-02.

[Giraud, G. and Quah, J.] (2004), "Heterodic Models of Aggregate Demand", *Berkeley Electronic Journal*.

[Grandmont, J.M.] (1978), "Intermediate Preferences and the Majority Rule", *Econometrica* **46**, 317-330.

[Grandmont J.M.] (1992), 'Transformations of the commodity space, behavioral heterogeneity and the aggregation problem', *Journal of Economic Theory* **57** , 1-35.

[Grandmont, J.-M.] (1993), "Behavioral Heterogeneity and Cournot Oligo- poly Equilibrium", *Ricerche Economiche* **47** (2), 167-187 .

[Grodal, B. and Hildenbrand, W.] (1992),'Cross-section Engelcurves, Expenditure Distribution and the Law of Demand', Essays in Honor of H.S. Houthakker, L. Philips and L.D. Taylor (eds), Dordrecht: Kluman Academic Publisher.

[Haerdle W., Hildenbrand, W., and Jerison, M.] (1991), 'Empirical Evidence on the Law of Demand', *Econometrica* **59**, pp. 1525-1551.

[Hicks, J.R.] (1953), "Value and Capital", Oxford: Clarendon Press, fourth edition.

[Hauser, J.] (1988), "Competitive Price and Positioning Strategies", *Marketing Science* 7, 76-91.

[Hauser, J. and Wernerfelt, B.] (1988), "Existence and uniqueness of Price Equilibrium in Defender", *Marketing Science* **7**, 92-93.

[Hildenbrand, K.] (1998), "On J.-M. Grandmont's Modelling of Behavioral Heterogeneity", Bonn Universität: *Discussion Paper* No. **A-580**.

[Hildenbrand W.] (1970), 'Existence of equilibria for economies with production and a measure space of consumers', *Econometrica* **38**, 608-623.

[Hildenbrand, W.] , *Core and Equilibria of a Large Economy*, Princeton: Princeton University Press 1974.

[Hildenbrand W.] (1980), 'On the Uniqueness of Mean Demand for Dispersed Families of Preferences', *Econometrica* **48**, 1703-1710.

[Hildenbrand W.] (1983), 'On the Law of Demand', *Econometrica* **51**, 997-1019.

[Hildenbrand W.] : Market Demand: Theory and Empirical Evidence. Princeton: Princeton University Press 1994.

[Hildenbrand W.] : Des preuves empiriques de la théorie de la demande. in L'économic devient-elle une science dure, d'Autume, A., Cartelier, J., Paris: *Economica* 1995.

[Hildenbrand W. and A. Kneip] (1993), 'Family Expenditure Data, Heteroscedasticity and the Law of Demand', *Ricerche Economiche* **47**, 137-165.

[Hildenbrand W. and A. Kneip] (1999a), "Demand Aggregation under Structural Stability", *Journal of Mathematical Economics* **31**, 81-109.

[Hildenbrand W. and A. Kneip] (1999b), "On Behavioral Heterogeneity", SFB 303 Universität Bonn: *Discussion Paper* N. **A589**.

[Houthakker, H.] (1955), The Pareto Distribution and the Cobb-Douglas Production Function in Activity Analysis, *Review of Economic Studies* **47**, 137-165.

[Jerison M.] (1982), 'The representative consumer and the weak axiom when the distribution of income is fixed', *Discussion Paper* **150**, SUNY, Albany, New-York.

[Jerison M.] (1984), 'Aggregation and Pairwise Aggregation of Demand when the Distribution of Income is Fixed', *Journal of Economic Theory* **13**, 1-31.

[Jerison M.] (1992), 'Optimal Income Distribution and the Nonrepresentative Representative Consumer', *Working Paper*, SUNY, Albany.

[Jerison, M.] (1999), 'Dispersed Excess Demand, the Weak Axiom and Uni- queness of equilibrium', *Journal of Mathematical Economics* **31**, 15-48.

[John, R.] (2001), "Equal Distribution of Consumers' Tastes and Perfect Behavioral Heterogeneity", SFB 303 Universität Bonn (mimeo).

[Jorgensen, J. and Slesnick, D.] (1987), 'Aggregate Consumer Behavior and Households Equivalence Scales', *Journal of Business, Economics and Statistics* **5**, 219-232.

[Kirman, A.P.] : Measure Theory with Applications to Economics. in : Handbook of Mathematical Economics. Arrow., K.J., Intriligator, M.D., North-Holland 1982.

[Kirman A.P.] (1991), 'Whom or What Does the Representative Individual Represent?', *Journal of Economic Perspectives* **6**, 117-136.

[Kirman A.P. and K.J. Koch] (1986), 'Market Excess Demand Functions in Exchange Economies with Identical Preferences and Collinear Endowments', *Review of Economic Studies* **53**, 457-463.

[Kneip, A.] (1999), "Behavioral Heterogeneity and Structural Properties of Aggregate Demand. *Journal of Mathematical Economics* **31**, 49-79.

[Kramer, G.H.] (1973), "On a Class of Equilibrium Conditions for Majority Rule", *Econometrica* **41**,285-297.

[Lane, W.] (1980), "Product Differentiation in a Market with Endogenous Sequential Entry", *Bell Journal of Economics* **11**, 237-261.

[Lau L.J.] (1982), 'A Note on the Fundamental Theorem of Exact Aggregation', *Economics Letters* **9**, 119-126.

[Lewbel A.] (1989), 'Exact Aggregation and a Representative Consumer', *Quarterly Journal of Economics* **104**, 622-633.

[Malinvaud E.] (1991), 'Voies de la Recherche Macroéconomique', Odile Jacob (eds), Paris.

[Malinvaud E.] (1993), "A Famework for Aggregation Theories", *Ricerche Economiche* **47(2)**,107-135.

[Mantel R.] (1974), 'On the Characterization of Aggregate Excess Demand', *Journal of Economic Theory* **7**, 348-353.

[Mantel R.] (1976), 'Homothetic Preferences and Community Excess Demand Functions', *Journal of Economic Theory* **12**, 197-201.

[Maret, I.] (1995a), Joint Distribution of Demand Functions and Price Expectation Functions, and Structural Properties of Market Demand, *Bonn Universität Disc. Paper No. A-483, C.O.R.E. Disc. Paper No. 9526*.

[Maret, I.] (1995b), Distribution of Demand Behavior and the Golden Rule Stationary State, *C.O.R.E. Disc. Paper No. 9565*.

[Maret, I.] (1998), "Heterogeneous Households' Intertemporal Characteristics and the Aggregation Problem", *Research in Economics* **52**, 133-157 .

[Maret, I.] (2000), "Erratum Note on Heterogeneous Households' Intertemporal Characteristics and the Aggregation Problem", *Research in Economics* **54**, 325-329 .

[Maret, I.] (2003), "Modeling Behavioral Heterogeneity in Demand Theory", in : Cowan, R. and Jonard, N. (eds), Heterogeneous Agents, Interactions and Economic Performance, Lecture Notes in Economics and Mathematical Systems. Berlin Heidelberg: Springer.

[Marhuenda F.] (1995), 'Distribution of Income and Aggregation of Demand', *Econometrica* **63,** 647-666.

[Mas-Colell A. and W. Neuefind] (1977), 'Some Generic Properties of Aggregate Excess Demand and an Application', *Econometrica* **45**, 591-599.

[Mas-Colell, A., Whinston, M.D. and Green, J.R.] , Microeconomic Theory, Oxford University Press, New-York, Oxford, 1995.

[Momi, T.] : Excess Demand Functions with Incomplete Markets — a Global Result. Graduate School of Economics, University of Tokyo, mimeo (2001).

[Plott, C.] (1967), "A Notion of Equilibrium and its Possibility under Majority Rule", *American Economic Review* **57**,787-806.

[Pollak R.A.] (1985), 'A transaction cost approach to families and households', *Journal of Economic Literature* **23(2),** 581-608.

[Prais S.J. and H.S. Houthakker] , 'The Analysis of the Family Budgets', 1st and 2nd edition, Cambridge University Press, Cambridge.

[Quah, J.] (1997), "The Law of Demand when Income is Price Dependent", *Econometrica* **65** (6), 1421-1442.

[Quah, J.] (2000), 'The Monotonicity of Individual and Market Demand', *Econometrica*, **68**, 911-931.

[Roberts, J., Sonnenschein, H.] : On the Foundations of the Theory of Monopolistic Competition, *Econometrica* **45** (1), 101-113 (1977).

[Rubinstein, A.] (1979), "A Note about the Nowhere Denseness of Societies having an Equilibrium under Majority Rule", *Econometrica* **47**, 511-514.

[Shafer W. and H. Sonnenschein] (1982), 'Market demand and excess demand functions', in K. Arrow and M. Intriligator (eds), *Handbook of Mathematical Economics*, Amsterdam, North-Holland.

[Shaked, A. and Sutton, J.] (1982), "Relaxing Price Competition Through Product Differentiation", *Review of Economic Studies* **49**, 3-13.

[Sondermann D.] (1975), 'Smoothing Demand by Aggregation', *Journal of Mathematical Economics* **2**, 201-223.

[Sondermann D.] (1976), 'On a Measure Theoretical Problem in Mathematical Economics', in: Springer Lecture Notes in Mathematics 541.

[Sondermann D.] (1980), 'Uniqueness of Mean Maximizers and Continuity of Aggregate Demand', *Journal of Mathematical Economics* **7**, pp. 135-144.

[Sonnenschein H.] (1972), 'Market Excess Demand Functions', *Econometrica* **40**, 549-563.

[Trockel W.] (1983), 'Market Demand is a Continuous Function of Prices', *Economics Letters* **12**, 141-146.

[Trockel W.] (1984), 'Market Demand: An Analysis of the Economics with Non-Convex Preferences', Berlin: Springer-Verlag.

[Tullock, G.] (1967), "The General Irrelevance of the General Possibility Theorem", *Quarterly Journal of Economics* **67**, 256-270.

[2]This terminology was introduced by Malinvaud (1993).

In: New Developments in Macroeconomics Research
Editor: Lawrence Z. Pelzer, pp. 177-192
ISBN 1-59454-663-0

Chapter 5

INFORMATION ACQUISITION IN REPEATED RELATIONSHIPS

***Axel Gautier*[1]* *and Dimitri Paolini*[2]**
[1]CEREC, FUSL & CORE (Belgium)
[2]DEST - Universita "G. D'Annunzio",
Pescara (Italy) & IRES - UCL (Belgium)

Abstract

This paper presents a new rationale for delegation. In a repeated relationship, when the principal gives up at time t the control over an action to the better informed agent, the decision taken by the agent signals his private information to the principal. The revelation of information is valuable to the principal only in a context of repeated relation where the principal can use the information at time $t+1$ to take another decision. In this paper, we present an example where delegation occurs only if the relation lasts for more than one period. In a single period context, if the agent has a bias in favor of one project, he does not have incentives to select a project that is not his preferred one; hence he does not disclose his private information and delegation is not valuable. While in a repeated relationship, it becomes costly for the agent to keep the principal non-informed and this counterbalances the agent's bias for one project. Shared-control (partial delegation) is then the preferred organizational structure when the interaction is repeated. Moreover, shared-control dominates an alternative mechanism where the principal centralizes all the decisions and the information is transferred through a message game.

Introduction

Economics of organizations concentrate on the design of incentive schemes to align the interests of the organizations' members and to promote the organizations' goals. Beyond

*E-mail address: gautier@core.ucl.ac.be., Address for correspondence: CORE Voie du Roman Pays 34, B1348 Louvain-la-Neuve, Belgium.

explicit monetary incentives such as performance related to pay scheme, the organization of the decision making process is by itself part of the incentive package. In particular, giving power to a subordinate affects the global performance of an organization. In this paper, we present a model that compares two organizational structures: delegation where the subordinate receives power from his supervisor and centralization where the supervisor retains the power. Obviously, when the subordinate has authority, the supervisor tries to limit the discretion of the delegate, especially when it is known that the delegates does not share the preferences of his supervisor. We explore a model where decisions should be repeatedly taken. In this case, the supervisor limits the power of the agent by allowing him to take a limited number of decisions. Delegation is then a shared control situation where the power is split between the two parties. We show that delegation to a subordinate even with biased preferences, could be the preferred organizational structure and lead to the first best outcome.

Model overview and results

This paper considers the problem of task delegation under asymmetric information. An organization composed of a supervisor (the principal, she) and a subordinate (the agent, he) should repeatedly select investment projects. The subordinate has superior information about the best project choice and he does not share the objectives of his supervisor who acts in the interest of the organization. The agent is biased toward some types of projects. In particular, there is one project that gives a larger private benefit to the agent. Such a divergence of interests between the two parties arises for example when the agent has a preference for empire and prefers to manage a larger firm (Jensen, 1986) or when a specific project leaves a larger private benefit to the agent.

To introduce delegation, we follow the incomplete contract literature [1] and assume that the principal and the agent cannot contract on the agent's private information and on the decisions.[2] However, control over the action is contractible. The project's choice is then a transferable control action[3]: an action than cannot be contracted for, neither ex-ante nor ex-post, but for which the control could be transferred. The contract signed between the principal and the agent then specifies who has the right to select the investment project at time t. Delegation in this context refers to a situation where the agent receives the control.

In a single period context, delegation of the project's choice to the agent entails a loss of control. Delegation is costly because the agent does not share the preferences of his supervisor. When the agent receives the control, he selects his preferred investment project ignoring the consequences on the principal's welfare. However, the benefit of an informed decider could countervail the loss of control. Despite the cost, it might still be efficient to delegate because the agent has superior information. The choice of delegating the task to the agent depends on the trade-off between the loss of control when the agent decides and the loss of information when the principal decides (Dessein, 2002). When the principal retains control, there is no bias in the decision but the principal is not or imperfectly informed.

[1]Tirole (1999).

[2]Contractibility would make the problem a standard adverse selection problem.

[3]Aghion, Dewatripont and Rey, (2002).

Under centralization, the agent could transmit part of his hidden information through non contractible messages.

In a two-period context, where the organization invests repeatedly in projects, there is an additional benefit of delegation: it becomes a way to transfer information from the agent to the principal. Delegation is efficient when the control over decisions is shared between the agent and the principal: the agent selects the project at time t, the principal at time $t+1$. Moreover, by observing the agent's decision, the principal learns (part of) the agent's hidden information. With shared control, the principal becomes informed if the agent's decision is contingent on his private information.

If, in the one period model, the agent always selects his preferred project, replicating this strategy in a repeated relationship is costly for the agent. When the agent always selects, whatever his private information, the same decision at t, the principal does not acquire information. Selecting his preferred project at t is costly if the decision of a non-informed principal at $t+1$ hurts the agent. Hence, the agent might not select his preferred project in the period one, in order to signal his private information to the principal. In this case, delegation is valuable as it implies a transfer of information from the agent to the principal (Gautier and Paolini, 2002).

Moreover, if the agent does not take a decision contingent on his private information, the principal is weakly better off if she retains control as she could replicate the agent's choice. The revelation of information is not only a property of delegation in repeated context, it is also a necessary condition for delegation to occur.[4]

The contribution of this paper is to give an example where delegation is not valuable in a single period context, but is valuable when the interaction is repeated. This example illustrates that in repeated relationships, delegation is valuable for the principal only because she acquires the agent's hidden information. Delegation is also preferred to an alternative mechanism where the agent transfers his private information through message and the principal then decides. Communication in the alternative mechanism is not complete: the principal imperfectly learns the agent's information. Hence, the principal prefers to learn the information by giving up control.

Related literature

In the standard principal agent theory, following the revelation principle (Myerson, 1982), delegation is always weakly dominated by a grand contract between the principal and all the agents. To speak about delegation in a principal agent setting, one needs to relax some assumption of the revelation principle. Melumad, Mookherjee and Reichelstein (1992) relax the assumption of perfect communication between the principal and the agents. When information transmission is noisy, delegation to one agent reduces the need of communication and improves the organization performance despite the divergence of interests between both parties. Laffont and Martimort (1998) assume that communication between the principal and the agents is imperfect and that side contracting between agents is feasible.

[4]Gautier and Paolini (2002) use the properties of signaling games to show that when the agent receives control, the decision he takes signals his private information i.e. the signaling game has a (unique) separating equilibrium.

When several agents have the possibility to collude against the principal, partial delegation to one agent reduces the stake of collusion.

Aghion and Tirole (1997), Dessein (2002), Ottaviani (2000), Gautier and Paolini (2002) and this paper assume that the contracts are incomplete. Incomplete contracting refers to situations where some variables cannot be part of the contract. A variable cannot be contracted upon, when it cannot be verified by a party outside the contracting relation (a court or a judge for example). If a third party cannot verify that a task has been correctly performed by an employee (and the circumstances under which this task has been performed), the contract governing the employer-employee relationship cannot specify a pay contingent on the achievement of this specific task. Non verifiability by outsiders could come from a prohibitive cost of writing a detailed contract. If the task performed by the employee has multiple dimensions, describing all of them in a contract would be extremely costly. Moreover, verifying if the task has been performed adequately would be even more costly. A prohibitive cost of writing detailed contracts is a justification for the incomplete contract hypothesis (Tirole, 1999).

A large part of the theory of organizations is built on the incomplete contract hypothesis. Explaining delegation, in particular, often relies on the hypothesis that the tasks performed by the delegate cannot be described in a comprehensive contracting framework.[5] In the incomplete contract models, delegation is associated with an effective control over the decisions: the delegate has the freedom to pick any action from an allowed set. While in a complete contract framework, even if the agent performs a task himself, he does not have any authority since everything has been specified in the contract.[6]

Dessein (2002) considers a one period principal agent relationship where both parties disagree on a project choice. The agent has a systematic bias and prefers larger projects than the principal. The relation takes place under asymmetric information. The agent has a piece of private information: he knows a state of the world parameter that the principal ignores. The state of the world determines the optimal project (for both the principal and the agent). Project choice and the state of the world parameter cannot be contracted upon, hence, the only feasible contract is to decide who decides. When the principal delegates the project choice to the agent, delegation is costly since a biased agent selects a project that is not the principal's preferred one. Because of the agent's bias, delegation is associated with a *loss of control*. However, the agent is better informed and this countervails the loss of control. If the principal retains control and asks the agent to advise her about the project choice, communication by the agent is imperfect i.e. he does not truthfully report the state of the world. Communication associated with a centralized decision by the principal is a cheap talk game. Following the Cheap Talk literature (Crawford and Sobel, 1982), communication is noisy. Hence, the principal will not acquire the agent's private information with a message game and communication is associated with a *loss of information*. Delegation dominates

[5]Roider (2003) is an exception. In his model, a simple delegation of authority is a solution to a complete-contracting problem with contractible actions both ex-ante and ex-post and unlimited transfer payments.

[6]Aghion and Tirole (1997) distinguish formal and real authority. Formal authority is conferred by contract or ownership, but it does not necessarily confer real authority that is effective control.

when the loss of control is lower than the loss of information. In other words, delegation is efficient when loss of control are relatively small, that is when the agent's bias is not too large.

Ottaviani (2000) also compares delegation to a better informed agent with strategic communication. He shows that reducing the agent's discretion by limiting his possible choices to a subset of the possible decisions increases the principal's utility. The reason is that reducing the agent's discretion countervails the agent's bias toward some types of projects and hence decreases the associated loss of control. Roider (2003) has a similar point: restricting the agent's discretion is meant to rule out extreme choices and thereby improves the organization performance. Armstrong (1994) considers the case where the agent has a multi-dimensional private information. The principal ignores both the preferences of the agent and the state of the world. Delegation with reduced agent's discretion is also the optimal organizational structure.

Gautier and Paolini (2002) and Legros (1993) study delegation in a two period model. In both papers, delegation is a learning process: by giving up control to the better informed agent in the first period, the principal learns part of the agent's private information. If in a single period model like Dessein (2002), the agent selects his preferred project whenever he receives control, it is not so when the interaction is repeated. In a multi-period relation, the decisions taken at the earlier stages have an informational content. The principal acquires information by observing the actions of the better informed delegate. Hence, when he chooses his action, the agent takes into account that his decision signals his private information to the other party. Delegation is then a signaling game between the agent and the principal (Spence, 1973). The first mover, the delegate, takes a decision based on his private information. Then, the principal observes the decision, revises her prior beliefs about the agent's hidden information and takes a second period decision. Delegation in first period becomes a signaling game only if the interaction is repeated. This is the main difference between repeated and single period models: it is only in the first case that the decision of the agent is strategic. When the relation lasts for one period only, the agent selects his preferred project whenever he has received the control. When the relation is multi-period, the agent trades off the immediate benefit of taking his preferred decision with the potential adverse effect it could have on the principal's information.

Legros (1993) considers the following problem: a politician delegates a policy choice to a delegate (a state agency for example) with unknown preferences. After observing the choice of the delegate, the politician either re-elects the same delegate or selects another delegate from the initial set. Legros (1993) shows that the agent partially hides his private information, in order to increase his probability of being selected as a delegate at the next period. If a delegate is too extreme in the first period, he has very little chance of being the next period delegate, hence he prefers to hide his information in the first period and he mimics less extreme delegates. The equilibrium in the signaling game is a partial pooling equilibrium. Second period delegation is used as a disciplining device. Even though the decisions cannot be contracted upon, the agent might be rewarded (or punished) for not being too extreme in first period by receiving control in second period too.

Gautier and Paolini (2002) consider the problem of Dessein (2002) in a repeated context. They analyze the equilibrium of the following signaling game: at a first stage, a better informed agent takes a decision, then, the principal observes the first decision and takes another decision. The agent has a bias toward larger projects and both decisions affect the welfare of the two parties. When there is a continuum of possible projects, delegation in the first period leads to a complete transfer of information if the state of the world can take two values. It means that the agent acts differently in the two states and the principal learns the true state of the world by observing the agent's decision. With more than two possible states of the world values, the equilibrium is not always separating (the agent could take the same action in two different states) but delegation always improves the prior knowledge of the principal. In technical terms, it means that the full pooling equilibrium where the agent selects the same decision in all states of the world does not exist. The results of Gautier and Paolini (2002) rely on the use of refinements of the Bayesian-Nash equilibrium and in particular the Cho and Kreps (1987) intuitive criterion.

This paper studies a similar problem in a simplified framework where the number of possible projects is limited. In this case, delegation to the agent is not always informative. The principal does not acquire any information if the relation lasts for a single period. With two periods, the principal learns information only if the agent's bias is not too large. It is only when the relation is repeated for a sufficiently long period that delegation is always informative.

Aghion and Tirole (1997) consider a problem where the information structure is endogenous. Both the principal and the agent have to perform an effort to learn information about potential projects. After the learning stage, a decision is taken either by the principal or the agent according to the contract. The incentive to acquire information increases when the party receives more control. For example, the agent has more incentives to be informed if he has both formal and real authority meaning that there is no threat that the principal overrules the agent's decision.

Aghion *et al.* (2002, 2004) show that a shared control over two decisions enhances cooperation between the parties. Two parties can either cooperate or not. If they do not cooperate, the party that has control implements his preferred project. In a shared control situation where the principal takes the first decision and the agent the second, the two parties prefer to cooperate as none of them could implement his preferred project. Cooperation could be achieved only if the control is shared. Similarly in this paper, shared control between the principal and the agent is meant to achieve information transfer from the better informed agent to the principal.

Applications

To illustrate our model, consider the following two examples:

Example 1: Manager-Shareholders relationship. Managers are supposed to act in the interests of the shareholders. However, since Berle and Means (1932), it is commonly agreed that ownership (shareholders) and control (managers) have different objectives. In practice, shareholders often transfer the effective control over the firm to the managers and rubber stamp most of the manager's main decisions. A reason for that is the managerial superior information about the firm and its environment. Contracts usually fail to reconcile the interests of the two parties. Thereby, to maximize the firm's value, shareholders have to decide which decisions they do leave to managers and which decisions they keep in hand. Whether or not shareholders rubber stamp the managerial decision depends on the information they have, and presumably the available information depends on the managerial past actions. For example, if the manager decides to acquire another firm in a new business segment, shareholders will allow the manager to diversify the firm as they do not have the necessary information. But, if the manager suggests additional acquisitions in the same field, shareholders have at that time more information to assess on benefits of such a merger and will exercise more control on this second merger decision. This shared control situation with information transfer is precisely what we describe in this paper.

Example 2: Advisors: Many organizations such as firms, governments or international organizations delegate research to experts like consulting firms or universities while they have resources to produce it. We can explain such a delegation by the fact that even if the consulting firms and/or universities have a different objective from those of the government (for example valuable academic research vs support to decisions), they have a better knowledge of the 'state of research' in some particular field. Part of this expertise is transmitted through the research output and the deciders can use it as a basis for their subsequent research that can be oriented more toward support to decisions.

The Model

We consider an organization composed of a principal and an agent. The organization should select an investment project that affects the welfare of both members.

There are three possible investment projects. One, denoted by S, is a safe project, the two others, denoted R_1 and R_2, are risky. The projects' characteristics (risk and return) are common knowledge. The project yielding the highest return, however, depends on the underlying economic environment. We represents this environment by a state of the world parameter θ which belongs to a set $\Theta \equiv \{\theta_1, \theta_2\}$. Only the agent knows the true value of θ, but it is common knowledge that $\Pr(\theta = \theta_1) = \eta_1$ and $\Pr(\theta = \theta_2) = \eta_2 = 1 - \eta_1$.

Asymmetric information is a key feature of organizations. Under full information, there is no reason to delegate the project's choice to the agent [7]; it is only because the agent is better informed that delegation could be valuable. There are plenty of examples of asymmetric information in organizations. In manager-shareholders relationship, the firm's manager, as an insider, has access to information that shareholders do not have. In multi-division firms, divisional managers, due to their greater proximity with their market, have private information about products, markets and investment opportunities. In employer-employee relationship, the employee acquires through on the job learning information that the employer does not have.

[7] Except for Zabojnik (2002) who finds that delegation may be optimal even if the principal is better able to choose a project. This results comes from the hypothesis that the agent's effort and the accuracy of project choice are complements.

Asymmetric information is not problematic by itself. If the information could be efficiently transmitted to the decision maker, delegation is again useless. Information will not flow efficiently within the organization when either proceeding information is costly or noisy[8] or when the members of the organization have conflicting objectives. In fact, there is no reason to assume that all the members of an organization share the same preferences. For example, in the manager shareholders relation, the manager does not necessarily selects the investment project that maximizes the shareholders' wealth. There are plenty of evidence that managers have preferences for empires. When shareholders want to maximize firms' value, managers have incentives to cause their firms to grow beyond the optimal size.[9] In this article, we will assume that in addition to asymmetric information, the principal and the agent disagree over the best project choice.

The returns of the risky projects depend on the economic environment θ while the safe project S has a return independent of θ. Whatever the state of the world, the safe project returns $s > 0$. The risky projects can either succeed or fail. When a project succeeds, it returns $v > s$ and it returns nothing when it fails. The probabilities that a project succeeds or fails depend on the state of the world θ.

The project R_i succeeds in state θ_i with a probability p and fails with the corresponding probability $(1-p)$. In the other state θ_j, the probability of success of project R_i is q. We assume that project R_i is more likely to succeed in state θ_i than in state θ_j: $p > q$. Conversely, failure of project R_i is more likely when $\theta = \theta_j$: $(1-q) > (1-p)$. The expected return of a risky project R_i is pv in state θ_i and $qv < pv$ in state θ_j.

We assume that in state θ_i, project R_i has the highest expected return and project R_j the lowest one:

Assumption 1: $pv > s > qv$.

The principal is supposed to be risk neutral. We assume that the utility is tied to the expected project return. Shareholders, for example, collect the final value of the firm. Hence, risk neutral shareholders want the firm to select the project with the highest expected return.

We denote by $U^P(y, \theta)$ the principal's utility in state θ when project $y \in \{S, R_1, R_2\}$ is implemented. Assumption 1 implies that in state θ_1, the principal' utility is such that:

$$U^P(R_1, \theta_1) > U^P(S, \theta_1) > U^P(R_2, \theta_1) \tag{1}$$

Similarly, assumption 1 also implies that in state θ_2, the $U^P(., \theta_2)$ is such that:

$$U^P(R_2, \theta_2) > U^P(S, \theta_2) > U^P(R_1, \theta_2) \tag{2}$$

If the principal is unaware of the true state of the world but only knows its prior distribution (η_1, η_2), we assume that her preferred project is the safe project:

Assumption 2: For $i = 1, 2$: $s > \eta_i pv + (1-\eta_i)qv$.

[8] Radner (1993) and Melumad *et al.* (1992).

[9] Jensen (1986).

Assumption 2 implies that for $i, j = 1, 2$:

$$U^P(S, \theta_i) > \eta_i U^P(R_i, \theta_i) + \eta_j U^P(R_i, \theta_j) \tag{3}$$

Hereafter we will refer to the first best situation when the principal manages to implement the project R_i in state θ_i.

The agent derives a private benefit that depends on the realized state of the world and the project's choice. The agent's preferences do not correspond with those of the principal. The agent has a systematic bias in favor of one project, say project R_1. We interpret the agent's bias as follows: there is one project that systematically leaves larger private benefits to the agent. These benefits could be for example, a higher visibility and thereby larger future employment (and pay) prospects, project R_1 could be easier to achieve for the manager due to a specific human capital linked to this project or the private benefits is simply on the job consumption.

Hence, in state θ_1, the agent's preferences correspond with those of the principal since they both prefer project R_1. Moreover, we assume that in state θ_1, the worst project for the agent is R_2.

If $U^A(y, \theta)$ represents the agent's utility in state θ when project $y \in \{S, R_1, R_2\}$ is implemented, we have the following preference relation in state θ_1:

$$U^A(R_1, \theta_1) > U^A(S, \theta_1) > U^A(R_2, \theta_1) \tag{4}$$

In the other state θ_2, due to the large private benefit, the agent's preferred project is R_1. But the next best choice of the agent is the principal's preferred project:

$$U^A(R_1, \theta_2) > U^A(R_2, \theta_2) > U^A(S, \theta_2) \tag{5}$$

For the agent, the preferred project is R_1 in both states. What changes from state to state is the worst project.

The agent is assumed to be liquidity constrained. Otherwise, the problem would have a simple solution where the agent buys the firm from the principal for a fixed upfront payment.

Delegation matters only if there is no complete contract governing the relation between the principal and the agent. Indeed, if it is possible to contract on the economic environment and on the actions, the following revelation mechanism where the principal designs a contract which associate to any report of the agent the corresponding action and payments leads to the first best project choice. However, it is costly for the principal since she has to transfer money to the agent. Hence, our non contractibility assumption is equivalent to a liquidity constraint for the principal.

We suppose that the state of the world parameter θ and the project choice cannot be contracted for, neither ex-ante nor ex-post. However control over the decision is contractible. The project choice is then a transferable control action (Aghion *et al.*, 2002)

Last, note that complete contract would not always be useful when the interaction is repeated because the principal will manage to implement the first best with a delegation contract. Before analyzing the repeated interaction model, we analyze a single period interaction.

Delegation and Communication in a Single Period Relationship

Suppose that the principal-agent relationship lasts for a single period. In this framework, there are two possible contracts: (1) **A-Control**: the principal delegates the project's choice to the agent and (2) **P-Control**: the principal retains control and chooses the project. Under P-Control, the agent could communicate information before the principal decides. Messages are not contractible. Hence, communication under P-Control is a recommendation or an advice from the agent to the principal.

If the principal transfers control to the agent, the latter selects the project knowing the state of the world parameter θ. Given the contract incompleteness, the agent cannot be rewarded or punished for his project choice. Thereby, in each state of the world, he selects the project which brings the largest payoff. When $\theta = \theta_1$, the agent's preferred project is R_1. When $\theta = \theta_2$, the agent's preferred project is R_1 too (by assumption). Hence, under A-Control, project R_1 is selected in both states θ_1 and θ_2.

Given that under A-Control, the agent's choice is independent of his private information, the principal is weakly better-off if she retains the control. Indeed, the principal could replicate the agent's choice under P-Control.

However, under P-Control, the principal will not select the risky project R_1, as the agent would do, but rather the safe project S. Ignoring the value of θ, the principal has a higher payoff if she selects the safe project. In a single period relation, facing a better informed subordinate is not sufficient to delegate the control because the agent has a bias in favor of one project. The agent's private information is not sufficient to make delegation valuable. [10]

Under P-Control, the principal could construct an alternative mechanism where she asks the agent to send a message before she selects a project. The principal and the agent plays a message game before the principal decides on the project. Following our assumption on the impossibility to base contracts on the state of the world realization, the agent cannot be rewarded nor punished for sending a "wrong" message. This kind of message game is a cheap talk game[11] where the informed agent sends a possibly noisy message based on his private information to the principal. Unlike the Spence (1973) signaling game, it costs the agent nothing to send a message.

Since the state of the world can only take two values, we analyze without loss of generality a cheap talk game where the agent could send two possible messages. We call them m_1 and m_2. Message m_1 (resp. m_2) means that the agent advises the principal that the sate of the world is θ_1 (resp. θ_2).

Suppose that, whatever the agent is doing in state θ_2, the agent sends the message m_1 in state θ_1. Indeed, it is in the interest of the agent in state θ_1 is to send a single message to inform the principal that the state of the world is θ_1. In the other state θ_2, if the agent also sends a single message (m_2 in this case), the principal learns the true value of θ and she implements the first best. By transferring the true information, the agent is better off in

[10]In Dessein (2002), there is not a single project preferred in all states but an agent bias for projects larger than the principal's preferred one. In this context, if the principal delegates, there is a trade-off between the size of the bias and the benefits of an informed decider and delegation could be optimal in the single-period model.

[11]Crawford and Sobel (1982).

both states compared to the non-informed principal case where the safe project is always implemented.

But in state θ_2 the agent can increase his utility further by randomizing over the two possible messages. Consider the following strategy: in state θ_2, the agent sends the message m_1 with probability σ and m_2 with probability $(1-\sigma)$. In state θ_1, the agent selects the message m_1 with probability 1. When the principal observes the message m_2, she is sure that $\theta = \theta_2$ and then she selects the project R_2. When the principal observes m_1, she revises her prior beliefs (using the Baye's rule). After receiving the message m_1, the principal's beliefs over the states of the world are: $Prob(\theta = \theta_1|m_1) = \frac{\eta_1}{\eta_1+\sigma\eta_2}$ and $Prob(\theta = \theta_2|m_1) = \frac{\sigma\eta_2}{\eta_1+\sigma\eta_2}$. Given these posterior beliefs, the principal selects the project R_1 if:

$$\frac{\eta_1}{\eta_1+\sigma\eta_2}U^P(R_1,\theta_1) + \frac{\sigma\eta_2}{\eta_1+\sigma\eta_2}U^P(R_1,\theta_2) \geq U^P(S,\theta) \tag{6}$$

Otherwise, the principal selects the safe project after observing m_1.

Condition (6) will be satisfied for σ sufficiently small. Therefore, for the agent in state θ_2, it is optimal to select the highest probability σ^* such that (6) is satisfied with equality. This optimal value σ^* is strictly positive given that (i) the left-hand side of (6) is decreasing in σ and (ii) for $\sigma = 0$, (6) is satisfied. With this strategy, the payoff of the agent in state θ_2 is

$$(1-\sigma^*)U^A(R_2,\theta_2) + \sigma^* U^A(R_1,\theta_2) > U^A(R_2,\theta_2) \tag{7}$$

The agent in state θ_1 cannot improve his utility by sending other combinations of the two messages, hence his equilibrium strategy is to always send message m_1.

The equilibrium in the message game involves randomization in state θ_2. It implies that the principal does not learn the true information. With cheap-talk game, the principal improves his knowledge of the unknown parameter θ but his information remains incomplete. This result is standard in cheap talk games (Crawford and Sobel, 1982). Under P-Control, the agent introduces noise in his message and the principal is not able to implement the first best.

Like in Dessein (2002) and Ottaviani (2000), there is a loss of control under A-Control and a loss of information under P-Control. However, in our framework A-Control is never optimal.

Delegation and Communication in Repeated Relationship

If, in the context of this model, delegation is not valuable in a single period, this section demonstrates that the principal could achieve the first best with a delegation contract when the relation is repeated twice. If instead of selecting a single investment project, suppose the organization invests repeatedly in projects. We consider a twice repeated version of the single period model. In period one, the organization selects a first investment project within $\{S, R_1, R_2\}$, and in period two, a second investment project is chosen within the same set. There is no reason to assume that the organization should select the same project in both periods but we suppose that a common state of the world parameter applies for these two periods.[12] Given that θ is time invariant, the first best choice implies that the same project would be selected in both periods. In particular, the first best is to implement project R_1 (resp R_2) in both periods when the state of the world is θ_1 (resp. θ_2). A change of project would mean that new information has become available before the organization selects the second project i.e. the project selected in first place was the wrong project.

Before the first period, the principal decides who will be in charge of the project choices. It means that the principal allocates the control over the projects before the first project choice.

The payoffs associated with the each project are described in equations (1) to (5). With a discount factor $\delta \leq 1$, the choice of projects y_1 and y_2 in periods one and two in state θ brings about a utility such that : $U^k(y_1, \theta) + \delta U^k(y_2, \theta)$, $k = A, P$.

Without communication, like in the basic model, if the principal keeps control over the two decisions (P-Control), she does not acquire information about the true state of the world and therefore, she selects twice the safe project. Similarly, if the agent receives the control over the two decisions (A-Control), he chooses twice the risky project R_1. Hence, like in the one period model, there is no reason to give full control to the agent in the repeated context since the principal could replicate the agent's choices.

But, when the interaction is repeated, the contracting possibilities extend and the control could also be shared between the principal and the agent. In a **Shared-Control** situation, where the agent selects the first investment project and the principal selects the second, the principal can acquire information by observing the agent's choice. Indeed, if the principal transfers the control, and if the agent invests differently in the two states, the principal learns the agent's private information by observing the project choice. The Shared-Control situation is a signaling game: the first mover (the agent) takes a decision that signals information to the principal who then revises her prior beliefs about the state of the world when taking the second decision. However, opposed to the cheap talk game, signaling the state of the world through the project choice is not cheap anymore.

Consider the choice of the agent in state θ_1. With Shared-Control, the agent's payoff associated with the choice of his preferred project R_1 in period one depends on the choice in the other state. If the agent also selects the preferred project R_1 in state θ_2, his payoff is $U^A(R_1, \theta_1) + \delta U^A(S, \theta_1)$. Alternatively if the agent selects a project in $\{R_2, S\}$ in state θ_2, his payoff is $(1 + \delta)U^A(R_1, \theta_1)$ since the choice of R_1 now signals to the principal that the state of the world is θ_1.

If instead of selecting project R_1, the agent selects his second preferred project S, the highest payoff for the agent is: $U^A(S, \theta_1) + \delta U^A(R_1, \theta_1)$ when the choice of S signals that the state is θ_1. If we compare the lowest payoff when the agent chooses R_1[13] with the

[12]This assumption is standard in dynamic incentive contract models (Laffont and Tirole, 1988). For our argument, we only need that the state of the world parameters are correlated in both periods, so that the information learned in the first period could be used in the second period.

[13]The lowest payoff is considered to be the case for which the principal does not acquire information after observing R_1. Payoffs would have been lower if the principal associates with the choice of R_1 posterior beliefs such that $\Pr(\theta = \theta_1 \mid R_1) = 0$. We discuss the robustness of these beliefs later.

highest payoff when he chooses S, the best choice for the agent is R_1 if:

$$U^A(R_1, \theta_1) + \delta U^A(S, \theta_1) \geq U^A(S, \theta_1) + \delta U^A(R_1, \theta_1)$$

$$\Leftrightarrow (1-\delta)U^A(R_1, \theta_1) \geq (1-\delta)U^A(S, \theta_1) \tag{8}$$

which is true given equation (4) for all $\delta \leq 1$. Hence, in state θ_1, the agent has a dominant strategy R_1.

Consider next the choice of the agent in state θ_2. If the agent selects his preferred project R_1, the principal does not acquire information, as we just established that the agent always selects the project R_1 in state θ_1. In a Shared-Control situation, the choice of R_1 in state θ_2 gives a payoff equals to: $U^A(R_1, \theta_2) + \delta U^A(S, \theta_2)$. If, instead of selecting his preferred project, the agent selects the second preferred project R_2, the principal learns the true state of the world after observing the agent's decision since the agent takes different decisions in the two states. The project choice then signals the state of the world to the principal and the principal, which is now informed, selects her preferred project in period two. With Shared-Control, the choice of R_2 by the agent in the first period is followed by a choice of R_2 by the principal and the agent's associated payoff is: $(1+\delta)U^A(R_2, \theta_2)$.

In state θ_2, the agent prefers to disclose his information (choosing project R_2) than hiding it (choosing project R_1) if:

$$(1+\delta)U^A(R_2, \theta_2) \geq U^A(R_1, \theta_2) + \delta U^A(S, \theta_2) \tag{9}$$

or differently if:

$$\delta(U^A(R_2, \theta_2) - U^A(S, \theta_2)) \geq U^A(R_1, \theta_2) - U^A(R_2, \theta_2) \tag{10}$$

The agent discloses his private information if the benefit of an informed principal in period two (the left hand side of (10)) is larger than the cost of informing the principal (the right hand side of (10)). To inform the principal, the agent renounces to select his preferred project, hence he incurs a cost.

Hence, in a Shared-Control situation, in state θ_2, the agent selects project R_2 if condition (9) holds and project R_1 otherwise.

Compared to the basic model, there is now a benefit associated with delegation: the principal learns the agent's hidden information if (9) holds. Hence delegating the first project choice to the agent could become valuable. Repeating the interaction modifies the agent's choice in state θ_2.

The signaling game under Shared-Control has another separating equilibrium where in state θ_1 the agent selects S and in state θ_2, he selects R_1 if:

$$U^A(S, \theta_1) + \delta U^A(R_1, \theta_1) \geq U^A(R_1, \theta_1) + \delta U^A(R_2, \theta_1)$$

But this second equilibrium is Pareto dominated. Moreover, it does not survive the Cho and Kreps (1987) intuitive criterion.[14]

[14] Gautier and Paolini (2002) use the intuitive criterion to show that delegation always implies an information transfer when there are two states of the world and the set of feasible projects is a continuous interval.

Proposition 1 *If condition (9) holds, the principal shares the control with the agent and the first best is implemented. If (9) does not hold, the principal retains control.*

In a single period context, the principal never delegates the project choice to the agent; when the interaction is repeated, transferring the control to the agent is valuable if the controlling party (the agent) transfers information to the non-informed party (the principal). Information is transferred, despite the agent's bias in favor of one project, when the loss associated with keeping the principal ignorant is large compared to the loss associated with canceling the choice of the preferred project to signal the hidden information. Sharing control creates incentives for the agent to disclose his private information. Note also that if there is no information transfer, the principal retains control. Information transfer is a new rationale for delegation but also a necessary condition for shared-control in a repeated relationship.

Like in the one period model, a mechanism in which the principal centralizes and relies on a message from the agent fails to inform the principal. Again, the agent randomizes his message in state θ_2. Hence, this alternative mechanism brings about a lower utility if (9) holds, but improves the principal's decisions if she retains control.

If the relationship lasts for $T > 2$ periods, the incentives to disclose information under shared control increase. Indeed, in a T times repeated interaction, there is an immediate benefit of hiding information in state θ_2, but there is a future cost: for the $T-1$ remaining periods, the principal remains non informed and implements the safe project. Repeating the interaction then increases the cost of keeping the principal ignorant (the left hand side of (10) increases). Thereby, for T sufficiently large, the equilibrium in the signaling is always a separating equilibrium. To be separating, the following condition (similar to (9)) should hold:

$$\sum_{t=0}^{T} \delta^t U^A(R_2, \theta_2) \geq U^A(R_1, \theta_2) + \sum_{t=1}^{T} \delta^t U^A(S, \theta_2) \tag{11}$$

The left hand side is the agent's utility when he signals that $\theta = \theta_2$ by taking selecting the project R_2, the right hand side is the agent's utility when he hides his information in the first period and let the principal takes the safe project in the remaining periods. Clearly, for large values of T, the condition is always satisfied.

Conclusions

In this paper, we show that delegation in repeated relationship is efficient only when the supervisor improves his knowledge of the unknown state of the world parameter. The principal gives up the control to the agent when she can learn the agent's private information. Without learning, delegation in repeated relations is valueless. Information acquisition is then a new rationale for delegation.

In the single period model, the agent does not use his private information and the principal then does not hand over control. The repetition of the interaction creates incentives for the agent to disclose his private information. It is because the agent may suffer from the ignorance of the principal that he has incentives to disclose his private information when receiving control.

The paper presents a simple example where delegation does not occur in a single period model but is the preferred organizational structure when the relation lasts several periods. In our example, the principal can implement her preferred project in both periods with shared control. Hence delegation does not cost anything for the principal. In more complicated frameworks like Dessein (2002) or Gautier and Paolini (2002), under delegation, the agent does not select the principal's preferred project and a loss of control results from delegation. But delegation in repeated relationships remains valuable only if the principal improves his knowledge of the state of the world parameter by observing the agent's decision. A necessary condition for delegation is then the existence of a separating equilibrium in the signaling game when the agent controls the first decision. [15] A separating equilibrium exists if the utility function satisfies the single-crossing property. [16]

Delegation is robust when we consider an alternative mechanism, compatible with the partial contracting set-up, where the principal centralizes all the decisions and the agent communicates a message before the principal decides. In this mechanism, communication is cheap-talk game. The equilibrium in cheap-talk is usually not separating (Crawford and Sobel, 1982, Dessein, 2002). Hence, the principal is not completely informed with the cheap-talk game, whereas he is fully informed with delegation if the equilibrium is separating.

References

[1] Aghion, P., Dewatripont, M., & Rey, P. (2002). On Partial Contracting. *European Economic Review,* **46**, 745-753.

[2] Aghion, P., Dewatripont, M., & Rey, P. (2004). Transferable Control. *Journal of the European Economic Association,* **2**, 115-138.

[3] Aghion, P., & Tirole, J. (1997). Formal and Real Authority in Organizations. *Journal of Political Economy,* **105**, 1-29.

[4] Armstrong, M. (1994). Delegation and Discretion.*Southampton University Discussion paper* **9421**, Southampton UK.

[5] Berle, A., & Means, G. (1932) *The Modern Corporation and Private Property.* MacMillan, New York.

[6] Cho, I.K., & Kreps, D. (1987). Signaling Games and Stable Equilibria. *Quarterly Journal of Economics,* **12**, 179-221.

[15]Gautier and Paolini (2002) prove the existence and the uniqueness of the equilibrium when there are two states of the world.

[16]For uniqueness conditions, see Fudenberg and Tirole (1991).

[7] Crawford, V., & Sobel, J. (1982). Strategic Information Transmission. *Econometrica,* **50**, 1431-52.

[8] Dessein, W. (2002). Authority and Communication in Organizations. *Review of Economic Studies,* **69**, 811-838.

[9] Fudenberg, D. & Tirole, J. (1991). *Game Theory.* Cambridge, MA: MIT Press.

[10] Gautier, A., & Paolini, D. (2002). Delegation and Information Revelation. Bonn Graduate School of Economics, Universität Bonn, *Discussion Paper* No. **18**/2002.

[11] Jensen, M. (1986). Agency Costs of Free Cash Flow, Corporate Finance and Takeovers. *Journal of Finance,* **76**, 323-329.

[12] Laffont, J. J., & Martimort, D. (1998). Collusion and Delegation. *The RAND Journal of Economics,* **29**, 280-305.

[13] Laffont, J. J., & Tirole, J. (1988). The Dynamics of Incentive Contracts. *Econometrica,* **56**, 1153-1175.

[14] Legros, P. (1993). Information Revelation and Repeated Delegation. *Games and Economic Behavior,* **5**, 98-117.

[15] Melumad N., Mookherjee, D., & Reichelstein, S. (1992). A Theory of Responsibility Centers. *Journal of Accounting and Economics,* **15**, 445-484.

[16] Myerson, R. (1982). Optimal Coordination Mechanism in Generalized Principal-Agent Problems. *Journal of Mathematical Economics,* **10**, 67-81.

[17] Ottaviani, M. (2000). *The Economics of Advice.* University College London.

[18] Radner, R. (1993) The Organization of Decentralized Information Processing. *Econometrica,* **61**, 1109-1146.

[19] Roider, A. (2003). Delegation of Authority as an Optimal (In)complete Contract. Bonn Graduate School of Economics, Universität Bonn, *Discussion Paper* No. **8**/2003.

[20] Spence, M. (1973). Job Market Signaling. *Quarterly Journal of Economics,* **87**, 355-374.

[21] Tirole, J. (1999). Incomplete Contracts: Where do we stand? *Econometrica,* **67**, 741-781.

[22] Zabojnik, J. (2002). Centralized and Decentralized Decision Making in Organizations. *Journal of Labor Economics,* **20**, 1-22.

In: New Developments in Macroeconomics Research
Editor: Lawrence Z. Pelzer, pp. 193-211
ISBN: 1-59454-663-0

Chapter 9

Bad Times, Bad Behavior: The Effects of Economic Conditions on Health-Related Behaviors among High School Students

Jeff DeSimone
Department of Economics, University of South Florida
National Bureau of Economic Research

Abstract

Previous research has revealed that among adults, behaviors such as smoking, drinking, physical inactivity, and overeating vary procyclically. Additional research finding procyclical fluctuations in mortality from sources such as heart and liver diseases, influenza and pneumonia, and homicide suggest that lifestyles become healthier as economic conditions worsen. In contrast, suicide appears to vary countercyclically. This chapter extends the hypothesis that economic downturns diminish mental health while otherwise prompting individuals to adopt healthier and less risky lifestyles to adolescents, who are presumably both less responsive to economic conditions and less risk averse than adults. In particular, I use pooled cross sections of data on high school students from the biennial 1991–2001 Youth Risk Behavior Surveys to examine the relationship between state unemployment rates and a large set of potentially health-reducing behaviors including riding a bicycle and motorcycle without a helmet, not wearing a seat belt, driving while drinking and riding with a drinking driver, carrying a weapon, being involved in physical fights, attempting suicide, using cigarettes, alcohol, marijuana and cocaine, having sex with one or more partners, while drunk or high and without birth control, being under or overweight and not exercising regularly. Controlling for age, grade and race as well as fixed effects for states and years, I find that, in contrast to the results of many recent studies of adults, almost all risky behaviors examined increase in prevalence as unemployment rises for at least one of the two genders. This suggests that economic downturns affect teenagers psychologically through substantive impacts on them or their families, allow teens more leisure time to engage in risky activities, or reduce their perceived opportunity costs of potential health reductions or entry into the legal system.

1 Introduction

Research on the effects of macroeconomic conditions on the health status of individuals dates back at least thirty years. Seminal work by Brenner (1973, 1975, 1979) showed that mental hospital admissions, infant mortality rates, and deaths from cardiovascular disease, cirrhosis, suicide, and homicide all varied countercyclically in aggregate time series data. This evidence suggests that on average health improves during economic upturns and worsens during economic recessions.

This relationship can potentially be explained with hypotheses from both psychology and economics. Straightforward psychological theory suggests that economic downturns, particularly those resulting in job loss, harm physical and mental health by producing stress over the possibility of not being able to support basic needs. These health effects are exacerbated by anxiety-induced risk-taking, such as "medicating" with alcohol, drugs or risky sex in order to alleviate psychological distress. Economic theory supplements this psychological reasoning in the sense that the opportunity cost of time spent in leisure activity falls during recessions, to the extent that unemployed individuals will have more time available to engage in unhealthy behaviors and sacrifice less if the outcome of these behaviors is illness or incarceration. Furthermore, economic expansions will likely improve health by making more money available to spend on health care and health-producing activities.

However, as Ruhm (2000) outlines, there are three reasons why health could deteriorate, and more specifically health-reducing behaviors could become more prevalent, during economic upturns. The first is the standard income effect of an outward shift in the budget constraint. Goods such as alcohol and cigarettes are likely normal, as are other potentially harmful goods and risky activities, so that their consumption will increase as more income becomes available. Another is that health could be an input into the production of goods and services. Just as the attempted relief of unemployment-related stress can increase the prevalence of potentially unhealthy behaviors during economic downturns, the physical or mental exertion of employment or job-related stress could lead to health-reducing consumption or behavior. Finally, leisure time available to engage in time-intensive health-producing activities, such as exercise, declines during economic upturns, meaning that the frequency of such activities will likely fall.

Indeed, several studies subsequent to Brenner's pointed out serious methodological flaws in his analyses, and studies correcting these problems were unable to replicate his findings. Moreover, recent studies examining the relationship between rates of mortality, which proxy for health, and unemployment, which reflect current economic conditions, have obtained the opposite result: health decreases when the economy temporarily deteriorates. This result is obtained using data on U.S. states from 1972–1991 (Ruhm, 2000), 50 Spanish provinces from 1980–1997 (Tapia Granados, 2002), 16 German states from 1980–2000 (Neumayer, 2002), and 23 OECD countries from 1960–1997 (Gerdtham and Ruhm, 2002). In these studies, a one percentage-point increase in unemployment is estimated to reduce total mortality by 0.3 to 1.1 percent. Furthermore, mortality variations are largest for those causes and age groups where behavioral responses are most plausible, suggesting that an increase in the incidence of potentially unhealthy behaviors is at least in part the source of these procyclical variations in mortality.

Much recent direct evidence, in fact, supports the implication that most potentially health-reducing behaviors respond procyclically to economic conditions. In an accompanying analysis of microdata from the 1987–1995 Behavioral Risk Factor Surveillance System (BRFSS), Ruhm (2000) finds that when the economy strengthens, smoking and obesity increase whereas physical activity is reduced and diet becomes less healthy. In earlier work, Ruhm (1995) finds that alcohol consumption and traffic deaths vary procyclically in a 1975 – 1988 panel of U.S. states. Subsequently, Ruhm and Black (2002) use 1987–1999 BRFSS data to confirm the procyclical variation in drinking and show that this largely results from changes in consumption by existing drinkers and that the decrease occurring during recessions is concentrated among heavy consumers. In addition, Ruhm (2005) shows in 1987–2000 BRFSS data that smoking and height-adjusted weight decline during temporary economic downturns while leisure-time physical activity rises, with the drop in tobacco use occurring disproportionately among heavy smokers, the fall in body weight among the severely obese, and the increase in exercise among those who were completely inactive. Using national data from the Natality Files from 1975 onward, Dehejia and Lleras-Muney (2003) find that babies conceived in times of high unemployment have a reduced incidence of low and very low birth weight and a reduced rate of neonatal and post-neonatal mortality. These health improvements are partially attributable to changes in behavior during recessions, as the use of prenatal care increases for all mothers and drinking decreases for black mothers, although smoking increases among white mothers. In contrast, Dee (2001) finds that binge drinking is countercyclical in 1984–1995 BRFSS data. Evidence that binge drinking increased substantially during economic downturns even among those who remained employed suggests that recession-induced increases in drinking prevalence to some extent reflect the influence of economic stress. Also, Raphael and Winter-Ebmer (1999) find that rates of specific violent crimes vary positively with unemployment in a 1970–1993 panel of U.S. states, while Ruhm (2000) finds that suicides increase during recessions, suggesting that violent and suicidal behavior might vary procyclically. A common element of these studies is that their regressions included fixed effects for the geographic unit at which unemployment is measured, so that effects of unemployment rates are identified by differences between geographic units in unemployment rate changes over the same time period.

This chapter further examines the relationship between economic conditions and health, concentrating on behaviors that potentially reduce health in the short or long run rather than on health status itself. It is similar to the studies on health-related behaviors summarized above in several salient ways: it uses the state unemployment rate as the measure of local economic conditions, analyzes the consumption of alcohol and cigarettes along with driving while drinking, diet and exercise patterns and violent and suicidal behaviors, and uses fixed state effects to control for state-level factors that are time-invariant and potentially correlated with both economic conditions and health-related behaviors. However, my study differs from those described above in two important respects. First, I examine the behavior of high school students rather than adults. Teenagers are well-known to be on average substantially more prone to engage in risk-seeking activities than adults, making it possible that their health-related behaviors are much less responsive than those of adults to external factors such as economic conditions. Furthermore, most high school students are somewhat more insulated from temporary changes in economic conditions than are adults in the sense that not only is their primary activity, attending school, unlikely to be affected by the state of the economy, but also many either are too young to formally work for pay or work part-time primarily for spending money rather than living expenses. Second, I examine some health-related behaviors, such as illegal drug use and sexual promiscuity, for which relationships with economic conditions have yet to be investigated, as well as some heretofore unused specific measures of broader previously-analyzed behaviors.

In contrast to most of the aforementioned results on adults, I find that a variety of potential health-reducing behaviors, including some that are apparently procyclical for adults, are countercyclical for high school students in the sense that they increase in prevalence as unemployment rates rise. Moreover, there is little evidence suggesting that any of the risky behaviors studied here are countercyclical. There are several potential explanations for these results. One is that economic downturns create anxiety for teenagers because of material effects on them, possibly through impacts on their parents, other family members or friends, and teens turn to activities that involve health risks but produce short-run pleasure or relaxation in order to alleviate this anxiety. Another is that students spend less time working for pay after school and on weekends when unemployment is higher, which allows them more free time to engage in risky behaviors. A third is that economic declines reduce teens' expected alternative opportunities sufficiently, perhaps partially because of short time horizons, to make activities with immediate benefits worthwhile even if they involve potential risks in terms of negative health shocks or arrest and imprisonment.

The remainder of the chapter proceeds as follows. The next section describes the data on risky behaviors among high school students that I analyze. Section 3 outlines my empirical methodology, which is quite similar to that of the aforementioned studies. Section 4 presents results in detail, and section 5 further discusses the results and concludes.

2 Data

I analyze data from the Youth Risk Behavior Survey (YRBS), a component of the Youth Risk Behavior Surveillance System established by the Centers for Disease Control and Prevention (CDC) to monitor the prevalence of youth behaviors that most influence health. The YRBS, which has been administered biannually to high school students in the spring of every odd-numbered year since 1991, focuses on behaviors that result in substantial mortality, morbidity, disability, and social problems. It uses a three-stage cluster sample design to produce a nationally representative sample of students in grades 9–12 in public and private schools. The first stage sampling frame contains primary sampling units (PSUs) consisting of large counties, sub-areas of very large counties, or groups of small, adjacent counties. A small subset of PSUs (e.g. 57 out of 1,256 in 2001) is selected with probability proportional to school enrollment size. At the second sampling stage, a number of schools (199 in 2001) are selected, again with probability proportional to school enrollment size except that schools with substantial numbers of black and Hispanic students are sampled at higher rates. The third sampling stage involves randomly selecting one or two classes of a required subject at each chosen school. Students who choose to participate complete a self-administered questionnaire in their classrooms during a regular class period. Although participation is anonymous, local parental permission procedures are followed before survey administration. The 2001 response rate of 63%, representing 75% of schools and 83% of students in responding schools, is similar to response rates for the 1990s surveys. Sampling weights, which I use both to calculate summary statistics and in the regressions, adjust for both non-response and varying probabilities of selection.

An important feature of the YRBS data is that state identifiers are reported for each respondent, in the public use files for 1993–1997 and in separate files obtained from the CDC for other years (although recently released 2003 data are not included because a version that includes state identifiers is not yet available). I therefore use state-level unemployment rates, which are available as monthly series from the Local Area Unemployment Statistics page of the Bureau of Labor Statistics (http://stats.bls.gov/lau/home.htm), to proxy for prevailing economic conditions. Given the sampling scheme described above, not all states are included in each YRBS year. Table 1 lists the number of YRBS respondents from each state and survey year. As the sampling scheme would suggest, generally the most populous states are sampled more frequently and have a larger number of respondents, while the least populous states have fewer respondents and either appear only sporadically or are not sampled at all. To the extent that the lack of balance in the state panel could potentially affect the results, I also show results for a balanced panel of only the eight states that are sampled in all six YRBS years, which are listed in bold in Table 1, and an intermediate sample that includes those eight states along with the nine states that are sampled in five of the six YRBS years, which are listed in italics in Table 1.

Table 1: Number of YRBS respondents from each state and year

State	1991	1993	1995	1997	1999	2001	Total
Alabama	*0*	*792*	*99*	*797*	*60*	*313*	*2,061*
Alaska	0	0	0	0	0	0	0
Arizona	0	438	0	1,116	132	411	2,097
Arkansas	0	397	290	364	0	0	1,051
California	**1,745**	**2,145**	**1,220**	**2,008**	**2,523**	**2,323**	**11,964**
Colorado	*141*	*262*	*105*	*272*	*0*	*667*	*1,447*
Connecticut	0	0	0	226	0	0	226
Delaware	0	0	215	0	0	0	215
District of Columbia	0	0	520	0	0	0	520
Florida	**1,179**	**532**	**549**	**681**	**866**	**1,076**	**4,883**
Georgia	**486**	**916**	**446**	**343**	**827**	**488**	**3,506**
Hawaii	0	0	0	0	314	0	314
Idaho	0	0	0	0	0	158	158
Illinois	*415*	*720*	*243*	*0*	*230*	*446*	*2,054*
Indiana	269	0	0	0	0	179	448
Iowa	0	0	243	790	0	0	1,033
Kansas	0	172	0	205	0	0	377
Kentucky	0	0	0	0	0	0	0
Louisiana	0	0	290	592	630	0	1,512
Maine	*0*	*249*	*152*	*238*	*204*	*208*	*1,051*
Maryland	213	145	0	830	0	0	1,188
Massachusetts	0	370	274	1,652	0	262	2,558
Michigan	**764**	**145**	**1,120**	**535**	**531**	**341**	**3,436**
Minnesota	0	323	0	0	0	0	323
Mississippi	**478**	**361**	**481**	**331**	**645**	**345**	**2,641**
Missouri	*248*	*185*	*558*	*0*	*563*	*471*	*2,025*
Montana	0	0	0	0	0	206	206

State	1991	1993	1995	1997	1999	2001	Total
Nebraska	0	397	0	0	0	0	397
Nevada	0	0	0	0	0	238	238
New Hampshire	253	0	0	0	0	0	253
New Jersey	455	0	0	738	239	227	1,659
New Mexico	259	665	0	283	0	156	1,363
New York	**376**	**1,259**	**508**	**359**	**740**	**323**	**3,565**
North Carolina	*0*	*300*	*116*	*341*	*516*	*673*	*1,946*
North Dakota	0	0	0	0	0	0	0
Ohio	**135**	**525**	**554**	**561**	**569**	**226**	**2,570**
Oklahoma	0	0	0	224	0	398	622
Oregon	0	188	0	0	0	184	372
Pennsylvania	*488*	*361*	*676*	*275*	*496*	*0*	*2,296*
Rhode Island	0	0	0	0	75	0	75
South Carolina	284	397	0	528	804	0	2,013
South Dakota	277	0	0	0	0	0	277
Tennessee	*0*	*530*	*354*	*581*	*266*	*615*	*2,346*
Texas	**2,517**	**2,772**	**1,711**	**951**	**2,763**	**2,068**	**12,782**
Utah	0	0	0	0	0	0	0
Vermont	141	0	0	0	0	0	141
Virginia	688	0	64	0	756	0	1,508
Washington	*424*	*380*	*85*	*110*	*0*	*55*	*1,054*
West Virginia	0	303	0	0	0	263	566
Wisconsin	0	0	0	299	556	238	1,093
Wyoming	0	0	0	0	0	0	0
Total	12,235	16,229	10,873	16,230	15,305	13,558	84,430

Table 2 lists the risky behaviors examined and shows their weighted means (and standard deviations for non-binary measures) by gender for the full sample that does not exclude observations from states sampled in fewer than five of the six survey years. The sample sizes shown pertain to the explanatory variables discussed below and are slightly smaller than table 1 implies because each variable is missing for at least a few respondents, but are slightly larger than the sizes of the regression samples which also omit observations for which dependent variables are unobserved. The table shows that the main advantage of using YRBS data is the plethora of health-related behaviors for which information is gathered. I examine only behaviors that are measured consistently in all six years of the survey during 1991–2001. These includes behaviors traditionally thought to be related to economic conditions, such as drinking and smoking, dietary and exercise habits, and violent and suicidal tendencies, as well as others not previously examined in relation to economic conditions, such as illegal drug use and sex. All frequencies are reported in categorical form and converted to numerical measures using midpoints of bounded intervals. Values for the highest-frequency categories that have no upper bound are chosen based on the span of the other intervals specified, the number of respondents within each interval and common sense, though results are insensitive to values used within reasonable ranges. Samples for variables that are defined only for those who engage in a specific behavior (such as substance use frequencies, injuries from fighting or attempting suicide, numbers of sexual partners and use of birth control) are restricted to those who report engaging in the corresponding behavior.

Table 2: Variable definitions and summary statistics

Variable	Males (*n* = 40,953)		Females (*n* = 42,511)	
	Mean	S.D.	Mean	S.D.
Dependent variables				
Rode bicycle without a helmet in past 12 months	.771		.641	
Rode motorcycle without a helmet in past 12 months	.202		.090	
Never wears seat belt when riding in car	.085		.038	
Never or rarely wears seat belt when riding in car	.234		.146	
Mostly or always wears seat belt when riding in car	.584		.681	
Always wears seat belt when riding in car	.309		.370	
Rode in vehicle with drinking driver in past 30 days	.366		.343	
Drove when drinking in past 30 days	.188		.103	
Carried a weapon in past 30 days	.316		.077	
In a physical fight in last 12 months	.466		.287	
If fought: needed medical treatment after fight	.111		.088	
Considered attempting suicide in past 12 months	.165		.284	
Planned suicide attempt in past 12 months	.127		.206	
Attempted suicide in past 12 months	.050		.114	
If attempted suicide: needed medical treatment after attempt	.348		.281	
Smoked cigarettes in past 30 days	.325		.316	
If smoked: number of cigarettes smoked in past 30 days	152.018	215.946	119.654	174.305
Used chewing tobacco or snuff in past 30 days	.172		.017	
Drank alcohol in past 30 days	.518		.474	
If drank: number of days drank in past 30 days	6.460	6.647	4.811	5.089
If drank: had 5+ drinks in a row in past 30 days	.666		.563	
If had 5+ drinks: number of days did so in past 30 days	4.963	5.439	3.614	4.003
Used marijuana in past 30 days	.258		.188	
If used marijuana: number of times used in past 30 days	19.209	21.686	11.910	16.734
Used cocaine in past 30 days	.038		.022	
If used cocaine: number of times used in past 30 days	14.243	20.058	7.034	12.141
Had sexual intercourse in past 3 months	.354		.368	
If had sex: had more than one partner in past 3 months	.366		.181	
If had sex: number of partners in past 3 months	2.070	2.129	1.329	1.008
If had sex: used alcohol or drugs before last experience	.292		.180	
If had sex: did not use a condom during last experience	.387		.522	
If had sex: did not use birth control during last experience	.221		.190	
Describe self as very underweight	.025		.018	
Describe self as very or slightly underweight	.214		.131	
Describe self as slightly or very overweight	.229		.378	
Describe self as very overweight	.027		.053	
Cardiovascular activity at least 20 minutes in past 7 days	.892		.789	
If cardiovascular: number of days did so in past 7 days	4.764	2.001	3.929	2.011
Exercised to strengthen or tone muscles in past 7 days	.780		.658	
If strength exercise: number of days did so in past 7 days	4.262	1.991	3.623	2.001
Explanatory variables				
15 years old	.227		.244	
16 years old	.265		.260	
17 years old	.253		.253	
18 years old	.167		.136	
In 10th grade	.251		.249	

Variable	Males (n = 40,953)		Females (n = 42,511)	
	Mean	S.D.	Mean	S.D.
In 11th grade	.246		.242	
In 12th grade	.249		.250	
White non-Hispanic	.675		.652	
Black non-Hispanic	.127		.145	
Hispanic	.097		.102	

As Table 2 reveals, risky behaviors are generally more prevalent for males than females. Boys are more likely than girls to ride bicycles or motorcycles without helmets, drive while drinking, carry a weapon, take part in a physical fight, binge drink, use chewing tobacco, marijuana and cocaine, have multiple sexual partners and use alcohol or drugs before their last sexual experience, and not wear seat belts. Boys who drink, smoke or use marijuana or cocaine also consume the corresponding substance more often than do girls who engage in the same behaviors. In contrast, boys are less likely to consider, plan or carry out a suicide attempt or describe themselves as overweight, and also exercise more often. Because occurrences of the behaviors examined here vary substantially across genders, I conduct separate analyses for males and females.

Table 2 also lists the explanatory variables included in the regressions (the categories excluded from Table 2 and the regressions are age 14, grade nine and all other races). The main disadvantage of the YRBS is that it reports information on very few plausibly exogenous factors that can serve as controls in the regressions. In particular, family socioeconomic status is not observed. Thus separating effects of changes in family income induced by changes in economic conditions from those directly attributable to changes in economic conditions is not possible, and the regression estimates are properly interpreted as reduced form effects of state unemployment rates on health-related behaviors. Students who are younger than age 14 or for whom information on age, grade, gender or race is missing, who as a group comprise somewhat less than half of one percent of the original sample, are omitted from the analysis.

The appropriate time frame for the state unemployment rate variable depends on the specific health behavior being examined. The time spans covered by these behaviors varies from the past seven or 30 days to the past three or 12 months. Although all YRBS waves were administered in the spring of the survey year, specific administration dates are not reported. I therefore assume that all surveys were completed at the end of March and use the unemployment rate from March of the survey year for behaviors spanning the past seven or 30 days, the average rate during the first three months of the survey year for behaviors spanning the past three months, and the average rate during the 12 months starting with the previous April for behaviors spanning the past 12 months. This ignores potential cumulative effects of further lags in the unemployment rate. Table 3 shows summary statistics by year for the three unemployment rate variables, weighted using the YRBS sampling weights for the combined full samples of boys and girls. As is well-known, unemployment rates rose sharply from 1990 to early 1993, fell steadily to historically low levels from then until late 2000, and then began to rise, though the sample period only encompasses the very beginning of the recent economic downturn that extended into 2003.

Table 3: State unemployment rate summary statistics

	Current month		Past 3 months		Past 12 months	
Year	**Mean**	**S.D.**	**Mean**	**S.D.**	**Mean**	**S.D.**
1991	7.192	1.223	7.175	1.046	5.925	0.875
1993	7.678	1.955	7.888	1.941	7.357	1.847
1995	5.777	1.264	5.985	1.292	5.760	1.338
1997	5.287	0.998	5.563	1.012	5.298	1.033
1999	4.653	0.714	4.850	0.733	4.592	0.761
2001	4.472	0.692	4.560	0.730	4.088	0.615

The current month rate is that from March of the indicated year, while the past 3 and 12 month rates are averages of the monthly rates counting backward 3 and 12 months, respectively, starting with March of the indicated year.

3 Methodology

The recent studies described in the introduction have a common methodological feature: their regression equations include fixed effects for years as well as the geographic unit at which the unemployment rate is measured, typically the state as is the case here. Fixed state effects automatically control for time-invariant factors that differ across states and prevent the effects of such factors from incorrectly being attributed to economic conditions with which they are spuriously correlated. For instance, a variety of potentially health-reducing behaviors such as drinking and smoking are much more prevalent in Nevada than in Utah because of lifestyle differences that vary little across the sample period. Without fixed state effects to absorb the effects of these lifestyle differences, the behavioral variation might be mistakenly attributed to economic fluctuations if unemployment rates are consistently higher in one of the two states. Fixed year effects, meanwhile, account for factors that vary uniformly over time across states, such as reductions in unprotected sex in response to growing information about the lethality of AIDS and ability of condoms to prevent infection with HIV. The impact of economic fluctuations is therefore identified by within-state variations in unemployment rates relative to unemployment rate changes occurring in other states.

The regressions that I estimate thus include fixed effects for states and years, and are consequently of the form

$$B_{isy} = \alpha_0 + \alpha_1 U_{sy} + X_{isy}\alpha_2 + \delta_s\alpha_3 + \gamma_y\alpha_4 + \varepsilon_{isy} \qquad (1)$$

where B represents one of the health-related behaviors in Table 2 for individual i living in state s and surveyed in year y, U is the unemployment rate in state s in year y, X is a vector of the age, grade and race indicators listed in Table 2, δ is a vector of indicators equaling one for state s and 0 for all other states, γ is a vector of indicators equaling one for year y and 0 for all other years, and ε is an error term that is assumed to be uncorrelated with U, X, δ and γ. In order to maintain consistency across the different behaviors under examination and make marginal effects of unemployment rate changes transparent, I use ordinary least squares for all regressions regardless of the form of the dependent variable. Results are similar when logit or probit regression models are used for binary dependent variables and when interval regression models are used with the original frequency variables reported in the survey. Standard errors are robust to heteroskedasticity of unknown form and allow for clustering by state, meaning that observations from different states are assumed to be independent but those from the same state, even from different survey years, are not.

4 Results

Tables 4–8 show the results of estimating equation (1) for the various health-related behaviors listed in Table 2. For brevity the tables show only the estimated coefficient and standard error of α_1, the effect of the unemployment rate on the corresponding behavior. The top and bottom panels show results for males and females, respectively. Within these panels, the upper estimates are derived from the full sample, the middle estimates are from the sample excluding observations from states surveyed in fewer than five of the six YRBS years, and the lower estimates come from the sample that includes only respondents from states surveyed in all six years. Each listing contains the coefficient in the first row, standard error in parentheses in the second row and regression sample size in brackets in the third row.

Table 4 lists estimated effects of unemployment rates on behaviors related to vehicle safety. For neither gender do economic conditions impact the propensity to ride a bicycle without a helmet, regardless of whether the sample includes all or a subset of states or all respondents or just bicycle riders. The same is true of riding a motorcycle without a helmet for males, but the roughly one-seventh of females who ride motorcycles become significantly less likely to do so without helmets as unemployment rises. Evaluated at the weighted mean proportion of female motorcycle riders in the full sample who have ridden without helmets, .504, the point estimates imply that a one percentage point rise in the state unemployment rate reduces without-helmet riding by about 12 percent. This turns out to be the only risky behavior examined here that exhibits statistically significant procyclical variation across all specifications for a specific gender. In the full samples, both genders become more likely to never or rarely wear a seat belt when riding in a car, and less likely to always wear one, as the economy worsens, though the effects are cut in half for males and become insignificant for both genders when samples are reduced to the balanced panel of eight states surveyed in all six years. The strongest countercyclical effect of economic conditions on vehicle safety behaviors, though, occurs for behavior related to drunk driving. For both genders, unemployment is positively related to both riding with drinking drivers and driving while drinking, with effects increasing in size as the panel of states becomes more balanced and significant in all cases except for female driving while drinking in the unbalanced panels. At the sample means, the balanced panel estimates imply that a one percentage point increase in the unemployment rate would increase propensities to ride with a drinking driver by nine percent for boys and 10 percent for girls and to drive while drinking by nine percent for boys and 12 percent for girls.

Table 4: Effects of unemployment rates on behaviors related to vehicle safety

Bike without helmet past 12 months		Motorcycle without helmet past 12 months		Wears seat belt				Drinking driver past 30 days	
Full sample	Riders only	Full sample	Riders only	Never	Never or rarely	Mostly or always	Always	Rode with	Drove
MALES – All observations									
-.002	-.004	.012	-.009	.011	.022	-.018	-.031	.022	.014
(.012)	(.005)	(.011)	(.016)	(.006)	(.011)	(.013)	(.010)	(.008)	(.005)
[39,952]	[30,606]	[40,247]	[11,450]	[40,864]	[40,864]	[40,864]	[40,864]	[40,838]	[40,115]
MALES – Observations from states surveyed at least five of six years									
-.001	.002	.015	-.007	.010	.020	-.012	-.028	.023	.014
(.017)	(.005)	(.013)	(.020)	(.007)	(.013)	(.014)	(.009)	(.009)	(.006)
[29,124]	[22,156]	[29,322]	[8,206]	[29,771]	[29,771]	[29,771]	[29,771]	[29,731]	[29,196]
MALES – Observations from states surveyed all six years									
-.007	.007	.003	-.032	.005	.009	.001	-.014	.033	.017
(.016)	(.005)	(.009)	(.023)	(.005)	(.010)	(.013)	(.011)	(.004)	(.005)
[21,548]	[16,310]	[21,688]	[5,870]	[22,013]	[22,013]	[22,013]	[22,013]	[21,988]	[21,606]
FEMALES – All observations									
.014	.000	-.008	-.061	.000	.015	-.018	-.020	.015	.004
(.012)	(.005)	(.005)	(.016)	(.004)	(.008)	(.012)	(.009)	(.008)	(.006)
[41,815]	[25,896]	[42,021]	[6,057]	[42,435]	[42,435]	[42,435]	[42,435]	[42,455]	[42,136]
FEMALES – Observations from states surveyed at least five of six years									
.019	.000	-.003	-.056	-.001	.014	-.019	-.018	.025	.009
(.015)	(.007)	(.006)	(.022)	(.005)	(.008)	(.014)	(.009)	(.007)	(.006)
[30,614]	[18,737]	[30,746]	[4,311]	[31,051]	[31,051]	[31,051]	[31,051]	[31,046]	[30,804]
FEMALES – Observations from states surveyed all six years									
.026	.008	-.008	-.062	-.003	.010	-.012	-.017	.035	.012
(.023)	(.006)	(.007)	(.039)	(.006)	(.009)	(.016)	(.011)	(.003)	(.003)
[22,376]	[13,573]	[22,466]	[3,046]	[22,686]	[22,686]	[22,686]	[22,686]	[22,682]	[22,495]

Each listing contains the OLS regression coefficient in the first row, the heteroskedasticity-robust standard error of the coefficient that also accounts for clustering by state in parentheses in the second row, and the regression sample size in brackets in the third row. All regressions include as explanatory variables the indicators for age, grade and race listed in table 2 as well as fixed effects for each state and year.

Table 5 indicates estimated effects of unemployment rates on violent and suicidal behavior. For males, weapon carrying is countercyclical: in the full sample, a one percentage point increase in unemployment raises the probability of carrying a weapon by almost six percent. Less than eight percent of females report carrying a weapon, about one-fourth of the analogous proportion for males, so it is not surprising that economic conditions are not related to weapon carrying by females. Physical fighting and needing medical treatment as a result of a fight are also countercyclical for both genders, with effects being particularly large for girls. In the balanced panels, a one percentage point rise in the unemployment rate increases the likelihoods of being in a fight by about eight percent for boys and 13 percent for girls and, among those who get in fights, of needing medical treatment because of fighting by 10 percent for boys and 23 percent for girls. Behavior related to attempting suicide, however, shows little relation to economic conditions despite the fact that suicide is one of the only sources of mortality that recent research has found to be countercyclical. Of the 24 estimated coefficients for the four suicide attempt-related outcomes in the three samples for each gender, only one is significant, that corresponding to suicide attempts by females for the balanced panel of states, with the direction of the effect supporting the previous evidence that suicide is countercyclical.

Table 6 shows results for past 30 day substance use, which is also countercyclical for cigarettes, alcohol and marijuana. A one percentage point increase in unemployment raises the probability of smoking by as much as five percent for boys and 14 percent for girls and the number of cigarettes that users smoke by up to 13 percent for boys and 16 percent for girls. For males, all four measures of drinking are significantly positively related to unemployment rates in all three samples, with a one percentage point rise increasing the probability of drinking and the number of days drinkers consume alcohol by five percent each, the probability that drinkers have five or more drinks at once (i.e. binge drinking) by three percent, and the number of days that drinkers binge by six percent. For females, drinking among all respondents is countercyclical in all three samples, with a one percentage point unemployment hike raising the probability of drinking by 10 percent in the balanced panel, but drinking among those who consume alcohol is unrelated to economic conditions other than a significant but small positive effect of unemployment on the probability of binge drinking for females. Using marijuana is also countercyclical, with a one percentage point rise in unemployment increasing the probability of using by seven percent for boys and nine percent for girls in the balanced panels, although frequency of consumption among users is only significantly related to economic conditions for boys and significance is more than marginal only in the balanced panel. Meanwhile, cocaine consumption does not vary with economic conditions and use of chewing tobacco or snuff is procyclical for both genders in the balanced panels.

Table 5: Effects of unemployment rates on violent and suicidal behaviors

Carried weapon	Physical fights past 12 months		Suicide attempts past 12 months			
past 30 days	In fight	Needed treatment (fighters only)	Considered	Planned	Carried out	Needed treatment (attempters only)
MALES – All observations						
.018	.019	.010	.001	.002	.004	.032
(.008)	(.008)	(.006)	(.007)	(.006)	(.004)	(.039)
[39,814]	[40,090]	[19,250]	[40,107]	[39,925]	[36,458]	[2,049]
MALES – Observations from states surveyed at least five of six years						
.017	.027	.005	-.001	.001	.007	-.003
(.007)	(.009)	(.007)	(.009)	(.009)	(.006)	(.036)
[29,041]	[29,161]	[13,966]	[29,171]	[29,020]	[26,476]	[1,539]
MALES – Observations from states surveyed all six years						
.010	.036	.011	-.003	-.004	-.001	.004
(.008)	(.008)	(.004)	(.009)	(.007)	(.006)	(.044)
[21,468]	[21,564]	[10,302]	[21,575]	[21,495]	[19,647]	[1,206]
FEMALES – All observations						
-.001	.009	.012	.004	-.001	.002	.008
(.004)	(.014)	(.005)	(.007)	(.006)	(.005)	(.025)
[41,949]	[42,038]	[12,648]	[41,964]	[41,658]	[38,794]	[4,753]
FEMALES – Observations from states surveyed at least five of six years						
-.002	.027	.015	.000	.002	.000	.016
(.005)	(.012)	(.006)	(.009)	(.007)	(.006)	(.021)
[30,731]	[30,723]	[9,313]	[30,650]	[30,401]	[28,278]	[3,495]
FEMALES – Observations from states surveyed all six years						
.000	.038	.020	.005	.004	.010	-.003
(.006)	(.011)	(.007)	(.009)	(.009)	(.002)	(.015)
[22,442]	[22,445]	[6,770]	[22,395]	[22,248]	[20,657]	[2,643]

Each listing contains the OLS regression coefficient in the first row, the heteroskedasticity-robust standard error of the coefficient that also accounts for clustering by state in parentheses in the second row, and the regression sample size in brackets in the third row. All regressions include as explanatory variables the indicators for age, grade and race listed in table 2 as well as fixed effects for each state and year.

Table 6: Effects of unemployment rates substance use in past 30 days

Tobacco			Alcohol				Marijuana		Cocaine	
Smoked cigarettes	# smoked (smokers)	Chewing or snuff	Drank	# days (drinkers)	5+ drinks (drinkers)	# days 5+ (bingers)	Used	# times (users)	Used	# times (users)
MALES – All observations										
.008	13.921	.007	.024	.327	.017	.301	.011	.959	.003	1.397
(.006)	(5.871)	(.009)	(.005)	(.152)	(.008)	(.128)	(.006)	(.617)	(.002)	(1.618)
[38,720]	[12,146]	[40,313]	[38,499]	[19,697]	[21,120]	[13,489]	[40,114]	[10,272]	[40,441]	[1,883]
MALES – Observations from states surveyed at least five of six years										
.017	12.060	.000	.022	.347	.017	.347	.019	1.086	.002	.411
(.006)	(7.853)	(.009)	(.004)	(.192)	(.009)	(.150)	(.007)	(.724)	(.003)	(1.270)
[28,215]	[8,738]	[29,292]	[28,010]	[14,413]	[15,455]	[9,853]	[29,179]	[7,610]	[29,393]	[1,428]
MALES – Observations from states surveyed all six years										
.011	19.449	-.012	.020	.349	.024	.283	.019	1.289	.002	-.595
(.007)	(8.307)	(.005)	(.005)	(.212)	(.011)	(.177)	(.008)	(.498)	(.003)	(1.107)
[20,875]	[6,432]	[21,670]	[20,699]	[10,756]	[11,525]	[7,385]	[21,581]	[5,455]	[21,695]	[1,202]
FEMALES – All observations										
.016	8.673	-.001	.021	-.058	.004	.078	.004	-.525	-.003	.478
(.013)	(7.898)	(.002)	(.009)	(.111)	(.009)	(.118)	(.006)	(.503)	(.005)	(.844)
[40,849]	[10,883]	[42,058]	[40,797]	[18,505]	[19,658]	[9,978]	[42,092]	[7,187]	[42,171]	[994]
FEMALES – Observations from states surveyed at least five of six years										
.035	18.623	-.002	.028	.015	.003	.134	.010	-.277	.003	-.714
(.010)	(6.365)	(.002)	(.011)	(.134)	(.008)	(.149)	(.006)	(.509)	(.002)	(1.186)
[29,920]	[7,715]	[30,687]	[29,800]	[13,461]	[14,332]	[7,147]	[30,766]	[5,224]	[30,776]	[736]
FEMALES – Observations from states surveyed all six years										
.044	17.138	-.004	.046	-.099	.011	.080	.016	.198	.006	.169
(.008)	(6.501)	(.001)	(.006)	(.166)	(.004)	(.188)	(.004)	(.257)	(.002)	(2.159)
[21,825]	[5,305]	[22,407]	[21,740]	[9,858]	[10,515]	[5,226]	[22,464]	[3,654]	[22,429]	[624]

Each listing contains the OLS regression coefficient in the first row, the heteroskedasticity-robust standard error of the coefficient that also accounts for clustering by state in parentheses in the second row, and the regression sample size in brackets in the third row. All regressions include as explanatory variables the indicators for age, grade and race listed in table 2 as well as fixed effects for each state and year.

Table 7 presents estimated effects of unemployment rates on sexual behavior. In the balanced and almost balanced panels, probabilities of having sex in the past three months among all respondents are also countercyclical, increasing by about six percent for each gender in response to a one percentage point rise in the unemployment rate. Similarly, the number of past three month partners among those who have had sex in that time is countercyclical with marginal significance for males and in the full sample for females, albeit with small effect sizes. Other risky sexual behaviors among those who are sexually active are largely invariant to economic conditions. The effect of unemployment on having multiple partners is insignificant in all specifications. Using alcohol or drugs in conjunction with sex and not using a condom both exhibit countercyclicality, but only significantly in one model out of six in each case. Economic conditions are also only related to not using any birth control in one of the six specifications, but in this case, the almost balanced male panel, the negative sign indicates procyclical variation.

Finally, Table 8 depicts results for self-described body weight and past week exercise. I use the 12 month unemployment rate in the weight regressions, which allows time for weight to fluctuate in response to economic conditions in the case that weight self-descriptions are accurate but does not eliminate the possibility that these self-descriptions in part reflect self-image rather than actual weight. In none of the weight or exercise variables are the effects of unemployment rates consistently significant. There is limited evidence that considering oneself either under- or overweight is procyclical for males, but unemployment is significant in only one of three specifications for three of the four weight indicators and never significant for the fourth. There is similar limited evidence that not engaging in cardiovascular exercise is countercyclical for females and not taking part in strength training exercise is countercyclical for males. It would potentially be more useful to study actual rather than self-described body weight, but this is not reported in the YRBS until 1999.

5 Conclusion

This chapter examined how a variety of potentially health-reducing behaviors vary with economic conditions among high school students in the biennial 1991–2001 Youth Risk Behavior Surveys. Unlike adults, who most recent studies have found adopt healthier lifestyles during bad economic times, YRBS teens appear to more frequently engage in unhealthy activities as the economy worsens. In particular, regressions that control for age, grade, race, and perhaps most importantly fixed effects for states and years, show that state unemployment rates are positively and significantly related to not wearing a seat belt, driving while drinking and riding with a drinking driver, carrying a weapon, involvement in physical fights, consumption of cigarettes, alcohol, marijuana and cocaine, having sex and not exercising regularly. The primary implication of the analysis is that any adverse economic effects of downturns in the economy are exacerbated by increases in risky behaviors among adolescents.

Table 7: Effects of unemployment rates on sexual behavior

		Among those who had sex past three months			
Had sex past three months	**Multiple partners past three months**	**# partners past three months**	**Used alcohol/drugs last experience**	**No condom last experience**	**No birth control last experience**
MALES – All observations					
.011	.009	.059	.012	.000	-.011
(.009)	(.009)	(.036)	(.010)	(.009)	(.016)
[38,630]	[15,746]	[15,746]	[15,830]	[15,589]	[15,408]
MALES – Observations from states surveyed at least five of six years					
.018	.004	.055	.021	-.008	-.033
(.008)	(.008)	(.033)	(.010)	(.010)	(.016)
[28,188]	[11,544]	[11,544]	[11,614]	[11,425]	[11,285]
MALES – Observations from states surveyed all six years					
.022	-.002	.044	.016	.001	-.009
(.007)	(.010)	(.028)	(.011)	(.013)	(.016)
[20,877]	[8,477]	[8,477]	[8,531]	[8,387]	[8,298]
FEMALES – All observations					
.006	.001	.031	.011	.008	.006
(.009)	(.004)	(.017)	(.009)	(.016)	(.005)
[41,104]	[15,825]	[15,825]	[15,854]	[15,699]	[15,531]
FEMALES – Observations from states surveyed at least five of six years					
.015	-.002	.014	.006	.012	.003
(.009)	(.004)	(.018)	(.010)	(.021)	(.006)
[30,132]	[11,523]	[11,523]	[11,539]	[11,429]	[11,296]
FEMALES – Observations from states surveyed all six years					
.024	-.001	.018	-.005	.026	-.004
(.008)	(.006)	(.022)	(.008)	(.010)	(.006)
[22,036]	[8,237]	[8,237]	[8,253]	[8,172]	[8,080]

Each listing contains the OLS regression coefficient in the first row, the heteroskedasticity-robust standard error of the coefficient that also accounts for clustering by state in parentheses in the second row, and the regression sample size in brackets in the third row. All regressions include as explanatory variables the indicators for age, grade and race listed in table 2 as well as fixed effects for each state and year.

Table 8: Effects of unemployment rates on weight and exercise

Self-described weight				Exercise in past seven days			
Very underweight	**Very or slightly underweight**	**Slightly or very overweight**	**Very overweight**	**Cardiovascular activity**	**# days (if activity)**	**Strength training**	**# days (if trained)**
MALES – All observations							
-.001	-.003	-.009	-.002	-.001	-.013	-.012	-.045
(.002)	(.007)	(.007)	(.002)	(.003)	(.036) [35,210]	(.006)	(.041)
[40,621]	[40,621]	[40,621]	[40,621]	[40,329]		[40,371]	[31,152]
MALES – Observations from states surveyed at least five of six years							
-.002	-.005	-.009	-.004	.000	-.011	-.008	-.048
(.002)	(.009)	(.006)	(.002)	(.003)	(.034)	(.006)	(.045)
[29,575]	[29,575]	[29,575]	[29,575]	[29,330]	[25,605]	[29,419]	[22,689]
MALES – Observations from states surveyed all six years							
-.002	-.014	-.019	-.003	.002	-.063	-.009	-.113
(.003)	(.006)	(.004)	(.002)	(.004)	(.050)	(.009)	(.041)
[21,867]	[21,867]	[21,867]	[21,867]	[21,642]	[18,878]	[21,794]	[16,828]
FEMALES – All observations							
.001	-.001	-.004	-.001	-.003	-.043	-.011	-.044
(.002)	(.006)	(.010)	(.004)	(.005)	(.030)	(.009)	(.047)
[42,358]	[42,358]	[42,358]	[42,358]	[42,091]	[31,286]	[42,173]	[25,655]
FEMALES – Observations from states surveyed at least five of six years							
.001	-.002	-.007	.001	-.007	-.042	-.012	-.021
(.002)	(.004)	(.011)	(.005)	(.005)	(.034)	(.012)	(.049)
[30,966]	[30,966]	[30,966]	[30,966]	[30,711]	[22,903]	[30,842]	[18,744]
FEMALES – Observations from states surveyed all six years							
-.001	-.002	-.018	.003	-.007	-.092	-.010	-.070
(.003)	(.002)	(.011)	(.006)	(.004)	(.036)	(.010)	(.044)
[22,619]	[22,619]	[22,619]	[22,619]	[22,372]	[16,593]	[22,570]	[13,591]

Each listing contains the OLS regression coefficient in the first row, the heteroskedasticity-robust standard error of the coefficient that also accounts for clustering by state in parentheses in the second row, and the regression sample size in brackets in the third row. All regressions include as explanatory variables the indicators for age, grade and race listed in table 2 as well as fixed effects for each state and year.

Why are behaviors that yield immediate gratification but involve substantial health risks in both the short and long term countercyclical for high school students? This finding has at least three possible explanations. First, economic declines produce tension by bringing about negative shocks to current budgets of teens' families or to teens' expected near-future budgets, and the kinds of activities in which teens take part to relieve this tension are intensely pleasurable in the immediate term precisely because they have the potential to cause health problems. Second, students either are less likely to hold part time jobs or work fewer hours in these jobs when economic conditions are bad, thus giving them more time to participate in activities that involve health risks. Third, deteriorating economic conditions have enough of a depressing effect on the perceived alternative opportunities of teens that behaviors bringing about instantaneous satisfaction become worthwhile in an expected value sense even if their potential consequences include addiction, disease infection, or entry into the criminal justice system.

A limitation of my analysis is that I do not make any attempt to control for prices, monetary or otherwise, for the behaviors examined. To the extent that within-state changes in prices and unemployment rates are correlated despite holding constant the demand factors controlled for in the regressions, omitted variable bias is opposite in sign to that of the correlation between prices and unemployment assuming that the correlation between own-prices and behavior is negative. If prices fall when unemployment rises, then the bias from omitting prices is positive: the true effect is more negative than the estimates reflect, i.e. behaviors appear more countercyclical than they truly are. In the extreme, this could be an important reason that this analysis obtains the opposite results to those of studies on adults. However, any such bias is mitigated by the likelihood that the price responsiveness of the activities studied here is small, especially in light of evidence from many studies of significant but small negative elasticities of substance use with respect to prices and risky sexual behavior with respect to AIDS prevalence, and that such prices vary minimally or even in the same direction as changes in unemployment rates.

Because state identifiers are not yet available for the 2003 YRBS, the sample period ends in spring 2001, just as the recent economic downturn began to manifest itself in the form of rising unemployment rates. For instance, the national seasonally adjusted unemployment rate rose from 3.9 percent in December 2000 to 4.3 percent in March 2001, and then continued to rise steadily until peaking in June 2003 at 6.3 percent, the highest unemployment rate since April 1994. The 1.5 percentage point rise in the unemployment rate between March 2001 and March 2003 is by far the largest increase in current (March) rates experienced between YRBS years during the sample period and portends, based on the results of this analysis and holding all else constant, a significant jump in the prevalence of many risky behaviors between the 2001 and 2003 surveys. Indeed, an examination of YRBS trends reveals that several behaviors, such as not wearing seat belts, riding with drinking drivers, getting in a physical fight and having sex, either increased markedly between 2001 and 2003 or held constant after steadily decreasing through 2001 (http://www.cdc.gov/HealthyYouth/yrbs/factsheets.htm).

The responsiveness of unhealthy behaviors by youth to economic conditions suggests several potentially fruitful avenues for future research. The Arrestee Drug Abuse Monitoring program of the National Institute of Justice has for over 15 years collected data on the results of urine screens administered to arrestees in various cities to test for illegal drug use, suggesting an investigation of the effect of metropolitan area unemployment rates on arrestee substance use. The Monitoring the Future (MTF) study has annually collected information on drinking and drug use as well as census region of residence from high school seniors since the 1970s, meaning that a long-term examination of the effects of regional unemployment changes on substance use by teens about to graduate from high school could be carried out. The YRBS has recorded the heights and weights of respondents since 1999, making possible an analysis of the effect of state unemployment rates on teen obesity. Finally, both MTF and BRFSS data on postsecondary school enrollment plans and status could be employed to study the effect of changing economic conditions on college attendance and completion.

References

Brenner, M. Harvey, *Mental Illness and the Economy*, Cambridge: Harvard University Press, 1973.

_______, "Trends in Alcohol Consumption and Associated Illnesses: Some Effects of Economic Changes," *American Journal of Public Health,* LXV (1975), 1279–92.

_______, "Mortality and the National Economy," *The Lancet*, September 15, 1979, 568–73.

Dee, Thomas S., "Alcohol Abuse and Economic Conditions: Evidence from Repeated Cross-Sections of Individual-Level Data," *Health Economics*, April 2001, 10 (3), 257–70.

Dehejia, Rajeev and Lleras-Muney, Adriana, "The Timing of Births: Is the Health of Infants Counter-Cyclical?" NBER *Working Paper* **10122**, November 2003.

Gerdtham, Ulf G. and Christopher J. Ruhm, "Deaths Rise in Good Economic Times: Evidence from the OECD," NBER *Working Paper* **9357**, November 2002.

Neumayer, Eric, "Recessions Lower (Some) Mortality Rates: Evidence From Germany," *Working Paper*, London School of Economics and Political Science, November 2002.

Raphael, Stephen, and Winter-Ebmer, Rudolf, "Identifying the Effect of Unemployment on Crime," *Centre for Economic Policy Research Discussion Paper* **2129**, April 1999.

Ruhm, Christopher, "Are Recessions Good For Your Health?" *Quarterly Journal of Economics,* May 2000, 115 (2), 617–50.

_______, "Economic Conditions and Alcohol Problems," *Journal of Health Economics*, December 1995, 14 (5), 583–603.

_______, "Healthy Living In Hard Times," *Journal of Health Economics*, March 2005, 24 (2), 341–63.

Ruhm, Christopher and William E. Black, "Does Drinking Really Decrease in Bad Times?" *Journal of Health Economics*, July 2002, 21 (4), 659–78.

Tapia Granados, José A, "Death Rates and Business Cycle Fluctuations in Spain at the End of the 20th Century: Further Empirical Evidence of Mortality Increase During Economic Expansions," *Working Paper*, New School University, 2002.

INDEX

C

D

M

N

O

W

X

Y

Z